Indigenous Peoples and the Nation-State: 'Fourth World' Politics in Canada, Australia and Norway

INDIGENOUS PEOPLES AND THE NATION-STATE: 'FOURTH WORLD' POLITICS IN CANADA, AUSTRALIA AND NORWAY

Edited by Noel Dyck

Social and Economic Papers No. 14

Institute of Social and Economic Research
Memorial University of Newfoundland

©Institute of Social and Economic Research
Memorial University of Newfoundland
St. John's, Newfoundland, Canada
ISBN 0-919666-44-2
1985

Canadian Cataloguing in Publication Data

Main entry under title:

Indigenous peoples and the nation-state

(Social and economic papers ; no. 14)
Bibliography: p.
ISBN 0-919666-44-2

1. Canada - Native races - Addresses, essays, lectures. 2. Australia - Native races - Addresses,
essays, lectures. 3. Lapps - Norway - Government relations - Addresses, essays, lectures.
I. Dyck, Noel. II. Memorial University of Newfoundland. Institute of Social and Economic
Research. III. Series.

E92.I62 1985   323.1'1   C85-098810-1

Contents

Acknowledgements

This book is based upon discussions among participants at a conference on, "The Politics of Representation in the Fourth World: Minority Indigenous Peoples in Canada, Australia and Norway," held at Simon Fraser University, January 6-8, 1982. The conference was generously supported by Simon Fraser University, the Social Sciences and Humanities Research Council, the Samuel and Saidye Bronfman Family Foundation, the Commonwealth Foundation and the British Council. Their contributions are gratefully acknowledged.

I also thank all those who took part in the conference and especially Isabel Emmett, Bruce Rigsby, Lorna Williams, Millie Poplar, Gary Patsey, Scott Clark, Gerry Gold, Beverly Gartrell, Heribert Adam, Steve Sharp and Ian Whitaker. The assistance of Bea Donald, Marianne Athey, Philip Moore, Herb George, Kathleen Nelson, Katherine Kuczerpa, Jean Jordan, Estela Racasa and Doug McKegney was essential to the organizing and hosting of the conference.

The appearance of this volume would not have been possible without the generous and unstinting assistance of Robert Paine. I also thank Sonia Kuryliw Paine for her valuable work on the manuscript and Jeanette Gleeson for preparing the manuscript for publication. Greg Spurgeon's timely assistance in obtaining photographs for the cover is much appreciated.

This book has been published with the help of a grant from the Social Science Federation of Canada, using funds provided by the Social Sciences and Humanities Research Council of Canada.

Aboriginal Peoples and Nation-States: An Introduction to the Analytical Issues

1

NOEL DYCK

The political problems of minority indigenous peoples encompassed within modern nation-states have received increasing national
and international attention in recent years. North and South
American Indians, Australian Aborigines, Saami in Scandinavia,
and aboriginal populations in other parts of the world are struggl-
ing variously to retain traditional lands, to cope with government
administration of their affairs and to survive as culturally distinct
peoples within nation-states. These peoples are, by and large,
politically weak, economically marginal and culturally stigmatized members of the national societies that have overtaken them and
their lands. Together, they comprise what has, in the past decade,
come to be known as the "Fourth World" (Manuel and Posluns
1974; Graburn 1981).

Unlike other ethnic minorities, Fourth World peoples are not
immigrants but the original inhabitants of lands that today form
the territories of nation-states. And unlike the peoples of the Third
World who can at least hope to take control of their countries one
day through strength of numbers, the tiny internal colonies that
make up the Fourth World are fated always to be minority populations in their own lands. In the present, as in the past, aboriginal
peoples are being subjected to government policies that, from one
country to another, range from genocide to forced assimilation,
from segregation to cultural pluralism. The form and substance
of their relations with national and state governments are matters
of fundamental significance in their everyday life and future prospects as indigenous peoples.

The essays in this volume examine the processes by which aboriginal peoples in three western liberal democracies—Canada, Australia and Norway—seek to manage their dealings and represent their political interests vis-à-vis the agencies of the nation-state. In some cases this has entailed the adaptation of traditional representational and leadership structures to new conditions, in others the generation of new forms and styles of representation. Governments, on their part, have sought alternately to elicit control of representations made by or on behalf of native peoples. Together, these concerns constitute the politics of indigenous peoples' struggle to survive as indigenous peoples, and governments' efforts to reconcile demands for special aboriginal status and rights with the existing institutional arrangements and ideological foundations of Western nation-states. The tension between these two positions lies at the heart of the issues—land claims, resource development, cultural rights, and constitutional issues—that have attracted the attention of government leaders, the news media and the public to the circumstances and aspirations of indigenous peoples in these countries.

Native peoples in Canada, Australia and Norway, in fact, account for only a small segment of any overall list of potential candidates for Fourth World status (cf. Graburn 1981); yet they have much in common in terms of their political demands and activities—commonalities which derive at least in part from similarities in their respective national political contexts. This commonality was recognized by the involvement of Australian Aborigines, Norwegian Saami and Canadian Indians in the recently formed World Council of Indigenous Peoples (WCIP), a body whose existence is predicated on the perception that aboriginal peoples in these—though not all—countries face essentially similar problems. In recent years, several types of links have developed between these three countries concerning native affairs. Native leaders have attended conferences in each other's countries; lawyers and government officials have begun to compare national policies in the fields of aboriginal land rights and the administration of native affairs. Ironically, anthropologists—who traditionally have specialized in the study of aboriginal peoples, and whose discipline proclaims the value of cross-cultural comparison—are only today beginning to grasp that an understanding of the contemporary political relations of indigenous peoples in any one of these geographically separated countries could be extended by a knowledge of native affairs in others.

Although many of the issues involving indigenous peoples date back to the eighteenth and nineteenth centuries, their recognition as matters deserving of national, and even international, attention is a relatively recent development. The rapid expansion of welfare-state programs in Canada, Australia and Norway following the Second World War had the effect of bringing to public attention the anomalous social and economic status of indigenous peoples. The postwar drive for international decolonization triggered a further rethinking of the appropriate place of aboriginal peoples within liberal democracies. Questions about how these tiny groups of often geographically remote subsistence hunters, reindeer herders, fringe dwellers, and reserve and mission residents were to exist within their respective national societies turned into public debates. Governments were forced to give their attention to these questions, which they often identified as the Indian, Aborigine or Lappish "problem."

The action that ensued from government's attempts to resolve these problems and from indigenous peoples' responses to official measures has prompted anthropologists to grapple with relations and questions that often had been ignored within the discipline. Anthropologists have also found themselves being drawn personally and professionally into dealings between governments and indigenous peoples, either through official requests for advice or through acts of advocacy performed in the course of field research at the behest of local aboriginal communities. As a consequence, we have acquired a certain familiarity with some aspects of the workings of different government agencies and the activities of indigenous peoples' representative organizations. But until recently, there remained a wide gap between this scattered and infrequently reported experience of individual anthropologists and the potential capacity of the discipline to foster systematic investigations and analyses of this complicated and often rapidly shifting field.

This gap is attributable in part to the scale, complexity and sheer geographic expanse of the overarching networks of relations that tie indigenous peoples to the nation-state. The recent attempt on the part of Canadian Indians to block patriation of the Canadian constitution (see Sanders' essay, this volume) provides an apt illustration of how an issue can simultaneously link scattered reserve communities with a national government and an international audience. The methodological and theoretical problems involved in examining developments such as these are considerable, but are neither entirely new to anthropology nor insurmountable.[1]

Our chief concern in these essays is to elucidate the range of formal and informal mechanisms employed at different levels by indigenous peoples to represent their interests to national governments. We shall also be asking to what extent certain similarities in the activities and demands of indigenous peoples in Canada, Australia and Norway reflect a political structure and agenda common to this type of nation-state. The volume in no sense entails an exhaustive areal comparison of native affairs, issues or peoples in the three countries; we do, however, seek to illustrate the potential advantages of a somewhat broader, extranational—if not global—perspective for investigating indigenous peoples' relations with the nation-state.

Specifically, Harvey Feit's essay considers the processes by which Cree communities in Northern Quebec organized to oppose the construction of a hydro-electric development on their hunting and trapping territories. Feit rejects the claim that the Cree were manipulated by either their leaders or by non-native advisers, and he also shows how the Cree resolved the dilemma of a negotiating mechanism by choosing one that reconciled pragmatic effectiveness with existing Cree notions of legitimate leadership. Feit's study illustrates—especially when compared with Weaver's essay—the differences between indigenous peoples' and governments' notions of what constitutes legitimate representation and leadership.

In the southern hemisphere, Jeremy Beckett traces the continuing evolution of a formal structure of representation for Australia's less-known indigenous people, the Torres Strait Islanders, within the state of Queensland. His essay focuses attention upon the role of native representatives who articulate relations between this officially recognized indigenous minority and state and national governments by ''knowing how to talk to white people.'' In a second paper from Australia, Basil Sansom analyses two recent land claims made by Aborigines in the Northern Territory and argues that the preparation of claims cases requires processual modelling whereby indigenous realities can be effectively translated into Western legislative and juridical concepts. His conclusions are reminiscent of Bateson's claim that there are two forms of colonialism: one type which says that "the natives have got to be like the colonists" and a second which says that "the natives have got to be like themselves and had better not change."[2]

Sally Weaver's essay identifies "representivity" as a basic political principle and a manipulable political resource that governments in liberal democracies use to influence and control indigenous peoples' representative organizations. She illustrates this claim with reference to relations between national governments and native peoples' organizations in Canada and Australia during the past two decades. Douglas Sanders investigates an international arena in his account of the Indian lobby which, between 1978 and 1982, sought to block, from Westminster to Ottawa, patriation of the Canadian constitution. His essay demonstrates that even though patriation did take place, the success of Indian, Inuit and Metis associations in garnering the support of an international audience and in insisting upon their right to participate in constitutional negotiations comprised an unanticipated political achievement.

Robert Paine's essay takes us to Norway and an analysis of protests staged by Saami in 1979 and 1981 in an attempt to halt the construction of a hydro-electric project that threatened Saami reindeer herders' lands. Paine identifies ethnodrama as an important means for Fourth World politicking and suggests some conditions for the staging of successful political drama by indigenous peoples.

Finally, in a brief concluding statement Dyck summarizes and readdresses the volume's main findings concerning representation and the Fourth World. As well as identifying some basic characteristics of the situation of Fourth World peoples, this essay considers the distinctive properties of Fourth World relations.

In the remainder of this introduction I shall consider more general concerns raised by the essays in this volume, including (1) the types of political claims being made by indigenous peoples and what these reveal about their relations with nation-states in

Western liberal democracies; (2) some of the means by which indigenous peoples are seeking to advance their interests; and (3) the paradoxical concept of a Fourth World, which purports to unite peoples from many countries who generally have been distinctive in their tendancies toward localism and the micro-scale of their communities and identities.

II

Indigenous peoples in Canada, Australia and Norway are today making essentially similar demands of their national governments, often in like fashion. The Dene Declaration of 1975,[3] which acknowledges the reality of the Canadian state but which insists upon the right of the Dene people of the Northwest Territories to be recognized as a distinct people and to exercise greater self-determination and control over their traditional lands, exemplifies the thrust of these claims. Land claims and the demand for recognition of a special status are distinctive political claims of indigenous peoples within liberal democracies. To appreciate why these particular objectives are being pursued we must direct our attention to the political, economic and ideological relations that bind indigenous peoples to the nation-state. Here we shall be especially concerned with the asymmetry and historical depth of these relations and the problems that they pose within liberal democracies.

Yet, before we turn to these matters, some comment is required concerning our analytical understanding of the nature of the state in liberal democratic societies. It is beyond the scope of this volume to provide a comprehensive discussion of the modern state, whose intricate complexity, in any case, is a matter for political scientists and political economists to analyse.[4] Our immediate concern is a more modest one; namely, to place our ethnographic studies of relations between indigenous peoples and governments within a framework that will afford us some degree of consistency in investigating this rather specialized sphere of state activity.

Briefly, our depiction of the state in Western liberal democracies is guided by three assumptions: (1) that the state has always played a leading role in facilitating the exploitation of lands and resources held by indigenous peoples; (2) that the state's subsequent involvement in administering minority indigenous peoples that have been largely or entirely dispossessed of their lands and resources has been governed historically by complex social and ideological considerations as well as by economic factors; and (3) that the modern state is not a monolithic structure, but consists of an assemblage of agencies, institutions and processes that are hypothetically capable of being—but that are often not—centrally coordinated and controlled. The result is that the actions of one government ministry are often offset by those of another ministry, level or body of government. The tactical considerations raised by these features of state organization with respect to indigenous affairs will be considered elsewhere in this introduction.

Relations between indigenous peoples and Western governments revolve largely around the fundamental asymmetry of the parties involved—a people and a state (Paine 1985). The one simply refers to a community of people; the other to a legal and political organization. In pluralist theory, at least, the liberal-democratic state represents the totality of its individual citizens, while an indigenous people consists of small, self-selecting communities whose members are bound to one another by dense networks of multiplex, face-to-face relationships. Indigenous communities are not, then, simply aggregates of separate individuals belonging to a category, but rather distinct groups that are usually associated with particular territorial bases. Indeed, the attachment of indigenous peoples to particular localities is one of their most notable and politically significant features, whereas, as Cohen notes (1982:7), identification of self with locality is anathema to the logic of modern political economy.

Because indigenous peoples retain a highly localized sense of identity and are often concerned with matters that do not readily correspond with the larger political agenda of the nation-state, it is difficult for them to achieve representation beyond the local level. The problems of translating their concerns into a format that will be comprehensible and plausible at the national level are unrelenting. Aboriginal land claims, for example, tend to be viewed by corporations and governments as issues involving control of access to valuable commodities, whereas for indigenous peoples these claims stand not only for a different set of economic interests but also for the protection of their culture and community. Feit's essay on the James Bay land agreement speaks directly to this issue.

Moreover, indigenous communities may, as Sansom's essay illustrates, also be of an organizational type not readily recognized by governments. In contrast to the increasingly centralized modern state, indigenous peoples are scattered over relatively large areas in small, dispersed and often informal communities. They exist for the most part on the margins of society, either pursuing some remaining subsistence pursuits or the benefits of welfare bureaucracies. In terms of their voting power in national elections they are insignificant. In this and other respects the asymmetry of relations between indigenous peoples and the state entails differences of scale as well as of type.

Although indigenous peoples are culturally and often geographically and socioeconomically distinct from the rest of the nation, government leaders in Canada, Australia and Norway today take great pains to minimize the perceived social and political differences between indigenous and non-indigenous sectors of the population. This situation, as we shall see below, marks a relatively recent stage in a long history of indigenous peoples' relations with the state in these countries.

As well as joining two quite different orders of social organization, relations between indigenous peoples and governments possess a historical dimension that plays an important part in shaping contemporary issues. Contrary to the impression often conveyed by government spokesmen in Canada, Australia and Norway, relations between governments and indigenous-peoples-as-distinct-communities are not recent inventions but rather long-established, though by no means unchanging, historical phenomena. This is clearly illustrated in Beckett's essay. Although indigenous peoples' claims have only recently achieved current public prominence, these issues are almost invariably rooted in some way—if only rhetorically—in past dealings with governments. That governments should now wish to dismiss the past as being irrelevant to contemporary concerns is ironic, and yet strategically significant.

The expropriation and settlement of indigenous people's lands in Canada, Australia and northern Norway were facilitated by the settlers' notions of their own racial superiority vis-à-vis the natives.

Yet, having swept native peoples away from their lands and con-fiscated their resources, they were faced with the question of what to do with the displaced peoples. Settlers were generally less in-terested in exploiting indigenous labour than in controlling their lands. Aboriginal peoples' inclination to retreat to regions less at-tractive to the newcomers offered one resolution; diseases which rapidly and savagely reduced native populations provided another. But always there remained some indigenous communities that, if they were not to perish on the settlers' doorsteps, had to be dealt with. In the countries we are concerned with two rather different modes of articulation developed between the state and indigenous communities.

Indians in Canada, Torres Strait Islanders in Queensland and Aborigines in some parts of Australia were formally distinguished and recognized as indigenous peoples by governments. They became wards of the state who were subject to special laws and regulations administered by separate government bureaucracies or, occasionally, by ecclesiastical authorities. The implementation of these quasi-colonial systems was based both on a pragmatic con-cern to ensure that native peoples did not become obstacles or a nuisance to settlement and on an official perception of indigenous peoples as ''primitives'' who would be quickly eradicated by Euro-pean settlers if they were not protected by authorities. In Canada, the negotiation of treaties in some regions marked a preliminary stage in Indian/government relations that was quickly superced-ed by a system of paternalistic reserve administration under the terms of the Indian Act. The agencies that oversaw indigenous af-fairs in both Canada and Australia sought to convert native peoples to Christian beliefs, the English language and the habits of sobriety, industry and self-sufficiency.

No less attention was given to the assimilation and 'Norwegianization' of the Saami, nor to the economic exploita-tion of Saami territories by Norwegians, but in this case the state did not formally and unambiguously recognize the existence of indigenous status. Instead, the administration of Saami com-munities was undertaken within the institutional and legal ap-paratus of a nominally homogeneous nation-state. Nevertheless, the continuing efforts of the Norwegian government in the fields of education, lands administration and agriculture to integrate

Saami communities into the national, cultural and economic spheres underscores informally articulated though persistently recognized differences between Saami and Norwegians.

Whatever might have been the intention, both of these modes of articulation served to strengthen and formalize the opposition of identities between settlers and indigenous communities in Canada, Australia and Norway. Government efforts to manage and integrate aboriginal peoples into national populations posed a constant threat to their integrity and to their very existence. Active and direct opposition to these government policies was undertaken by aboriginal leaders, but their efforts proved to be generally fruitless and potentially costly. As an alternative, many indigenous communities developed various forms of indirect and symbolic opposition that spoke loudly to the members of the community, invoking them to remain committed to their community, identity and culture, but that did not unduly provoke government officials. Notable among these forms of indirect opposition were various manifestations of cultural conservatism, reinforced by passive resistance and strategies of indirect competition (cf. Schwimmer 1972; Henriksen 1983) that asserted the dignity and value of an indigenous community and culture.

The sustained and often aggressive efforts by governments to assimilate indigenous peoples, combined with indirect opposition served to generate within indigenous communities[5] a remarkable persistence and deep sense of grievance and injustice—the key elements that formed the basis of the political claims that they began to make openly and directly in the postwar period. Yet, given the fundamental division established in the past between indigenous communities and governments, there exist two separate understandings of their past and present relationship: the view of government officials who have traditionally defined the nature of the so-called indigenous "problem" and the views and experience of native peoples who have long been deemed to be problematic.

Since 1945, governments in all three countries have discontinued or amended practices that were becoming increasingly out of place in a postwar international order dedicated to decolonization and the protection of human rights. In Canada the permit system that regulated virtually all aspects of reserve agriculture was quietly dropped in the 1950s, and Indians were finally granted the federal franchise in 1960. At the same time, governments in these liberal democracies continued with schemes to speed up the integration or assimilation of indigenous peoples. This, then is the context within which native peoples in the 1950s, '60s and '70s began to assert their claims for land rights and special status, and to criticize governments' past and present policies toward indigenous peoples.

III

The various means adopted by native peoples in Canada, Australia and Norway to represent their interests to governments reflect not only the asymmetry and historical particularity of these relations, but also a fundamental divergence of views with respect to their needs and rights. Demands for land claims are part of the long-standing effort on the part of indigenous peoples to achieve greater control over their communities by securing a territorial base. Similarly, efforts to enshrine one or another form of special legal and political status aim to ensure the survival of discreet indigenous communities. Yet nation-states tend to discount land claims as being opportunistic in motive and, furthermore, assert the principle that there should be only a single category of citizenship within a nation. They seem inclined to view their past relations with indigenous peoples as being regrettable—perhaps—but largely irrelevant to the contemporary situation.

Indigenous peoples' increasingly pressing socioeconomic difficulties have received somewhat more sympathetic attention than previously from governments in the West, if not resolution. Since the end of the Second World War these governments have endeavoured—largely in response to growing public sensitivity to these problems—to introduce measures to reduce anomalies of life expectancy, income and educational and living standards between indigenous peoples and other citizens. To this end, native spokesmen, along with academics and bureaucrats, have been invited to advise government bodies.

Aboriginal leaders have gradually come to recognize the inherent limitations of such consultative arrangements and have insisted that they be permitted to initiate consultations with governments and to draw up the agenda for discussions. Their success has led to the development of a variety of formal representational channels between aboriginal communities, representative organizations and governments, a process documented at the national level in Australia and Canada by Weaver (this volume) and at the local level in the Torres Strait Islands by Beckett (this volume).

The growth of organizations at the local, regional and national levels in the 1960s and '70s—whose aims are to represent the interests of indigenous peoples to governments—raised several issues, some of which may be peculiar to liberal democracies. One of these involved the not infrequent practice of funding indigenous peoples' organizations. Ostensibly, the independence of a political organization may be seriously threatened by any financial reliance upon the governments with which it seeks to negotiate. Moreover, even in the case of organizations that do not receive substantial government funding, there is the further question of the basis upon which these bodies are accorded recognition by governments as having a legitimate right to speak and act on behalf of the communities they purport to represent. As Weaver's essay demonstrates, "representivity" constitutes not only one of the prime political values of Western liberal democracies, but also an essential resource that can be strategically either attributed to native organizations or denied by government leaders.

The leaders of native organizations find themselves operating within representational arenas that are governed by the rules of the nation-state. Although they have worked assiduously to discover the procedural means, the inconsistencies in official policies and the institutional divisions that can, with patience and experience, be exploited, they are only too aware of the various levers that can in turn be manipulated by bureaucrats and politicians to contain and control action. The demands involved in endeavouring to bridge the organizational and cultural gap between the indigenous communities and various levels of government are onerous and unrelenting. As well as having to satisfy governments, indigenous leaders, as Feit's essay shows, are also obliged to respect their communities' particular understandings of what constitutes legitimate representation on their behalf.

Participation in different types of consultative and representational structures has given indigenous leaders considerable experience and insight into the workings and assumptions of the institutions of the nation-state. They have learned at first hand just how deeply ingrained are the values of individualism and equality of citizenship. Governments in Canada, Australia and Norway stoutly uphold the principle of human rights and officially deplore the poverty of indigenous peoples, but they are reluctant to entertain the notion of a minority population's possessing special rights by virtue of aboriginal status. Yet, to escape falling victim to the agencies of the welfare state, it has been necessary for indigenous leaders to reject the presumption that their people are simply poor and disadvantaged members of their respective national societies, and to insist upon being recognized and dealt with as indigenous people.

The implications of asserting an indigenous status rather than being deemed members of an ethnic minority or a disadvantaged sector of the population, are twofold. First, insistence upon indigenous status—"We were here first!"—permits the formulation of arguments based on the legal consequences of prior occupancy of a territory. This is not so much an appeal to the laws of aboriginal peoples in opposition to those of liberal democracies, as an appeal based upon major inconsistencies in the historical treatment accorded by imperial, colonial and national legal systems to indigenous peoples, especially with respect to their lands and the taking of these for settlement. The Western legal system has been far from predictable in its recent handling of indigenous peoples' claims. This is because the courts have been dealing in an area clouded with historical ambiguity, an area of law that depends upon long and often contradictory state practice with respect to indigenous peoples and their lands.[6]

Arguments of indigenous status also evoke a moral dimension. Although the paternalistic and racist assumptions that for so long guided Western nations' treatment of indigenous communities are no longer fashionable, the moral premise and cultural distinctions fundamental to relations between indigenous people and the state have not simply disappeared. Instead, an inversion has occurred: indigenous peoples are insisting upon retaining their historically distinct status as an essential means for achieving their aims and improving their situation. Nation-states, nevertheless, are today equally adamant in defending the principle that there should be only a single category of citizenship within a country.

In response, indigenous leaders have developed the tactic of contrasting the past and present treatment of their peoples with other ideals of liberal-democratic societies. This approach has provided indigenous peoples with some surprisingly effective leverage in a number of cases that have involved appeals either to the courts (see Feit's and Sansom's essays, this volume) or to the public (see Paine's and Sanders' essays). Whereas it could be said that the gains registered by indigenous peoples in these cases are relatively minor within the overall scheme of national politics, the point is that these results have often been obtained by appeals to a special status and rights. Such appeals challenge the nation-state's authority by denying fundamental tenets about the presumed equality of citizenship and rights within a society. The demonstrated persistence of indigenous peoples in resisting assimilation and opposing unpopular government initiatives, combined with increasing official recognition of special rights, pose formidable problems for national governments in the future—difficulties of which government leaders are becoming aware.

Governments are also discovering that simply refusing to consider the claims of native peoples can have a quite different effect than one that may have been intended. Historically, relations between indigenous peoples and governments have revolved around a sense of differentiation and opposition of identities and purposes. The traditional means of opposition undertaken by indigenous communities that had been dominated by colonial powers were indirect, largely symbolic and commonly expressed in terms that did not provoke a punitive response from governments; indeed, messages and acts of opposition aimed primarily at members of their own communities were often not even detected, or understood, by government personnel. In contrast, the opposition tactics of today are open and, as often as not, decidedly provocative. The development of political organizations, the issuing of legal challenges and the use of the mass media are all means by which indigenous spokesmen can appeal directly to governments and the public. Moreover, actions that, from a government official's perspective, may constitute an unreasonable demand and elicit a negative response may, from the perspective of the indigenous community, provide fresh evidence of the perfidy of governments and of the community's need to organize behind its leaders. In short, instances both of direct and indirect opposition may serve to heighten the people's sense of their being distinct from other citizens and to reinforce their boundaries.

The political rhetoric that indigenous spokesmen use to support their claims and to express their opposition to government policies and practices exhibits several distinct features. In terms of content, it combines notions of special status and rights with a historical critique of the manner in which past governments have denied them ordinary civil rights. In tactical terms, it is rhetoric that seeks to move governments and publics by what might be termed "the politics of embarrassment." In effect, indigenous leaders endeavour to construct and make relevant a set of moral claims against the nation-state, past and present. What they strike for is the perception on the part of government officials that indigenous claims might be accepted as factual and legitimate by politically significant sectors of the public. Non-native individuals and associations can, as Paine's essay shows, play an essential part in supporting the moral claims constructed by native spokesmen.[7] In this respect, the moral and the symbolic have been transformed into pragmatic means by which indigenous communities in Canada, Australia and Norway can pursue their interests vis-à-vis governments.

Aboriginal peoples' political undertakings are also facilitated by certain disparities of scale between their communities and the nation-state. Relatively few individuals serve as representatives of these numerically small communities. This situation places substantial burdens on the shoulders of individual leaders, but it also provides them with some advantages in dealing with government officials. Leaders at the local and regional levels can stay in close contact with their communities and with each other and are able to share information and coordinate action more quickly and efficiently than disparate government ministries.[8] As well as benefiting from the multiplex relationships within their communities, individual leaders commonly deal with a broad range of government agencies and officials. Thus, in a relatively short period of time they acquire an up-to-date understanding of a wider spectrum of state institutions than does the ordinary citizen or, for that matter, than do most bureaucrats. Indigenous representatives have discovered the diversity of institutions and interests that exist within the modern nation-state and often use it to obtain resources and support from one government agency while actively opposing the activities of another. What these and other factors provide indigenous leaders with is a growing ability to exercise influence and to initiate action within the scope of their communities' relations with the nation-state. The extent of their influence is, of course, largely contingent upon the willingness of the state to permit it to be exercised. But the state within a liberal democracy is not, in practice, all-powerful.

The important questions then are, how do indigenous peoples select their claims, justify their grievances and present their issues? As we have seen, the principal objectives of indigenous peoples in Canada, Australia and Norway have been to achieve greater local control over their communities (see Feit, Beckett and Paine, this volume) and to recodify their status and rights politically and legally within these societies (see Sansom, Weaver and Sanders, this volume). The first aim reflects the extent to which local communities comprise not only political units, but also the locus of cultural identity, economic opportunity and ethnic sanctuary for indigenous peoples. The second objective arises from the difficulty of translating essentially local concerns and identities into the operational format of national and international political arenas. These include both the existing political and representational channels that link indigenous peoples to the nation-state and a variety of other situations and techniques that can be manipulated by native peoples; namely, the innovative use of national and international courts to pursue native land claims and the staging of protests and ethnodramas both locally and supranationally to exert moral pressure upon recalcitrant governments. In practising the politics of embarrassment, native peoples take care to highlight the power differentials that distinguish them from the government bodies and corporations that jeopardize their interests. Attention is also given to generating sympathy and support among interested non-native groups and individuals both at home and abroad.

These and other political approaches developed by indigenous leaders hardly rival the powers of the nation-state; however, used skilfully they have influenced governments in Canada, Australia and Norway. In comparison with electoral politics, these are rather marginal and vulnerable political pursuits that exploit subtle differences of political micro-cultures and competing structural interests within the nation-state. Large interest groups within these countries employ their numerical (in terms of voters) or financial power to force government to respond to their demands. Lacking such resources, minority indigenous peoples have had to adopt a more patient approach and to demonstrate the persistence and ingenuity typical of hunter-gatherers in making the most of opportunities others might deem nonviable.

Another significant aspect of the contemporary political situation of indigenous peoples in these countries is the expectation on the part of governments that native representatives ought to speak on behalf of a united and essentially undifferentiated constituency. Whereas this may be a criterion of legitimate representation within liberal democracies, it hardly corresponds to the realities of indigenous communities. In fact, national indigenous populations are made up of many small communities spread over large areas, and they may be linguistically and culturally distinct from one another. Historical processes of settlement of their lands and the effects of government assimilation programs have been experienced at different times and in varying ways by these communities. Moreover, in all three countries there is an increasing number of individuals of indigenous ancestry living in urban centres whose links to communities may be becoming tenuous, but who, nonetheless, must cope with the stigma that their identity bears in the view of the majority population. All of these factors have served to exacerbate cultural, economic and geographical differences between native peoples within a nation-state.

The public expression of such differences can raise serious difficulties for native spokesmen seeking to make representations to governments. For instance, indigenous peoples' interests in land claims tend to be highly localized, since those who depend upon the land (or water) for a significant proportion of their livelihood are usually a minority among indigenous populations. The actions of rival native spokesmen who may dispute or simply refuse to support such claims may, as both Sansom's and Paine's essays illustrate, permit government to question just how representative these claims are.

To resolve inherent problems of divisiveness and factionalism, native leaders must ensure that local and particular interests are balanced by a broader set of concerns that will tend to unite rather than to distinguish the various communities they represent. What all sectors of a national indigenous population have in common are the majority society and the nation-state; a common sense of grievance vis-à-vis the attitudes and actions of non-native citizens and governments can provide a powerful means of mobilizing an indigenous constituency beyond the local level.[9] Symbolic opposition directed against the state may thus serve the pragmatic organizational purpose of creating a community of interests and an overarching indigenous identity that can be employed —if only defensively—to support particular claims. Although Paine shows that such an outcome is by no means a certainty, the general point is that the other side of a politics of embarrassment aimed at the state and at non-indigenes is a politics of grievance conducted within the indigenous sector in order to inhibit and control factionalism.

IV

Two other preliminary matters remain to be considered. One involves the development of the concept of a Fourth World of minority indigenous peoples and the difficulties of determining who, according to what criteria, ought to be included in this category. Since this entails more than simply defining one's terms, discussion of it will be deferred for the moment. The other matter concerns the nature and significance of supranational strategies and cooperation among Fourth World peoples.

The very notion of supranational action by minority and indigenous peoples is, on the face of it, paradoxical. These are not multinational corporations with portable business interests nor interchangeable technocrats who can be relocated around the world at a moment's notice; these are communities that are distinguished from others by their members' commitment to particular localities and ways of life. And yet, native peoples in Canada, Australia and Norway have, in the last decade, become politically active at the international level and have formed bodies such as the World Council of Indigenous Peoples. Why are these supranational undertakings being pursued? How can indigenous peoples from different nations—indeed, from different continents—advance their particular interests by cooperating with one another?

Appeals made to international bodies, such as the agencies and commissions of the United Nations and to audiences in other countries, represent an extension of the kind of indigenous people/state politics that has developed within liberal-democratic nation-states. Supranational activity offers indigenous peoples an additional source of potential influence and leverage with which to advance their particular claims and interests; international audiences and tribunals that are asked to hear and judge for themselves the legitimacy of native peoples' claims may provide a new set of 'friends' who could exert some pressure on national governments merely by publicly expressing circumspect support for indigenous peoples' aspirations. Governments in Canada, Australia and Norway are sensitive about their image in the international community, especially at a time when human rights have become such a charged political issue. Although governments have little to fear from international bodies beyond possible embarrassment, they are clearly anxious to avoid, wherever possible, international discussion of what they regard as domestic, national concerns. Thus, during the 1981 tour of Europe by Canadian Indians opposing repatriation of the Canadian constitution, Canadian diplomats in France, West Germany, Belgium, and Britain worked to mitigate the effects of the generally sympathetic hearing received by the Indians. Evidently, the news coverage that Indian spokesmen initiated in Europe *was* monitored closely in Ottawa. The founding of organizations such as the WCIP and the International Indian Treaty Council (formed in the 1970s by the American Indian Movement) by indigenous peoples from different countries was a comparatively recent development which awaited the recognition of similarities between indigenous peoples in different nation-states. Having discovered, in their travels, the common opposition of interests and of identities between native peoples and nation-states, political innovators such as George Manuel (see Manuel and Posluns 1974), former president of the National Indian Brotherhood of Canada, returned to promote the adoption of a broader frame of reference and the more general category of Fourth World. This in turn has complemented efforts to recodify the status of indigenous peoples within individual countries.

These types of political endeavours and the general eschewing of violence as a political means stand in sharp contrast to the activities of various groups representing individual "nations without states" in Europe (cf. Foster 1980) and reflect basic structural distinctions between the two types of minorities. Minority indigenous peoples are seldom territorially isolable in any effective sense. Unlike groups such as the Basques in Spain, indigenous minorities in Canada, Australia and Norway are comprised of small, geographically dispersed groups seeking neither to opt out of existing nation-states, nor to set up their own countries, but rather to acquire greater local control within existing national frameworks (see Asch 1984). Aboriginal peoples are, in consequence, constrained to operate *within* the bounds of the nation-state.[10] Activity at the international level offers another means of creating space for manoeuvering within the confines of national political systems.

The extent to which supranational activity provides a viable political strategem for minority indigenous peoples will, nonetheless, depend upon the nature of the nation-state within which they are located. Canada, Australia and Norway represent a distinctive type of national setting; they are part of a recognized block of western European and North American nations that, along with countries such as New Zealand, belong to the highly developed, capitalist, liberal-democratic First World. The political realities that face minority indigenous peoples either in socialist block countries such as the U.S.S.R. and China or in Third World countries such as Guatemala, Brazil or the Philippines, are likely to differ substantially from those discussed in this volume. At the same time, the influence exercised by the First World over Third World affairs—as evidenced by the World Bank's recent insistence upon some form of settlement of indigenous land claims as a condition for the granting of loans for developing territories in the Amazon basin—opens the possibility of supranational political activities on the part of South and Central American members of the WCIP.

Future comparisons of minority indigenous peoples in the First, Second and Third Worlds will no doubt reveal just how extensively their aspirations and activities have been shaped by the particular economic structure and political ethos of their national settings. Even in the case of Canada, Australia and Norway, countries that have much in common when contrasted with less liberal regimes, there are characteristic national features that distinguish the administration of indigenous affairs between them: Australian administrative systems tend toward decentralization and multiplicity compared with those in Canada, whereas Norwegian politicians tend to assume a national cultural homogeneity that is obviously absent in Canada. Notwithstanding differences between countries, we may also discover certain striking parallels in the situations of minority indigenous peoples, regardless of their national surroundings. The persistent oppositional processes by which indigenous peoples in these countries distinguish themselves from the majority population (cf. Spicer 1971) may prove to be remarkably widespread among aboriginal peoples and similar in purpose, if not always in form and particulars.

Will subsequent comparisons of indigenous peoples/state relations in various national settings be aided or impeded by the adoption of a category of a Fourth World of minority indigenous peoples? This will depend upon the manner in which the term is understood and used. Although it has already been employed to refer to a range of different phenomena,[11] the most common anthropological usage of "Fourth World" is that of Manuel and Posluns (1974): peoples who have special non-technical, nonmodern exploitative relations to the lands which they still inhabit and who are disenfranchised by the nations within which they live.[12] Adopting this definition, Graburn (1981:68) includes in the "IV World" the Indians and Inuit of North America, the Lapps (Saami) of Scandinavia, some Africans, the Ainu of Japan, Maori of New Zealand, Aborigines of Australia, tribal groups in India, some of the peoples of New Guinea, the Indian peoples of Central and South America, and indigenous minorities within the U.S.S.R. He notes that the inclusion of the Welsh and other "nations without states" has also been suggested.

This typological approach to defining the Fourth World raises questions about the analytical utility of such a concept, especially in view of the existence of sharply varying uses of the term. What, it is asked, is paramount about this particular usage: indigenous status (i.e., nationality, in Marxian terms) or class factors such as economic exploitation? Furthermore, how can a Fourth World be said to exist if it is not recognized by more than a handful of activists among the populations who are said to swell its ranks? On these and other bases it could be argued that the notion of a Fourth World and the question of which peoples ought to be included in it, and for what reasons, will rapidly become as problematic and misleading as has become the concept of Third World.

Yet, as Worsley has noted (1967:283) with respect to the notion of a Third World,[13] the definition and composition of such a term are always situational and complex, for this is an operational rather than an analytical term. Anthropologists will do well to remember that in the first instance, the notion of a Fourth World was popularized by native leaders (especially George Manuel) and is still being circulated by them for validation. It has not yet been either successfully launched or discredited. Our task should be to examine the rhetorical and practical use made of the term, the characteristics of the people employing it and the contexts within which it is being used, rather than simply to assume its utility and appropriate it as an analytical category.[14]

In asserting their own identities within national settings, indigenous peoples have embarked upon a campaign for recodification of their status and rights—a campaign that has now been extended supranationally through Fourth World political identification activity. To put it another way, the Saami, when they were Lapps, did not recognize the Inuit when they were Eskimos.[15] To explain how the Lapps have 'become' Saami and how even *some* Indians, Torres Straits Islanders and Aborigines have also come to speak of themselves as "Fourth Worlders" is to explain, in part, the processes central to the political transformation that has been occurring in indigenous peoples/state relations. The notion of a Fourth World, like the assertion of indigenous status, denies the assumptions of the nation-state. It declares that indigenous peoples are no longer merely minorities within liberal democracies. They are members of these nation-states, but they will no longer accept being recognized as anything less than distinctive members with special rights. As Fourth Worlders, they escape the image of being known either as members of groups defined by their poverty or as just another ethnic group. The political image of the Fourth World rejects these images and asserts a supranational character for these peoples; in effect, they seek to go over the head of the nation-state and to claim recognition at a higher level of political organization.

Understandably, then, the definition and composition of the Fourth World have become central political organizational concerns for the WCIP. At the founding conference of the WCIP, held in Port Alberni, British Columbia, in 1975 (see Sanders 1977), Canadian Indians, Australian Aborigines and Norwegian Saami quickly discovered that their experience of Western, liberal-democratic, industrialized nation-states was roughly equivalent. The experience of Indian delegates from Latin America was found to be remarkably uniform but, in many respects, quite different from that of indigenous peoples within liberal democracies. Hence, from the outset a major internal problem for the WCIP has been to bridge the experience and concerns of these two divergent groups. This accounts for the reluctance of the WCIP to admit into its membership peoples from other regions such as Asia or the Middle East, or African liberation movements whose priorities, it was felt, would rapidly submerge the less dramatic concerns of indigenous peoples in other countries. To begin with, at least, the WCIP would seek to work out relations between its two constituent groups before proceeding further.[16]

In view of these types of considerations, we are perhaps best advised to treat the Fourth World as a concept produced by a particular historical moment, as an artifact of the form of welfare capitalism that developed in Western liberal democracies following the Second World War. The similar histories of relationships between indigenous peoples and nation-states in countries such as Canada, Australia and Norway have provided a comparative framework that has been recognized not only by indigenous peoples and anthropologists, but also by government administrators, lawyers and even multinational corporations.[17] Indeed, one might even surmise that the Fourth World has been called into existence as much by the policies and procedures of governments as by the innovative actions of indigenous leaders. The development of a distinctive Fourth World category seems to reflect the same processes by which minority indigenous peoples have been shaped within their respective countries and subsequently identified in terms of their colonial histories. This has been

recognized by the WCIP, for in contrast to Manuel's (1974) definition of Fourth World peoples (cited above), it adopted a definition of indigenous peoples that jettisons as a criterion the continuation of archaic cultures and emphasizes instead their status as
previous occupants of the lands taken by colonizing nation-states
and as peoples who lack self-determination.[18]

There is, therefore, little need for anthropologists to agonize
over the existence or the definitional adequacy of Fourth World.
It has been proclaimed by indigenous leaders and is currently being used. It is not a term that should be either discarded or
employed uncritically as an analytical category. Instead, we should
be concerned with the practical use made of it by others, bearing
in mind the possibility that this recent concept, and the activities
constructed in terms of it, may just as quickly change or disappear in the future. The people who today describe themselves as
being of the Fourth world are not the same as their forefathers
were forty or a hundred years ago; they, like their ancestors, are
the products of historical processes. To our mind the more interesting question is not, then, who ought to be classified as belonging to the Fourth World but rather, what is being accomplished
by whom by means of this operational category?

The processes revealed by such investigations will, it is hoped,
have significance beyond the particular Fourth World situations
and peoples dealt with in this volume. The political processes that
are occurring under the banner of the Fourth World may well be
similar to the processes found in relationships and situations other
than those involving indigenous peoples and the nation-state. In
this sense, our examinations of various aspects of Fourth World
politics are intended to be neither definitive nor exhaustive, but
preliminary and open-ended.

Notes

1. Evidence of this is available in recent publications dealing with in-
    digenous peoples in each of the three countries we are concerned with
    here (e.g., Brody 1975; Eidheim 1971; Howard 1978, 1982; Paine 1977,
    1982). Moreover, recent studies of ''nations'' and ''states'' in Europe
    (Grillo 1980) and of social organization in British rural cultures (Cohen
    1982) deal with analytical problems of broadly similar order.
2. Bateson, as cited in Brand (1973:37).
3. A copy of the Dene Declaration is reprinted in Elliott (1983:32-33).

4. As just two examples out of a literature that is becoming vast and increasingly specialized, see Panitch (1977) and Grayson (1980). For an interesting discussion of relations between the state and indigenous peoples in the United States see Bee and Gingerich (1977).

5. See Spicer (1971) and Castile and Kushner (1981) for discussions of cultural persistence and strategies of opposition.

6. The Calder Case in British Columbia (Sanders 1973) provides an example of legal legitimation of Indian land claims' preparing the way for a greater degree of political legitimacy. See also Sanders (1983).

7. For a list of support groups in different countries that assist indigenous people's organizations, see Bodley (1982:218-20).

8. See Dyck (1983) for a Canadian example. I recognize, however, that this is not an invariable outcome.

9. See Dyck (1983) for further development of this theme.

10. Even the Dene Declaration calls for independence and self-determination *within* the country of Canada (cf. Elliott, 1983:32-33).

11. As Graburn (1981, 67ff.) notes, the term Fourth World has been variously applied to victims of group oppression, economically indigent or ''basket case'' nations and to the imprisoned, the poor, the sick, the elderly and underaged in America. McCall (1980) applies the term to ''nations without states.'' Worsley (1967:283) reports a distinctive use of the term by the Chinese.

12. As summarized by Graburn (1981:67).

13. Worsley also noted that, ''Such oscillations of meaning are not by any means mere academic definition-spinning; they are the stuff of everyday international relations'' (1967:285).

14. I thank Beverly Gartrell for making this point.

15. I am indebted to Robert Paine for this formulation of the point.

16. These groups are broken down further into five regions within the WCIP: North America, Central America, South America, Northern Europe, and the South Pacific (Australia and New Zealand).

17. For example, the Amax Corporation has recently been involved in disputes concerning the impingement of its mining developments on aboriginal land rights both in Western Australia and British Columbia.

18. Note the shifts in the definition of indigenous peoples from Manuel and Posluns (1974) to the definition incorporated into the Charter of the WCIP in 1975:

> Indigenous peoples shall be people living in countries which have a population composed of different ethnic or racial groups who are descendants of the earliest populations which survive in the area, and who do not, as a group, control the national government of the countries within which they live (Sanders 1982:2).

And compare these definitions to the draft International Covenant on the Rights of Indigenous Peoples, adopted for discussion at the Third General Assembly of the WCIP at Canberra in 1981:

> The term Indigenous Peoples refers to a people (a) who lived in a territory before the entry of a colonizing population, which colonizing population has created a new state or states to include the territory, and (b) who continue to live as a people in the territory and who do not control the national government of the state or states within which they live (*ibid.*:2-3).

Legitimation and Autonomy in James Bay Cree Responses to Hydro-Electric Development

2

HARVEY A. FEIT

INTRODUCTION

This paper examines analytical and methodological problems encountered in evaluating Fourth World political processes, specifically; in analysing the autonomy of representations from the Fourth World.[1]

Because indigenous peoples have found themselves increasingly threatened by intrusions of nation-states and international economic interests, their participation in protests, political and legal mobilizations and complex organizations has also increased in order to oppose these intrusions. As Fourth World political opposition accelerates, one demand put upon anthropologists is to evaluate these experiences so that others—indigenous peoples, administrators, politicians, and social scientists—will be informed about the consequences and effectiveness of the strategies of opposition and resistance.

In order to meet this demand, anthropologists have turned to the analytical tools of political and administrative sciences, and economics. These tools have clearly strengthened the analysis (e.g., Weaver 1981; SSDCC 1982), but in the process there has been a tendency to omit the traditional anthropological emphasis on local-level processes, cultural/symbolic factors and traditional/historical contexts. In scaling their tools to the complex levels of national, political and economic structures, anthropologists have often lost sight of the local-level actions that shape micro-level responses to macro-level interventions and contribute to the final determination of events (Feit 1982).

A case in point are the evaluations that have been made of the James Bay Cree responses to hydro-electric development in northern Quebec. In November, 1975, the James Bay Cree and Inuit of northern Quebec signed the first modern aboriginal claims settlement in Canada—the James Bay and Northern Quebec Agreement (JBNQA). Their leaders called it "a great victory." In the two months that followed, ratification meetings in the Cree villages demonstrated an overwhelming predominance of opinion in favour of the agreement.[2]

Yet, outside the Cree communities the agreement was widely condemned by natives and non-natives, alike. Native opposition, which took the form of condemning the Cree for signing the agreement, was motivated in part by the intention of the federal government to use the agreement as a model for other native claims (Feit 1980). The most common charge was that Cree representational processes had failed: the agreement was a sellout by the native leadership, or it was a sellout by the non-native advisers who controlled their clients, or it was a trick by the government negotiators who duped the native peoples.[3] The assumption that representation broke down is still widespread, and probably still dominates perceptions of those events, although present-day views are often more tempered and thoughtful than the original versions.

The most extensive account of James Bay Cree representational processes is *Negotiating a Way of Life* (LaRusic et al. 1979), which attempts to evaluate the initial James Bay Cree experience with the administrative structures arising from the agreement. Among the key questions raised by the authors is the role the new Cree regional leadership has in its own policy-making and administrative structures, and in particular the leaders' position vis-à-vis the consultants. They argue that in the post-agreement period, evidence suggests that the Cree control the more routine aspects of administration, but that the key decisions and policy-making power reside "under the determining influence of consultants in general, and legal advisers in particular." This situation is attributed to necessity (pp. 20-21, 32, 47f., 51), to consultants' brokerage interests (pp. 38, 51, 53), and to the history of the court case and negotiations (pp. 10, 20-21, 42, 46).[4]

LaRusic et al. argue that the representational processes by which the Cree opposed the hydro-electric development, negotiated a land claim settlement, and established a regional Cree government were ineffective, in the sense that they did not reduce dependency on external agencies or individuals. Their argument, in summary, is that dependence was transferred from government agencies to individual and corporate consultants.

They claim further that before the court hearings commenced in December, 1972, the Cree did not have independent political or administrative structures that could be called "their own." The authors state that the court proceedings demanded the involvement of consultants and a high level of organizational skill and sophistication. "Band councils were inefficient, cumbersome and controlled by Indian Affairs . . ." and so they "could not have been viewed as useful to the lawyers," and no other organization such as the provincial Indians of Quebec Association (IQA) was suitable (p. 46). A new organization, the James Bay Task Force, was therefore set up to fill the need. This was initially "a structure where the managerial and directive positions were largely assumed by consultants" (p. 47). The authors describe the role of this organization in shaping Cree leadership and policy as follows:

> The Cree leadership which emerged through their work in this organization had as their principal role that of a liaison between the scattered Cree communities and the consultants who needed rapid and efficient access to the body of data available only at the community level. Initially, the Cree had only to express to the public a general demand that the James Bay Project be stopped; the role of the consultants was to choose the grounds upon which the battle would be fought (p. 47).

Lawyer Douglas Sanders reaches similar conclusions in his account of Cree mobilization against the James Bay hydro-electric project and the role of non-Cree lawyers. Sanders notes that when the Cree appeared in court, their initial position was to stop the project completely. He infers that the lawyers' aim was to establish a bargaining position, and he bases this on the following press quote of one of the lawyers advising the Cree: "This is the most difficult thing I will have to say to you, but when the white man wants something he takes it" (Sanders n.d.:13). Sanders concludes that the lawyers had to convince their Cree clients that the project could not be stopped, and that therefore the Cree had to abandon a position of complete opposition to the project. Thus, when the Cree entered into final negotiations in early 1974, "they were following legal advice to accept a negotiated settlement . . . . There was a young leadership for the Inuit and the Cree who were clearly involved throughout the process. But one only has to start to read the final agreement to know, without question, that it is the product of lawyers. It is not a document which could be communicated in its detail to northern Indians and Inuit" (n.d.:19).

The problems that I see in the analyses of Sanders and of LaRusic and his associates rest on a failure to examine data that traditionally have been the core of anthropological analysis and to link these to the newer forms of macro-political and economic analysis. Sanders' analysis, for example, depends on inferring the lawyers' motives from press reports of their statements, and the views of Cree villagers from formal statements made in a courtroom setting. His interpretation of limited local-level participation is based not upon an account of the process of reaching the agreement, but upon the highly legalistic text of the agreement, which itself was the result of a strategic decision to express the outcomes of negotiation processes in formal legal drafts. The lack of data on community-level processes makes his overall interpretation fragile at best. Thus, whether the lawyers' advice was consistent with community opinion or not, whether it was influential and whether there was a shift in community goals remain essentially undocumented.[5]

The root of the analytical problem inherent in these assessments of autonomy is the failure to distinguish between two distinct perspectives on Fourth World representation: the relationships of the representatives to those whom they represent, and to those to whom representations are made. These two perspectives highlight different dimensions of the representation processes; the former emphasizes the legitimacy of the representation, whereas the latter emphasizes the effectiveness of the representation. LaRusic et al. discuss extensively the relationship between representors and those to whom representations are addressed, be they judges, politicians, bureaucrats, or consultants. According to them, the need for these representations to be effective placed real constraints on Cree leadership, and it was this need that determined the predominance of consultants.

The second dimension of representation, namely the legitimacy of the representation as determined in the relationship of the representors to the represented, receives almost no attention in their analysis of this period.[6] Because this dimension was neglected, their analysis of Cree autonomy is incomplete and misleading. The failure to consider community/leader relations strengthens their conclusions that the emerging Cree leadership was dominated by its consultants.

In this paper I question the claim that James Bay Cree responses to the hydro-electric project were determined by advisers, and that these advisers set the stage for the development of a regional leadership, structures and organizations that were dependent on consultants. In particular, I look at the initial opposition to the hydro-electric scheme from May, 1971, to May, 1972.[7] The Cree began mobilizing opposition to the development in May, 1971, when the Quebec government refused to take their interests into account in the design of the hydro-electric project and in the planning for the development of the region. In late 1972, the Cree sought an interlocutory injunction to stop all work on the project, utilizing a number of fortunate anomalies in Canadian law. They won the court case in late 1973, and although appeals immediately delayed implementation of the court ruling, the stage was set for negotiations. Although construction continued, putting pressure on the Cree, the disruptions caused by the appeals made potential investors wary of continuing to fund the project, which put pressure on the government. Negotiations between the James Bay Cree, the Inuit of northern Quebec and the governments of Quebec and Canada began early in 1974 and continued for nearly two years. They covered modifications to the project; the protection and development of the indigenous society, culture and economy; allocations of rights to the territory and its resources; indigenous control of Cree communities, services and organizations; indigenous participation in the government, administration and development of the territory; financial benefits; and new structures of articulation between indigenous peoples and senior governments. These negotiations culminated in the JBNQA of 1975.

This paper examines the historical and cultural context in which the opposition was organized, and shows how the trends initiated during the first year of political mobilization were not in the direction of increased dependency.

CULTURAL AND HISTORICAL PERSPECTIVES ON CREE
LEADERSHIP

Anthropological discussions of traditional leadership and authority
in contemporary Cree and eastern Algonquian societies have emphasized a consistent and pervasive set of themes: the communal
and egalitarian principles on which the society is organized; the
dependence of a leader's actions on already existing consensus;
authority based on influence, usually won by demonstrating ex-
ceptional competence; the short-term duration of leadership; and
the ability of followers to change allegiances if and when a leader's
performance did not conform to values. Although I do not disagree
with this analysis, I believe it simplifies the dynamics between communal interests and leadership initiatives in Cree society, and it
suggests that leadership was somewhat more transitory and
unstructured than my data indicate.

To understand Cree models of leadership and authority it is
necessary to examine day to day leadership patterns *within* the community. The most widespread form of formal leadership in Cree
society occurs in hunting groups that live together from three to
nine months a year in bush camps. It is this form that is crucial
to our understanding of Cree leadership in general.

Hunting-group formation and leadership are influenced by
rights to defined areas of land called "hunting territories." The
Cree region of Quebec is divided into approximately 300 con-
tiguous tracts of land, each ranging from approximately 230 km^2
to several thousand km^2 and together averaging about 1200 km^2.
Access to, and use of, the hunting territories are defined by a
system of rights and obligations encompassing various categories
of individuals.

Each hunting territory is said to be "owned" by an individual
"boss," whom I shall call a steward. Although the term for the
relationship of stewards to their hunting territories is "ownership"
in English, the relationship is not one of ownership by Western
standards. The steward appoints his successor, but he cannot
dispose of the land by sale or transfer. The Cree say that land was
created by God and can neither be owned nor disposed of in the
way in which Euro-Canadians are accustomed. The steward is
therefore the temporary custodian of a portion of the community
and kin-group patrimony. He is under obligation to see that the

land is used in ways that sustain its productivity, and to protect the land for posterity.

The steward exercises a broad mandate and considerable authority vis-à-vis his contemporaries. He has the right to decide whether the hunting territory is to be used for an extended period of time, that is, whether it can be harvested intensively and, to some extent, by whom. He can decide which and how much of the big-game species can be hunted, as well as where and when. Spiritual sanctions support his authority, and animal spirits communicate their willingness to be caught through dreams and signs.

In practice, a steward exercises much less day-to-day direction than this formal account implies; allowing a hunter to use a hunting territory often carries an implicit or explicit agreement on the overall size of the harvest and the area to be harvested, and no more direction than that may be required. Often, direction takes the form of an impersonal commentary on a situation, or a suggestion in accordance with the ideology of egalitarianism.

Other rights pertain. Hunters acquire a long-term right of access to one or more hunting territories in which they have grown up or hunted over an extended period of time. If a steward decides a certain hunting territory will be used, then those people with a long-term right of access to it may use it without having to be invited to join the steward's hunting group. Their use of it, however, is still subject to the steward's supervision. In addition, a hunter may be granted the privilege of using a hunting territory for a specified period of time—for several months or for a hunting season.

An individual occupies the role of steward for several decades, typically between the ages of 40 to 60. Thus, leadership is exercised by a relatively stable and limited number of individuals. There are about 300 stewards in the James Bay Cree area among a population of 8,600.

The authority of stewards derives not only from being a skilled hunter, but also by having direct control of information and access to intensively used resources. This means that a limited number of men exercise considerable authority over the activities of others in the name of the community and in the common interest, as well as the interests of themselves and their immediate kin. I would emphasize that both community and kin-group interests must be harmonized so that neither will be served exclusively.

The steward's authority is, in principle, sanctioned spiritually, which while making it powerful also obligates him to protect and improve the resources, and to share them with the community. If these values are not respected, the spirits and the animals will not provide a good hunt. Stewards are generally expected to accommodate hunters without land, and in so doing they reinforce egalitarian and communal values. When a steward uses his authority according to Cree values, he wins public approval and prestige. The system works most of the time.

The key elements of this system are the following: (1) a communal and inalienable interest in the use and protection of all land resources; (2) the existence of a limited and relatively stable set of leaders whose detailed knowledge of, and spiritual ties to, particular tracts of land are the basis of their authority over those lands; (3) community expectation, sanction and encouragement of leaders to exercise authority with a view to protect communal and family needs and intergenerational continuity. This model coincides fundamentally with the classical accounts of Cree leadership (e.g., Rogers 1965), but it does differ in its emphasis on the resources that leaders control and the durability of their status, and in specifying a more complex means by which leadership is exercised and constrained.[8]

The dynamics of traditional leadership are also more complex than has often been suggested. The power of leaders does not simply decline because they lose followers. When they lose support they still retain control of important resources, and many people will not, or cannot, cut their ties and join other leaders. It is easier for those who depend on invitations to cut ties. The more serious challengers of a steward's authority are his close kinsmen and associates who have primary rights of access to his territory. When leadership breaks down, they are likely to engage in a kind of civil disobedience: they begin challenging publicly the steward's management. If this fails to bring about accommodation, they may make parallel claims of ownership to part or all of the territory, claiming their personal ties to his predecessor and to the spirits as their authority. Calling on public opinion for support, they may declare that 'ownership' should be split or transferred, since it had been wrongly assigned. If such conflicts are not quickly resolved, the challengers start to use the land under their own direction with informal public sanction, thus undermining an errant steward's authority.

From the present perspective, the above model of leadership is significant when applied to the role of the new leadership whose mandate encompasses external arenas, resources and action. The new leaders are the chief and band council and the regional leaders.

Chiefs and band councils came into being during the 1930s and '40s in various Cree communities when governments set up administration of the region, and when the first band membership lists were prepared by the federal Indian Affairs Branch. Chiefs and councils appear to have existed for a decade or more prior to this in some communities; they resembled the earlier trading chiefs appointed by the Hudson's Bay Company (HBC) during the previous two centuries (cf. Morantz 1982). Government recognition of chiefs and councils brought them officially under the Indian Act. This national legislation authorized the council to act for the band as a whole, but at the same time delegated considerable authority to the federal minister of Indian Affairs. This distribution of authority did not reflect Cree political culture. With regard to the band council, this was not usually a problem because, as I indicate below, its authority was restricted. However, the authority of the minister was a source of conflict.

My limited data on these early leaders indicate that they were generally chosen from among the elders of the various extended kin groups, who were appointed by the Hudson's Bay Company trader and/or the resident missionary (cf. Kerr 1950; Honigmann 1962; Rogers 1965). Later, the Indian government agents, who were often former HBC traders, tended to use these same elders for the tasks of identifying band members, receiving requests for aid and distributing social assistance, just as the HBC had done before. When elections were held, the same men used by the agents were often elected to positions of chief and band council. Sometimes the agents themselves chose the candidates or intervened to disallow election results with which they were dissatisfied (cf. Pothier 1967; Najmi n.d.).

Within the community, elected leaders had legitimacy because most had already been active leaders in the community. Some were

stewards or hunting group leaders; others were elders who organized community-wide activities and church ceremonies and mediated
social conflicts (Preston 1971; Kupferer 1966; Honigmann 1962).
However, election to titled positions was sometimes ridiculed and
on occasion, highly respected individuals refused such a position
(Kerr 1950; Preston 1971).

The main responsibility of this elected leadership was to represent the community to external agencies—primarily the government but also the church and fur traders. In this respect, the expectations and legal mandates of the elected chiefs conflicted with
their structural position. LaRusic (1972) indicates that the elected
chief and council had limited knowledge of the outside world and
were therefore dependent for information and resources on the
very persons to whom they made representation: the Indian agent,
the minister and trader, all three of whom shared certain interests
and exchanged personnel. The chiefs therefore had limited information and means for making demands on and responding to external agencies (e.g., Preston 1971).

As a result, by the 1960s the band council was, with occasional
exceptions, simply the recipient of benefits and services decided
on by external agencies. As such, the role of the chief and band
council was to serve the needs of the external agencies by, for example, approving programs and services offered by government
departments. Thus, during the 1960s, when the road and rail networks were opened in the southern Waswanipi area, when mining towns were built, when forestry operations were begun, and
when the Hudson's Bay Company closed its trading post on the
newly granted reserve, the band council had no response to the
decisions (LaRusic 1972).[9]

This pattern was not easily accepted by the chiefs, many of
whom resented their dependence on non-natives and sometimes
expressed their frustration (Kupferer 1966; Preston 1971). By the
mid-1960s, therefore, the chiefs and band councils in several Cree
communities began initiating responses and demands (LaRusic
1972; Kupferer 1966; Preston 1968, 1971; Hyman 1971; Robbins
1967; Barger 1980). The impetus for change appears to have been
the return to communities of young adults who, during the 1950s
and '60s, acquired a higher level of education than any generation before them. As external influences on community life increas-

ed, this generation began to be elected to positions of chief and council because of a widely expressed need to have representatives who could speak English (and occasionally French), who were not reticent with whites, and who understood the ways of governments. This trend continued for a decade so that eventually traditional leaders shared official positions with the younger men (LaRusic 1972; Barger 1980).

Also significant during this period was the emergence of a provincial Indian association in 1967, under the stimulus of the Department of Indian Affairs (LaRusic 1972). Despite its origins, the Indians of Quebec Association (IQA) provided a forum in which chiefs and councillors from bands across the province could get together and learn by sharing their experiences. For younger leaders from the more northerly, isolated bands, the contact with southern Indian leaders broadened their knowledge in dealing with outside agencies and provides a basis of comparing southern and northern reserves (cf., LaRusic 1972). Because the IQA had a small staff and limited organizational and financial resources at this time, only occasionally was it able to help band leaders, but the effect of its bringing together Indian leaders was pervasive (LaRusic 1972; Barger 1980).[10]

As a result of the above developments, not only was there a steady increase in political action, but also an elaboration of political ideas. Kenneth Barger, working in Great Whale River, identified three themes underlying Cree concerns in their discussions with government officials in the late 1960s: self-government, claims to the land and the preservation of their culture. In addition, the Cree demanded increased government services and socioeconomic development (Barger 1980:202-03). The form of expression that these demands took derived in part from outside contacts, but the concerns themselves were deeply rooted in community values. The new leaders were expressing community-wide concerns within the framework of Indian rights, demands that were becoming known in the wider Canadian society. Political activism united both young and old, and it opened up communications of a new order—initiated by the bands rather than the government. But it did not guarantee success.[11]

The new band leaders inherited the same broad mandate, based on autonomy, as that exercised by stewards. They, also, were expected to exercise this autonomy to serve community interests. The nature of their authority was modified by the new conditions, but in important respects it remained consistent with that of stewardship. Band leaders, for example, had the authority to allocate resources; and those who were closest to a leader were often the first and the most vocal in expressing discontent. A form of civil resistance occurred, for example, when close kinsmen opposed the re-election of a leader, or when community members criticized a leader in front of the government authorities with whom the leader had to maintain credibility. In addition, just as stewards could not alienate land, so too the new leaders could not alienate or control land or land-based resources; they were expected to refer such matters to the community. The important point here is that the new leaders added a leadership structure to community organization without supplanting the old form of community leadership. The new leaders thus inherited a relationship not only to the community at large, but also to the stewards, who retained their authority over land and resources. The stewards, elders and chiefs became interdependent leaderships. Such developments resulted in some control being retained by the community over its leaders and in a leadership whose exercise of autonomy was constrained by community interests. In the period from 1971 to at least 1980, the relatively stable leadership reflected the general success of this model from the perspective of both band members and leaders.

The hydro-electric project strengthened this interdependence because it made clear to the elders and the stewards that the land and resources were threatened by the intervention of Euro-Canadians whom they could neither influence nor communicate with effectively, unless they worked in cooperation with the younger leaders. Furthermore, credible opposition to the hydro scheme required that younger leaders be able to demonstrate the support of the elder hunters, whose lives would be most affected. The younger leaders also depended on being able to draw on the elders' knowledge of the land and of Cree history in order to assess the long-term implications of the project for native/white relations in the region.

THE LEGITIMACY DIMENSION—ESTABLISHING REGIONAL REPRESENTATION

Self-Selection of the Emerging Regional Leadership

When, on 30 April 1971, Premier Robert Bourassa announced that the James Bay hydro-electric scheme would begin immediately, he had neither consulted Indian representatives nor set in motion any consultation process.

A collective Cree response to the announcement was not immediate. There were as yet no leaders with a regional mandate to speak for the James Bay Cree as a whole and so a unified response was impossible. Initial reactions therefore came from various levels, both band and provincial. Billy Diamond, the chief of Rupert House, said he would fight the project, in a *Montreal Star* interview a few days after the premier's announcement. His objections were many: the project would have an impact on Cree hunting; it was to be built on Indian land; there had been no consultation; the jobs created by the project would not last; and so on. He went on to say, "I think it's the feeling of all the chiefs on James Bay that the Indians will get nothing out of this project and will be ruined completely" (*Montreal Star* 4 May 1971). He said he wanted the help of all Quebec Indians, who should fight for their rights. And he indicated that he wanted to stall the project or get compensation for Indians whose land and livelihood will be affected. Other chiefs began calling band meetings in May to discuss with their band members the responses they should make, although official details of the project were as yet unknown.

At the provincial level, the IQA also took an immediate stand against the project. Chief Max Gros-Louis, secretary-treasurer of the IQA, was quoted as saying that Quebec Indians would block the James Bay project and go before the courts if necessary (*Montreal Star* 4 May 1971). The association also had legal counsel, James O'Reilly, send a letter to the federal minister of Indian Affairs, stating that it was essential that the territorial rights of Indians be dealt with immediately, before the project went any further (Diamond 1972; Rouland 1978:210).

It is noteworthy that each of these stands was taken independently of one another, and none was related to an existing community or leadership consensus on strategies of response to the project. Diamond's statements aimed at creating a consensus, not expressing one.

Another initiative was taken by a young councillor of the Mistassini band, Philip Awashish, who decided to call a meeting of Cree band leaders at Mistassini to discuss possible regional responses to the proposed project. He went about this using both formal and informal channels of communication: through ties with former classmates at residential Indian schools, but seeking first the permission and assistance of the Mistassini chief and the participation of other chiefs. This meeting is regarded as the starting point of a new regional representation process, a new leadership and eventually a new organization among the James Bay Cree. Looking back on this meeting Chief Diamond commented:

> For the first time in history, the Cree sat down together to discuss their common problem—the James Bay Hydroelectric Project. But we found out much more than that—we found out that we all survive on the land and we all have respect for the land. Our Cree Chiefs also found out that our rights to the land, our rights to hunt, fish and trap and our right to remain Crees were considered as privileges by the governments of Canada and Quebec (Diamond 1977:3).[12]

The funds needed to arrange the meeting were sought first from the Department of Secretary of State, but the request was refused because the IQA had already been provided funds for such meetings (LaRusic 1972:34). The Cree organizers, who saw the meeting as preparatory for adopting a position at an upcoming IQA general meeting, did not go to the IQA for funding. They planned to use band funds, but received funding from the Man in the North Programme of the Arctic Institute of North America, then located on the campus of McGill University, where Awashish had been a student.[13] When the IQA executive heard of the meeting, they arranged to transport a large contingent of Cree chiefs and councillors to Mistassini by chartered aircraft, as well as to send an IQA executive member and IQA legal counsel (LaRusic 1972). A total of 35 people from seven communities attended the three-day meeting.

The Cree initiators originally envisaged an informal meeting of Cree leaders, to be conducted in Cree, at which information on the James Bay project would be shared and potential responses to it discussed. However, because of the non-Cree in attendance, extensive translations were needed and long discussions took place in English, with few inputs from unilingual Cree (LaRusic 1972:35). There was little information about the project itself, but it was pointed out that (1) the project would cause severe damage to the land, the animals and to the Cree communities; (2) that the project would serve whites not Indians, and those who would benefit from the jobs would be whites first and Indians second; nor would the jobs last. It was unanimously decided to oppose the project (Anonymous* 1971).[14]

The meeting ended on 1 July 1971 with a resolution addressed to the minister of Indian Affairs and Northern Development:

> We, the representatives of the Cree bands that will be affected by the James Bay Hydro Project or any other project, oppose to these projects because we believe that only the beavers have the right to build dams in our territory, and we request the Minister of Indian Affairs and Northern Development to use his legal jurisdiction to stop any attempt of intrusion of our rightful owned territory by the Government of the Province of Quebec or any other authority (quoted in Diamond 1977).

The resolution was given to the IQA representatives to be delivered to the minister.

Building Community Consensus in Favour of Opposition

When the community leaders returned to their villages, many called meetings to report on the Mistassini discussions. This period was critical because the leaders not only had to inform the communities of developments but also to unify community opinions. Data drawn from two villages, Waswanipi and Fort George, illustrate the process.[15]

At meetings held in summer of 1971 the Waswanipi band members were presented with a brief account of what were then thought to be the main features of the project and the legal and political grounds for opposition. They were asked to support their chief's initiative to oppose the project. In reply, they expressed a widespread and deeply rooted scepticism about the practical

---

*Unpublished sources cited in the text are listed at end of essay. Published citations are included in the bibliography at end of volume.

possibilities of effective opposition to the project. At this time, they discussed the short-term goals of stopping or delaying the project and/or receiving compensation.

The data available from Fort George for this period generally support this picture.[16] Only slowly did a response of indignation and consensus to oppose the hydro-electric development grow through the summer and fall of 1971, following several inputs from the chiefs and councillors who attended the Mistassini assembly.

The importance of the change from quiescence to a consensus on opposition is easily overlooked, as is the role of the emerging regional Cree leaders in the creation of that consensus. Evidence of these processes does not appear widely in the public documents of the period; indeed, it would have been politically dangerous if it had. However, this development becomes obvious in a comparison of statements made at Waswanipi band meetings immediately before and after the Mistassini assembly.

At the meetings held in two Waswanipi settlements on May 15 and 20, Chief Peter Gull did most of the talking. He informed the people of the government's decision to build the project without consulting the Cree. He impressed upon them the need to express their views about the project and to think about how they wanted to respond. He had already been in touch with Philip Awashish and Billy Diamond, and a 'moccasin telegraph' of information was already established. The chief showed maps (unofficial) of the lands to be flooded and discussed problems that would be encountered by hunters traversing the reservoirs and the problems of flooded hunting areas and burial sites. He reported that efforts were under way to secure a film on the effects of flooding on Peace River. He emphasized that the band members could not be passive in the face of the development, that the project must be stopped—but ''if we can't stop them I want to be sure we will get something out of it'' (Waswanipi 1971a).

Few band members spoke at these meetings, but those who did were decidedly pessimistic about the possibilities of stopping the project. When some members noted that it might bring direct benefits, the chief agreed, specifying money, electric power, roads, and tourism benefits. However, he warned that above and beyond any benefits that might result, they had to think of their land; he emphasized that wildlife and hunting would be disrupted

(Waswanipi 1971a and b). Unfortunately, it is difficult to judge how much of the technical project data and of the political situation was understood by community members at this stage.[17]

At the meetings held after the Mistassini assembly, the chief met with a mix of support and scepticism from band members. On the one hand, some opposition to the project was voiced: people cited its detrimental impact on the land, the animals and on their hunting, and they repeatedly cited the fact that they should have been consulted about the project before it was begun. On the other hand, opposition was not unanimous, even among those Waswanipi who had attended the Mistassini assembly.[18] Several people expressed the view that the government never listened to them before, and that things had already gone too far, given the intensity of surveying and exploration work already in progress. Others commented that the project would not "be all bad for us," and that the government had helped the Indians, and they expected more help in the future: ". . . I don't think we should complain what the government wants to do with this land because I don't think he [they] will leave us completely in need." Nevertheless, there was more opposition to the project than had been evident at previous band meetings (Waswanipi 1971c and d).

The chief repeatedly stressed that opposition was possible. He referred to the legislative basis of Indian rights to the land and specifically to the failure of the Quebec government to fulfil the obligations under the 1912 Quebec Boundaries Extension Act. "It's only right that they should ask the Indians first when they want something from our land and it is time we should get something for it too," he said (Waswanipi 1971d). He went on to explain how the project could be made opposed:

> Over half the money comes from the U.S. Maybe it will cost about $7 billion . . . So maybe if we can hold this thing back for 2 or 3 years, the people that are putting their money in for it will not like their money going to waste not knowing if they are going to continue with it or not. They want to make money with this. If they quit putting their money for it I don't think [the] Quebec government will continue to do it alone. This thing is not too certain yet (Waswanipi 1971d; cf. 1971c).

Although the chief could not dispel the scepticism with such arguments, nonetheless, a position was expressed by a band member that made a consensus possible: "All we can say is we don't want it [the James Bay Project] because we are not sure if it will be good for us or not" (Waswanipi 1971c). Although this view did not reconcile the growing opposition with the widespread scepticism, it proposed a position from which opposition could proceed in the face of what seemed to many band members to be a hopeless case. In short, they could oppose because there was no better alternative.

By the time Billy Diamond and Philip Awashish polled the communities in early 1972, they found that the Cree were united in opposition to the project.

Establishing the Legitimacy of the Emerging Leadership Structure

Cree leaders not only had to develop a consensus on the need for action, but they also had to establish the legitimacy of regional structures for coordinating action and the legitimacy of the individuals who would occupy the new regional leadership roles. The opportunity to pursue these objectives was provided by the widely perceived need in the Cree communities for more information on the project and on the possible responses to it. This need led, at the insistence of the emerging leaders, to the funding of two full-time communications workers in October 1971.[19] Billy Diamond and Philip Awashish began work in January 1972 (Anonymous 1973) after a second meeting of regional leaders, this time in Val d'Or, Quebec, sanctioned their appointment.

The funding of these communications workers provided the first opportunity for a regional tour of the communities by Cree leaders. Their first task was to establish their legitimacy and that of the regional meetings of chiefs and councillors. This was accomplished in the following way.

Billy Diamond began by meeting with the chief and band council of each community he visited, asking whether they wanted him to speak to their people about the project (Diamond 1972). He told them that his own role and that of the IQA depended on the authorization and support of the band council. This made it clear that the legitimacy of the communications workers and the IQA derived from the band level; accordingly, the workers and the program were under the ultimate control of the band councils.[20] Communicating the data collected on the project established the potential usefulness of regional personnel to the chiefs and councillors who were responsible for keeping their people informed. Thus the skills and resources Chief Diamond brought to his position were presented as resources available to the existing leadership.

This mutual support between regional and band leaders also helped the communications workers establish their legitimacy with their public—the band members. They had to do this in opposition to the Cree James Bay Development Corporation (JBDC) liaison workers, who had visited the communities prior to Chief Diamond's arrival. The JBDC workers, however, failed to establish their legitimacy because they had not received band-council support, had spoken informally to people in the communities and had called meetings of band members on their own initiative.

That Chief Diamond's procedure was considered appropriate by the councils is reflected in their approval and organization of public meetings, in their agreeing not to say very much, "but rather give the public the opportunity to say all they wanted about the project," and in officially introducing Diamond at the general meetings (*ibid.*).

In his presentations to the communities, Diamond sought to legitimate the new regional political structure. He also gave a description and history of the James Bay project, a report on the responses and decisions made at previous meetings by the chiefs and leaders, and an outline of IQA actions and support.

Initially, in each village there was "confusion and bewilderment as to our [IQA communication worker] position" in relation to the JBDC, to the project and to the Cree (1972:5). Chief Diamond had to explain the differences between the IQA and the JBDC, which he found difficult to do effectively since people had little contact with either. However, he saw an occasion for this in the presentation of the JBDC reports on the environmental impacts of the proposed project to the communities.

In his own community of Rupert House, Chief Diamond had the full English report and the Cree-English summary read to the community. The omission of several erroneous and derogatory comments on the Indian people, which had appeared in the full report but not in the Cree summary, was pointed out. These included claims that Indians were "economically and politically, strongly dependent on white man's society," and that "the Indians are no longer as economically dependent on [wildlife] as some people think" (Federal-Provincial Task Force 1971a). As Chief Diamond reported (1972:7):

> Some of the people could not believe the report after the comparison was made and as Chief of the Rupert House Band, I asked my people. . . what shall we do with the report? The first reaction was from the crowd, Mr. Andrew Salt said let us burn the reports. . . . Then one hundred and twenty-five copies of the reports were burned in the stove and others were taken outside and burned as well.

Other communities simply mailed the reports back to the corporation. These meetings established for the communities who could legitimately be seen as working for the Cree people.

Chief Diamond's meetings thus established not only the legitimacy but also the usefulness of regional-level representation. They also revealed a willingness among the Cree to adopt a consensus on the key issues. Even in those communities that thought they would not be as affected by the project as others, there were clear statements of regional solidarity. For example, a band member from Paint Hills said: "Of course, we will unite with our brothers of Fort George, Eastmain, Rupert House, Waswanipi and Mistassini to stop the James Bay Projects" (Diamond 1972). And in Great Whale River the Inuit who thought they would be less directly affected than the Cree stated they would stand behind the Indian people.

The meetings were also an opportunity for the community to express their views regarding regional leadership mandates. This was happening as early as the summer of 1971 at meetings held by Chief Peter Gull. When he urged his people to speak up and help their chief to represent them, several band members agreed: "You need to know what they [other band members] think." But a former chief felt differently: "You chiefs get together and talk to each [other] about this instead of asking us. Then whatever you think, we'll agree to your idea. You're the ones that [are] supposed to know" (Waswanipi 1971d).

These two views—that chiefs should listen to the people, and that chiefs should take the initiative to make decisions—are complementary components of a Cree leader's mandates. This was reflected in a comment by a Fort George band member: "Our Chiefs and Indian leaders have a RIGHT to voice their opinions on our behalf against the Project because they know that the Project is no benefit for the Indians" (Diamond 1972). In other words, leaders are expected to speak their *own* ideas; the reason they must do so is because they are *knowledgeable;* and they are expected to do so *on behalf of the community.*

Leaders are expected to be competent in serving their communities at the same time as community members are expected to guide their leaders in decision-making. The two sides of this model are united in process, but not through a formal sequence of steps. Consensus does not necessarily precede any leadership action, and leaders do not just present their decisions as *faits accomplis.* Their mandate is to lead and not just represent their people. By confirming and consulting the community, the community participates in the ongoing decision-making, and the final authority rests with the community.

THE AUTONOMY DIMENSION: CHOOSING STRATEGIES AND DEFINING GOALS

Cree goals and objectives emerged only in the process of working out a strategy of opposition to the hydro-electric scheme. A gradual development of goals is to be expected when a crisis occurs before political mobilization has taken place. I emphasize this point, because it is easy to neglect the state of mobilization when looking back from the present perspective. Unlike native groups in Canada today who face development schemes after a decade of nation-wide political mobilization on the issues of aboriginal rights, northern development and self-government, the Cree were forced to mobilize without having yet determined their goals. The Cree, I hasten to add, were not alone in this position in 1971; as yet there had been no supreme court ruling on the Nishga case, no Morrow caveat, no Berger inquiry, no Malouf judgment. Native peoples across the Canadian North at this period were living more or less autonomously and only occasionally in public conflict with the state.

Taking the Initiative to Define Strategies

The Mistassini assembly, in June 1971, was the first opportunity for Cree leaders to discuss their options for opposing the project;

specifically, whether it could be stopped, whether it could be delayed as the oil pipeline had been in Alaska, or whether to demand compensation from governments. Advice was offered by Chief Max Gros-Louis, the IQA representative, and Jacques Beaudoin, a legal counsel for the IQA.

Chief Gros-Louis emphasized the need for Indians to present a united front to the government at the band, provincial and national levels, and he proposed a statement of solidarity between Cree chiefs with the other Indians of the province, which was signed by the Cree chiefs (IQA 1974). Second, he argued against taking a case to court where a white judge would hear the case and cause the Indians to lose. Third, he recommended mobilizing Indian and non-Indian support, throughout Canada and beyond, suggesting that if other countries knew what was going on they would try to help.

Beaudoin's advice covered the possibilities of legal action. He stated that normally the government could take the land without Indian consent, and that a court case would be very difficult to file against the government. Dealing with the province would be difficult, for although the authorities needed the permission of the minister of Indian and Northern Affairs to go ahead with the project, they were already certain of federal support. Therefore, the province would only discuss compensation and not a change in project plans. He suggested communicating with the minister, possibly by means of a resolution opposing the project, and urging him to use his powers, on behalf of the Cree. In response to a question from a chief asking what they could do if the minister decided not to stop the project, the lawyer implied that the only thing that could be done was to establish the value of the claim for compensation (Anonymous 1971).[21]

The assembly did not make a clear choice between suggestions made by the IQA executive member and the lawyer. Rather, the leaders kept the options open by acting on both of the suggestions. They drafted and sent off to the minister the resolution cited above, requesting that he use his legal powers to stop any intrusion of Cree-owned land. They also proceeded to mobilize support from Indian organizations.

The general meeting of the IQA, held in Quebec City the following month, supported opposition and received messages from many Indian associations.[22] Only part of a day was devoted to the James Bay project, however, and discussions focused on trying to stop it (Waswanipi 1971d).[23]

During the meeting a press conference was held by the executive of the IQA and the James Bay Cree chiefs "to make it clear that the Indians of Quebec were opposed to the James Bay project" (Anonymous 1973). The executive stressed that their opposition to the project was aimed at establishing consultations with the Quebec government at the cabinet level (*Montreal Star* 29 July 1971).

The IQA position was consistent with its long-term strategy, which was to negotiate a series of agreements with the province on questions of aboriginal rights. To this end the IQA had submitted to the Government of Quebec in the last several years three position papers on territorial rights, hunting and fishing rights and taxation. A negotiated agreement on hunting and fishing rights had been reached by early 1970 (LaRusic 1972), but a change in government resulted in its never being finalized and implemented (LaRusic *et al.* 1979). The submission on territorial rights was made in 1969 to the Quebec Royal Commission on the Territorial Integrity of Quebec—the Dorion Commission. The province refused to negotiate until the commission's report was submitted on 5 February 1971, shortly before the announcement of the James Bay project. Reaction to the project was therefore linked to the long-term IQA goal of establishing senior-level negotiations on Indian territorial rights (IQA 1974). The objectives of the IQA were not entirely clear, but their submission mentioned that "without prejudice to any future re-evaluation, we consider that our rights have been alienated in the amount of five billion dollars, exclusive of damages" (IQA 1972).

The commission's report recognized the possibility of serious implications resulting from Quebec's failure to settle Indian rights, particularly the rights to hunt, fish and trap in large areas of the province (Leger 1971:44). These included the areas affected by the James Bay project for which jurisdiction had been transferred from the federal to the provincial government in 1898 and 1912, with a specific proviso in the latter transfer that the province deal with aboriginal rights (Savoie 1971:38). The report responded to IQA submissions and recommended that the Government of Quebec

sign an agreement with the Indians of Quebec to abolish all rights
and debts whatsoever (cf. Savoie, p. 41). It implied that $34 million
dollars was a starting point for discussions.

The IQA approved the report's recognition of Indian rights but
rejected its interpretation of the nature of those rights and their
political solution. Its statement indicated that the rights included
land, hunting and tax exemption (IQA 1974). Following the release
of the report, the IQA requested that negotiations begin with the
provincial government (Savoie, p. 38). The first session took place
on 27 September 1971.[24]

Thus it is clear that the Dorion Commission Report and IQA
initiatives were important sources of support for opposing the
James Bay project, and also that opposition to the project would
influence the province-wide negotiations. Nevertheless, there were
differences in perspective between the Cree leaders and the IQA
executive. For the Cree leaders the aim of mobilizing federal
government support was to get the province to discuss the project
with the Cree. For the IQA the aim of mobilizing federal and public
support was to get meaningful negotiations underway on territorial
rights and compensation for all Quebec's native peoples. The two
aims were perceived to be linked but it was also recognized that
they could come into conflict.

During the summer and fall of 1971 the Cree leaders waited,
observed and evaluated the effectiveness of their decisions made
at the Mistassini assembly. Little or no concrete response was forthcoming from the government. Meanwhile, exploration and
preparatory construction work on Cree lands accelerated. Hunters
expressed their concern upon their mid-winter return from their
bush camps, and people became bitter when they realized the construction work had begun without their having been consulted
(Awashish 1972a).

The meeting of the Cree leaders with two executive members
of the IQA in Val d'Or in mid-January, 1972, was the occasion
that the leaders took to assert their own goals and strategies. It
had also been the first occasion at which the leaders met a senior
representative of the JBDC, and they were upset by the failure of
the JBDC representative to do more than inform them of project
plans. This, together with the failures of the minister of Indian Affairs to respond to their resolution and of the Quebec government

to discuss the project, in the face of growing opposition in the villages, led them to insist the IQA take out an injunction to stop the project. A request for an injunction was drafted and signed by the Cree chiefs and delegates on 13 January 1972, and the IQA was asked, via the two IQA executive members present, to proceed immediately with the court action (Awashish 1972a).

When Chiefs Diamond and Awashish visited the Cree communities in February and March, they reported these decisions to the band members, and asked the band councils to pass resolutions supporting the court action and requesting the IQA to take immediate action on it.

In making this decision they went against the priorities of the IQA executive. During the fall of 1971 the IQA had begun negotiations with Quebec's minister of Natural Resources. There had been little progress on the question of territorial rights, since the minister refused to begin discussions on the basis of the $5-billion claim and asked the IQA to itemize its demand (*Montreal Star* 4 March 1972). However, progress was being made on the question of taxation and by late February, an order-in-council was prepared, exempting Indians in Quebec from the provincial sales tax. IQA lawyer Beaudoin was quoted as saying that this was "a sign of good faith by Quebec that they're interested in bargaining seriously" (*ibid.*).

The Cree leaders, for their part, began to see a conflict between the IQA role of carrying out a mandate to oppose the James Bay project and the IQA interest in negotiating with the province. Several Cree individuals accused the IQA of selling James Bay for tax concessions (*ibid.*), and in February several Cree band councils "warned the Indian association they want a firmer stand against the project" (*Montreal Star* 29 February 1972). Events over the next couple of months tended to heighten Cree fears. Chief Andrew Delisle, president of the IQA, said the association would not discuss James Bay in their negotiations because the IQA did not have a mandate from the Cree. But he also said that the IQA told the Quebec government: "you can't talk about a project to be built on our territory until you settle our claims" (*Montreal Star* 4 May 1972). The most serious breach of cooperation occurred when it was revealed that the IQA did not forward to the federal minister the resolution passed the previous July in Mistassini until 14 April 1972 (Rouland 1978:211; Chrétien 1972).

Mobilizing Support and Deciding on Tactics

Having chosen a strategic course of action, the Cree needed organizational, financial, legal, political, and technical support and information, which, during this period, came from a range of sources: citizen protest movements; university-based researchers and journalists; as well as from the IQA executive and legal advisers.

A protest meeting at McGill University in January led to the formation of the James Bay Committee, which, along with the Society to Overcome Pollution, the Canadian Wildlife Federation and the Sierra Club, organized public protests against the hydro-electric project and researched the bases for opposition. By July 1972, one book by a journalist, six pamphlets by citizens' groups, as well as numerous newspaper commentaries criticized the project (Richardson 1972a, 1972b; Berkes *et al.* 1972; James Bay Committee 1972a, 1972b; LaJambe 1972; Parti Québécois 1972; Spence 1972; Spence and Spence 1972). Discussions and protests took place at public meetings of, for example, the Canadian Zoological Society and the Canadian Preparatory Committee for the United Nations Conference on the Human Environment. The anthropology journal *Recherches amérindiennes au Québec* published a special issue on James Bay in the fall of 1971. And the Programme in the Anthropology of Development at McGill University began a study of the social implications of the project late in 1971 for the JBDC, and it organized open seminars, among whose participants were several Cree (Salisbury *et al.* 1972).[25]

However, Cree leaders still felt the need for organizational and financial support and for legal advice. The success of the IQA in obtaining funding for the Mistassini meeting and the communications workers demonstrated the effectiveness of dealing with the government through an organization. This realization, plus a desire to cooperate with other Indians, led the Cree to pressure the IQA and its advisers to assist with an injunction.

Thus, when the leaders visited the communities in February and March, their task was twofold: to mobilize support for their decision to initiate court action and to request band-council resolutions in support of IQA aid with the injunction. The resolutions at Mistassini and Waswanipi demanded that the IQA proceed immediately with the injunction (Awashish 1972a; Waswanipi 1972).

In preparation for taking action, a meeting of the IQA Board of Directors was scheduled for 18-20 April 1972 in conjunction with a meeting of the Cree leaders and representatives of the Inuit of northern Quebec. According to Awashish, the first issue to be resolved was what the IQA was prepared to do to support legal measures against the James Bay project (1972b). While the communications workers were mobilizing community opinion on the matter in preparation for the meeting, the IQA legal advisers were asked to prepare specific recommendations on the means of proceeding with an injunction and implementing the strategy of accelerating opposition.

At the meeting, IQA lawyers O'Reilly and Beaudoin presented an analysis of the options open to the assembled leaders. First, they argued that if the IQA could negotiate quickly, important concessions might be gained. But if this could not be achieved, then the Cree might be left with only a claim for damages when the project was completed. A court injunction on aboriginal rights was one alternative, the lawyers claimed, but the chances of Indians acting alone in court were not good because injunctions against the Crown were difficult to execute and because of the complications in determining the nature of native rights. It was noted that the enforcement of native rights was at that time being tested by the Nishga in British Columbia. The lawyers pointed out that the chances of success were greater if the federal government could be persuaded to take an injunction against the province, but that given the political situation the federal government was unlikely to do so. Rather, the federal government was likely to pressure the Cree to negotiate a settlement (Awashish 1972b).

The lawyers offered a fourth alternative: court action based on the unconstitutionality of Bill 50, the legislation that set up the crown corporation to develop the region, for violating federal jurisdictions;[26] or court action against the province and contractors for working on navigable waters without federal authorization under the Navigable Waters Protection Act. The lawyers indicated that such legal actions would show the seriousness of Cree opposition and might make the project negotiable—if that was the Cree objective. If these legal actions failed, court action on native rights could then be considered, but with the realization that if the case were finally lost, there would be no recourse against the project (Awashish 1972b).

Awashish (*ibid.*) reported that having received this advice concerning the four possible alternatives,

> The native people of James Bay and Mistassini-Waswanipi area requested the following:
> (a) That Jean Chrétien [minister responsible for Indian Affairs] be pressured into undertaking an injunction against the Provincial Government of Quebec. Support would be mobilized from various groups and resolutions collected;
> (b) That legal action proceed under the basis of Bill 50 and the Navigable Waters Protection Act.
> A press conference would be held following the presented actions. Everything was to be ready by May 1, 1972. . . .

The IQA was mandated to take whatever legal measures were necessary to block the project until "a satisfactory settlement could be achieved" (Diamond 1977). In addition, the James Bay Task Force was established under the coordination of Chief Billy Diamond and the IQA to evaluate both Indian rights and the impact of the James Bay project.

Commitment of the Cree to the IQA was indicated at a follow-up meeting of Cree chiefs and lawyers held on 28 April, at which the Anglican bishop of the Diocese of Moosonee offered to assist the opposition by sponsoring communications workers. The Cree leaders decided the church could assist by declaring publicly that it supported the stand taken by the Cree and the IQA, and by writing letters to Prime Minister Trudeau and Premier Bourassa protesting their governments' handling of native issues raised by the James Bay project. But they did not accept the organizational participation of the church.

At this same meeting the lawyers reported on the legal actions they had drafted: the first one, against the attorney general of the province and the crown corporation, asked the court to declare Bill 50 unconstitutional. The second, against the contractors, asked (if Bill 50 were proven unconstitutional) that the court issue a permanent injunction forcing them to cease all work. The lawyer noted that the constitutionality of Bill 50 could be seriously challenged. He also indicated that the possibility of action under the Navigable Waters Act was still being researched; in the meanwhile a letter requesting federal intervention had been sent to the appropriate minister. The assembled Cree leaders agreed on the two court actions.

A week later, a series of meetings and press conferences were held in Ottawa by the Cree chiefs, leaders and band representatives, the IQA board of directors and legal counsel, with officials of the Department of Indian Affairs. The court actions were launched.

About the same time, the Mistassini band council requested the minister of Indian Affairs to report on his responsibilities and power with respect to the hydro-electric project and Indian interests. They also asked him how he had used this power in the past, and how the Cree could initiate its use again.

Defining the Goal

The intensification of opposition pushed to the forefront the question of what the Cree wanted specifically. The question was raised by the minister of Indian Affairs at the May meetings, and the legal counsel for the IQA asked the Cree leaders whether they were totally against the project.

Until the hydro-electric project began, then, the Cree commitment to a distinctive economic, social and cultural way of life had not been previously questioned. The young Cree collectively discovered the viability and extent of their commitment to the renewable resource-based economy in the process of opposing the project. However, although this commitment was widely shared, it was not part of an explicit ideology; nor was it clear how this way of life could be threatened—or protected—for example, whether the project would have to be stopped completely or only modified to make its socioeconomic impact survivable. Similarly, that the whole issue of aboriginal rights was the goal of the opposition was not envisaged at the beginning; rather, aboriginal rights looked like one possible basis for the main task, which was to oppose the project and protect existing Cree autonomy.

As noted above, the Cree leaders had decided to block the project until "a satisfactory settlement could be achieved." This phrase originated in many of the band-council resolutions passed during Diamond's and Awashish's tour. For example, the Mistassini resolution authorizing the IQA to proceed with an injunction stated: "The purpose of this court injunction was to stop all works and constructions until an agreement has been reached between the affected Indians and the Provincial Government of Quebec'' (Awashish 1972a).[27]

A more precise definition of the goal of opposition was encouraged by the lawyers, who asked: ''What did people of the area mean by an 'agreement'?'' Awashish (1972b) reports that after some discussion,

> . . . most of the Chiefs felt that they would accept some form of hydro development under conditions that would be acceptable to the native people of the area. A negotiable development project would be the goal. Therefore, all Chiefs of the bands involved were opposed to the James Bay Development Project as it is or has been presented by the Provincial Government of Quebec.

According to Awashish, it was obvious that specific details concerning possible agreement would have to be worked out before proceeding with negotiations.

During the first tour of the villages in February and March, statements by nearly 100 members of various bands had been recorded and summarized by the leaders. Although these statements were united in their expression of opposition, they contained many diverse views of the possible goals of opposition (Diamond 1972). Thus, when the leaders returned to the villages in March and May, they sought advice from the elders. In effect, the reports of their discussions represent a summary of the elders' understanding of Cree/white conflicts, of their ''ideology'' regarding whites and of how the present crisis fitted into this historical perspective.[28] The elders talked about governments and developments and of the historic context within which the current crisis had to be understood. Summarizing their views, Awashish (1972f) wrote:

> [The present pattern was] started by the arrival of the first white man to the area and still continues to this very day.
>
> Development has been solely in the hands of people outside the region.
>
> The James Bay Development Corporation in its plans to develop the area has given little or no consideration to the resources which are important for subsistence to the Cree people . . . .

> The region has been utilized almost exclusively by the Cree people
> who have no voice in the decision-making body which [is now]
> planning the development of resources in the area.

The desirability of negotiation with the government was
reflected in the following statement by a Waswanipi elder:

> This is the way it appears. Things are being done behind the backs
> of the Indian people. Things are so secret. There has simply . . .
> been no talk at all. Perhaps if they had started to consult the
> Indians about the benefits of the James Bay Project, there would
> be less opposition to it. So now we have no other way but to
> oppose it (Waswanipi 1972).

The elders' resentment against government development practices
repeatedly focused on the lack of previous consultation, concern
for the ecology of the area, concern for the future of Cree communities, and the abrogation of the traditional rights. These
statements make it clear why a complete stop to the project was
not the main goal for the Cree. Cree elders viewed the hydro-
electric project in the broader historical perspective of long-term
relationships with whites; the project required that relations between Cree and whites be restructured. The goals encompassed
both a modified project and a new relationship with governments
that had to include the recognition of a Cree role in determining
the development of their land. The means to these ends was
negotiation, and the tone was conciliatory, although immediate
opposition seemed essential to achieve these ends.

The regional leaders' responses, as they sought to define the
goals of opposition, were thus informed by the developing consensus among the elders on the long-term objectives. The leaders
articulated this growing consensus: opposition until agreement is
reached and a demand for participation in the development of the
area. Awashish (1972f) argued that:

> Indian people from the area must be involved in the planning
> body of the development of the area. It is not . . . enough to have
> experts from outside the region to study the situation of the Cree
> people and plan the development of the region . . . . [it is]
> require[d] that the native people be meaningfully involved in the
> planning for the use of the resources of the area.

It took three and one-half years of political mobilization, court
action and negotiation to achieve this goal. Although the strategies

decided on in the spring of 1971 did eventually pressure the government to negotiate an agreement, this did not occur until a year-
long injunction hearing, based on the plausibility of the claim for
aboriginal rights, was won.

CONCLUSIONS

The first year of Cree mobilization against the hydro-electric project set into gear several distinct but interrelated processes of
representation. The process of creating Cree regional political structures had begun, and an *ad hoc* meeting of local leaders and several
active young Cree had, by the spring of 1972, given birth to a
regional decision-making forum based on key elements of Cree
political culture. The new Cree leaders, largely self-selected, began
developing their skills cooperatively to meet the task at hand. They
did not set up a formal organization but used the existing provincial Indian association for administrative, financial and general
organizational support. The new regional structure made use of
the already existing organization of chiefs and band councils and
thereby avoided being imposed by, or claiming authority from,
outside authorities. As such, the regional structure complemented
and enhanced the growing autonomy of local band councils, a process that, as I have indicated, had begun several years earlier. This
trend was critical to the events that followed.

Vis-à-vis the communities, the regional leadership initiated an
information program aimed at consensus-building, and established the legitimacy of regional decision-making. Providing information to the communities was a priority of the regional structure,
which 'recognized that only an adequately informed public could
effectively participate in decision-making. On the one hand, the
extent of political and legal information available to the Cree
leaders from diverse sources was impressive; on the other, technical
information on the hydro-electric project was very restricted and
constantly changing as the plans themselves developed. The leaders
systematically and repeatedly communicated this information to
the communities, but it is clear that they found effective communication to band members to be an elusive and difficult task.
Many people could not conceptualize the scale of the hydro-electric
project and its associated structures, and it was also difficult for
them to comprehend the complex macro-political processes behind

the project, as well as those involved in opposing the project. But the regional leaders renewed their commitments to the information program and initiated changes for its improvement (Awashish 1972a). It was to be a complex, long-term project. The important point here is that this was recognized by the regional leaders right from the start, and they were committed to the task from the start.

Community feedback to the regional leaders did not take the form of clear directives, but rather was expressed in general consensus on broad orientations. The critical points of consensus centred on the need to oppose the project as it was then proposed and on the legitimacy of the new decision-making forum and of the self-appointed incumbents in regional leadership roles. The communities also supported the initiation of legal action and the request that the IQA act on behalf of the Cree. However, it is difficult to assess whether, at this stage, these were more than *pro forma* approvals of the strategies recommended by the regional leaders.

More specific direction was provided by the elders, who interpreted the hydro-electric project crisis in terms of their perception of the history of Indian/white relations, specifically the problems created by whites for maintaining Cree social and economic autonomy. Thus, when the regional leaders sought guidance with respect to the long-term goals of opposition, the elders advised them not to view the project as an isolated instance, but as part of an ongoing conflict over control of the development of the region. This attitude influenced the leaders to seek an agreement with the government rather than oppose the project outright. Whereas this broader goal was consistent with opposing the specific project at the strategic level, the elders' view also reflected a desire to achieve long-term reconciliation rather than ever-increasing confrontation. The important point here is that community elders played a key role in giving direction to the regional leaders' emerging position regarding the long-term goals of political action.

During this first year the regional leaders also established contact with individuals and organizations at the provincial and national levels that could provide them with information, advice and infrastructural support. It is clear that the leaders had decided to work most intensively with the IQA executive and legal counsels. From the beginning, the leaders were aware that their priorities

were not identical with those of the IQA; but they were also concerned to link Cree interests to those of all native people. During
the course of the year, the differences between the Cree and the
IQA over the need for court action and over the urgency of immediate opposition increased. Partially as a result of this, the Cree
leaders began to assert a stronger and more independent voice in
the choice of strategies while continuing to work with the IQA executive.[29] With respect to legal advice, the leaders gave priority to
those strategic options that the lawyers advised were potentially
effective, although they did not follow precisely their recommendations or IQA priorities. The lawyers provided the leaders with
a comprehensive set of options, given the current state of legal opinion on aboriginal rights. Thus, it was local-level concern for dealing with the hydro-electric project and the elders' concern for dealing with it in the broad context of controlling development in the
region that guided the leaders in making choices of strategy and
goals—rather than any imposition of choices by legal advisers.

This conclusion differs from that reached by LaRusic *et al.*
because they did not examine the legitimacy component of
autonomy and thus they failed to record or analyse the critical
micro-level activities of the emerging regional Cree leadership: initiating community consensus; creating and legitimating a regional
structure; mobilizing information, advice and support from external sources; choosing strategies and tactics of opposition; and articulating Cree goals through dialogue with community elders.
Without a consideration of these activities, any assessment of Cree
autonomy is incomplete and erroneous.

In conclusion, it is my hope that this case study has illustrated
the complexity of evaluating autonomy in Fourth World representation and the impossibility of omitting consideration of micro-
level legitimation processes in the analysis. The methods of traditional anthropological analysis, though not sufficient, remain
essential to the study of politics of indigenous communities in
modern nation-states.

Notes

1. The research on which this paper is based was funded by grants from
   the Social Sciences and Humanities Research Council, the Canada

Council Killam postdoctoral research program and the Arts Research Board of McMaster University. I wish to thank Noel Dyck, Peter Hutchins, Sonia Paine, Ignatius LaRusic, James O'Reilly, Richard J. Preston, Robert Paine, and Richard F. Salisbury for their comments on various versions of the paper; Chiefs Billy Diamond, Philip Awashish and Peter Gull for their aid; and the Cree Regional Authority and the Grand Council of the Crees (of Quebec) for allowing access to their archives.

2. In a ratification vote in Cree communities, 922 signatures supported the agreement, and one opposed it (Diamond 1977) out of a resident adult population of 2,540. The low turnout was due to the fact that many Cree did not see the need for a ratification vote in view of the extensive consultations and the official approvals given in each community before the signing of the agreement (Feit, field notes; Rouland 1978:51). In the Inuit communities the ratification results were more complex: two-thirds of the population voted 96 percent in favour of the agreement; however, in three of the 14 communities that were strongly opposed to the agreement, only 15 percent voted, most people preferring to boycott the ratification process (Rouland 1978).

3. An example of the sellout theme appeared in the *Native Press* on 18 November 1974 under the headline *$150,000,000 James Bay Sellout*. The term was also used by a lawyer who condemned the agreement and ridiculed the legal opinions influencing the Cree strategy (Cumming 1977). *Le Monde diplomatique* accused the government of trickery and native leaders of exploitation (Dommergues 1976).

4. LaRusic *et al.* suggest that this pattern is not invariable and that there are signs of stronger Cree roles in some areas, which could expand (cf. LaRusic 1979:26-27; 36-38; 53). They, nevertheless, claim the pattern is a general one.

5. The question of what advice the lawyers actually gave their clients when negotiations were resumed in 1974 is beyond the scope of this paper. It is important to note that many of those involved in the events would not agree with Sanders' evaluation that the legal aim was to establish a bargaining position.

6. Elsewhere LaRusic has analysed the pre-1972 period in detail, and I draw on these studies in the body of this paper.

7. Although I did not play an active role in the events of the year covered by this paper, I was involved with the Cree response from December 1972. An analysis of the later stages of this process is envisaged to extend the present analysis.

8. A fuller account of this system is in preparation.

9. A similar picture of the period up to the early 1960s is provided for the other Cree communities of the period (cf. Kerr 1950; Honigmann

1962, 1964; Johnson 1962; Rogers 1965; Kupferer 1966; Pothier 1967; Knight 1968; Preston 1968, 1971; Barger 1980).

10. Other factors in this shift were diverse, but they were all linked to outside interventions. One factor was the availability of alternative channels of information and assistance. Another factor was the increasing takeover by provincial governments of former federally administrated programs (cf. Preston 1968, 1971; Sam 1968; Barger 1980). The short-lived Indian Affairs community-development-officer program in the mid-1960s provided the opportunity for non-natives to teach government policy and structure without being committed to a career position in that structure (McDonald *et al.* 1965; McDonald 1966). Also important was the new funding of native centres and organizations, which opened up new links to government, paralleling those of the Indian Affairs Branch. And the relatively recent presence in the villages of young Euro-Canadian teachers and social service administrators similarly increased access to new knowledge and resources. Of long-term importance in this development was the Indian Affairs policy of transferring some administrative services to the bands, which created full-time salaried Indian band managers, so that some band members were then able to gain experience of government operations (Preston 1971).

11. In Waswanipi, the demand for a new reserve went unresolved despite band decisions on this matter in 1964 and 1965 and a clear agreement on a site by the band members in 1967 (cf. Najmi n.d.; and LaRusic 1972). Similarly, the resistance to provincial government involvement in schooling was not satisfactorily resolved at Rupert House (Preston 1971), nor was the issue of provincial administration of services settled at Great Whale River (Barger 1980). As wider demands for self-government and land rights were articulated, these two met with implacable sympathy and inaction. At Great Whale River the calls for self-government received comments from federal government agents such as: "If the Indian and Eskimos after getting the necessary knowledge can administer their own affairs, I feel that both Quebec and Ottawa would be happy to allow them to do this" (quoted in Barger, 1980:205).

12. Looking back, Chief Diamond cited the personal implications of this and subsequent events that followed this meeting:

> Through my twelve years of experience in dealing with the White government and also in talking with my own people, it became clear that political representation in the outside world was necessary at a very early stage. I decided to make that my very own career . . . . But if you make a decision

for one specific career, I think you should evolve and become
a perfectionist the same way a hunter becomes a perfectionist
and I decided to become a politician (Diamond 1981).

13. The programme, then headed by Eric Gourdeau, provided $1,000 for
the meeting on the understanding that it be permitted to use the occasion to present its research program to the assembled leaders
(LaRusic 1972:34).

14. Only brief minutes are available of this meeting. This and subsequent
analyses are based mostly on unpublished documents recording
statements by Cree leaders and by members of the Cree communities.
I have distinguished between community members' views, leaders'
views and the views of non-Cree participants.

15. LaRusic taped five Waswanipi band meetings, two in May 1971, two
in August 1971, and one in March 1972. A report based on translated
transcripts of these meetings was written by LaRusic (1971), who kind-
ly provided me with copies of the transcripts on which I based my
account.

16. A summary of informal community discussions and reactions at Fort
George has been published by Yves Leger, a Quebec social administrator who lived in the community in the summer of 1971. The
opinions of these two communities are most critical, for when the
James Bay project was first announced, it was thought that the
southern complex (Nottaway-Broadback-Rupert) would be the first
one built and Waswanipi was likely to suffer the most extensive impact from it. In the spring of 1972, when the decision was made to
proceed first with the northern complex (LaGrande), Fort George
became the community to suffer the most extensive impact.

17. At this time there was virtually no official data on the project, and
in fact the location of the first phase of construction work had not
yet been decided. However, considerable unofficial information was
available.

18. At Fort George, Leger noted that although everyone expressed concern about the impact of the project on the land and about Cree territorial claims, this concern was mixed with a widespread non-
involvement. Furthermore, among those who were active a considerable variety of responses were expressed, from rational opposition, to prophetic pleas of doom, to sympathetic support for the project, all in the context of inadequate information about the project
and about ''politico-economic manoeuvres of Whites'' (1971:43,
48-50).

19. The Cree leaders had pressed for information on the project at the
July 1971 meeting, but the IQA executive had not been willing to
join the James Bay Development Corporation (JBDC) in a communica-

tion project for fear that the corporation would try to "sell" the project to the Cree people (Leger 1971:44). The Cree chiefs and leaders supported this position, while pressing the IQA to set up its own information program. Action toward this goal was slow until the JBDC hired Cree liaison workers during the fall to prepare a Cree summary of a report on the potential impacts of the project and to take these to the communities. In January 1972 meetings were held to coordinate the JBDC visits with those of IQA representatives, but this failed and the JBDC workers made the tour themselves.

20. The derivation of authority from the band council was IQA policy at that time, and Chief Diamond told each band council that the assistance of the IQA had to be formally requested by a band-council resolution before the IQA could take any action to assist the communities.

21. Anonymous notes of a meeting of Cree chiefs and representatives in Mistassini, 30 June - 2 July 1971. However, the notes at this point include a number of question marks and so may incompletely report his remarks.

22. A dissenting opinion on the desirability of opposition to the project was publicly expressed by a Montagnais leader (Diamond 1977:5; citations of press headlines in National Indian Brotherhood 1973), but the general pattern was one of wide native support.

23. The general meeting, attended by 75 Indian leaders from all of Quebec, including representatives from all James Bay Cree bands, provided an opportunity for information communication and discussions. The Montagnais leaders present provided the Cree with firsthand accounts of the environmental, subsistence and employment effects of the Manicouagan and Churchill Falls hydro-electric developments (Waswanipi 1971c). In addition, information on potential sources of political leverage was exchanged. The Cree chiefs were appraised of the legal status of their lands and of the potential effects of delays to, or disruptions of, the project that might worry potential investors. The IQA lawyers reaffirmed that if the project could not be stopped, then the Indian people should get monetary compensation (Waswanipi 1971c).

24. Prior to the submission of the commission's report, the government had created a new negotiating committee on Indian Affairs in the provincial Department of Natural Resources, under the chairmanship of a former secretary of the commission. In March 1971 the premier recognized the IQA as the privileged spokesman on all questions regarding Quebec Indians (Savoie 1971:38).

25. Draft versions of the report were circulated for comment (cf. Awashish 1972b).

26. One of the provisions of Bill 50 stated that "this Act shall in no way affect the rights of Indian communities living in the territory."
27. This wording probably originated with the lawyers, but it is significant that the resolution received support in the communities before it was incorporated into the leaders' decisions about goals.
28. For a recent account of Cree ideologies of whites, see Scott 1983.
29. This tension continued for several years, culminating in 1974 in the formation of a separate Cree political organization, the Grand Council of the Crees (of Quebec).

Unpublished Sources

The empirical data for the above analysis was based on the following unpublished sources, as well as published sources listed in the bibliography:

ANONYMOUS
1971 Anonymous notes of a meeting of Cree chiefs and representatives in Mistassini, June 30 - July 2, 1971.
1972 "Brief on Recent Developments in James Bay." Circa September 1972.
1973 "Crees of Quebec, Indians of Quebec Association, Northern Quebec Inuit Association, Opposition to the James Bay Hydro-Electric project."

AWASHISH, PHILIP
1972a "The Cree Indian people of Mistassini-Waswanipi Area and the James Bay Development Project." 20 March 1972.
1972b "Report of Philip Awashish, Communications Worker Indians of Quebec Association on the James Bay Development Project, April 10 - May 5, 1972;" Huron Village, 11 May 1972.
1972c "Report of Philip Awashish, Communications Worker, Huron Village. May 18, 1972."
1972d "Memorandum, From: Philip Awashish, Communications Worker, To: Executive Director, Subject: Communication Work. Date: May 24, 1972."
1972e "Philip Awashish, Communications Worker, Indians of Quebec Association. Meeting on James Bay Project. June 15, 1972. Montreal."
1972f "Report of Philip Awashish, Communications Worker. James Bay Development Project. Huron village. June 23, 1972."

DIAMOND, BILLY
1972 "Report from: Chief Billy Diamond, Communications Worker, on the James Bay Project. February 15, 1972 - April 3, 1972."

GULL, PETER
1972 "Report of Peter Gull, Communications Worker. August 29, 1972." Indians of Quebec Association, Huron Village.

INDIANS OF QUEBEC ASSOCIATION (IQA)
   1972 "Second Report on the James Bay Project. October 11, 1972."
   1973a "Third Report on the James Bay Project. February 7, 1983."
   1973b "Fourth Report on the James Bay Project. May 3, 1973."

MCDONALD, RICHARD
   1966 "Report to the Indian Affairs Branch on Community
   Development at Mistassini, Chibougamau and Lac Dore."

NAJMI, M. A.
   n.d. "Legitimation of Power and Leadership Among the Quebec
   Cree." Report to the McGill-Cree Project.

O'REILLY, JAMES
   1972 [Letter to] "The General Assembly of the Indians of Quebec
   Association, Mistasini, Quebec. Re: James Bay Project."

SANDERS, DOUGLAS
   n.d. "Indians and Lawyers." Unpublished manuscript.

SPENCE, J. A.
   1972b "I.Q.A. James Bay Task Force. Proposal for Environmental
   Impact Studies on the James Bay Development."
   1973 "Summarizing Report. Research carried out in 1972 by the James
   Bay Task Force of the Indians of Quebec Association and Northern
   Quebec Inuit Association."

WASWANIPI
   1971a Transcript of band meeting, 15 May 1971.
   1971b Transcript of band meeting, 20 May 1971.
   1971c Transcript of band meeting, 8 August 1971.
   1971d Transcript of band meeting, 15 August 1971.
   1972 Transcript of general meeting, 3 March 1972.

resources of their discipline should also feel bound to draw on their
professional competence to supply a sociological appreciation of
the very business of anthropological representation. To show how
I have come to hold these views and in order to contribute toward
an understanding of the anthropological representation of Fourth
World issues, I have written this paper about Aborigines, anthropologists and Leviathan, drawing on my experience of two
Australian cases—both of land claims entered in the Northern
Territory.

There was, first, the matter of Finniss River—a land claim
entered under the provisions of the Aboriginal Land Rights (Northern Territory) Act 1976—and this was a fractious business. For
the first time the Aboriginal Land Commissioner heard a case in
which separate and rival groupings of Aborigines pressed claims
to the same tract of land. The people concerned joined to form
two antagonistic parties. The members of each party argued that
they and they alone made up the band of "traditional owners"
of a disputed piece of black soil plain located to the west of Darwin. The other case is of an aborted claim, entered on grounds
of *de facto* occupancy, long association and need on behalf of the
people of a small outlying cattle station that rejoices in the name
of Humpty Doo.

In the shorthand terms that those concerned with Territory
Land Claims now all tend to use, Finniss was a "rights claim,"
whereas Humpty Doo was grounded in "needs." The contrast is
significant because "rights claims" and "needs claims" call for
quite different types of argument and open themselves to distinct
kinds of anthropological representation. In rights claims, the anthropologist, when called to court, is an expert witness on
tradition—its provisions, its discriminations, the processes of traditional politics, and the processes by which tradition is created and
recreated to pass from people of preceding generations to their
heirs. In claims of need, the anthropologist is called upon to make
representations concerning the lifestyle of a set of claimants, and
must produce a brief ethnography structured to define a predicament of social deprivation. I have chosen to write of Humpty Doo
and Finniss because the first can stand for the association of jural-
ly defined need within an anthropology of social conditions,
whereas the second concerns the reconciliation of a statutory

definition of "traditional owners" with those actual, living traditions that the abstract legal definition is supposed to reflect and
therefore to be able to encompass.

To deal either with claims of need or with claims of right in
Northern Australia, a particular sort of anthropological modelling is required in order to comprehend the dynamics of group formation and reformation which are essential to Aboriginal social
life. Aborigines of the region describe the realities of day-to-day
association by saying that they are people who "run with mobs."
When individuals tell their own life stories, they give their lives
as serried "times" spent with first this located mob (that mob at
Blue Grass Station) then with that other mob down at the Estuary
and so on. Mobs are fluctuating groups that belong to the time
and place of their realization. Because these essential units of and
for association do not have an enduring and fixed existence, the
structural anthropology of corporate groups and enduring positions of status within such groups must yield to an anthropology
of social organisation in which analysis of the exigencies of recur-
rent recruitment substitutes for analysis of perduring structures
made up of relationships of status. In such modelling of process,
the contemporary circumstances of a particular set of claimants
are related either to the perduring trends of action that produce
the fluctuating group or to the ways in which social shifts and
changes are entertained in a tradition that accommodates change.
In the terms supplied by Mayer (1966), processural modelling is
the analysis of the formation of quasi-groups which are more-or-
less consolidated through repetitive recruitment of their members
to form action-sets in order to fulfil some nominated purpose.
While the "mob" of Aboriginal English translates as Mayer's
"quasi-group," his "action set" finds its equivalent in Aboriginal
English as a "company for business." The processes to be com-
prehended in the modelling of group dynamics in the Australian
North can now be characterised. They are the processes by which
mob members are organised to form companies for business and
by which the repetitive formation of companies for business is con-
stitutive of a mob.

My prime message, then, in brief is that anthropological
representation of Aborigines to government agencies in Australia
requires processural modelling on the anthropologists' part, if the

representations made are to survive the hard scrutiny of the lawyer, or the bureaucrat, or of the parliamentarian who is a member of, say, the Standing Committee on Aboriginal Affairs. The truly teasing questions asked in judicial, administrative or political contexts always concern how things happen and how they come to be. Time and time again, the hard questioning returns to the issue of the production and reproduction of social forms.

To turn the cases to general effect, I relocate time-bound and regionally confined acts of representation to a wider world of discourse that is Fourth World—a community of discussion and focused interest on the position and destinies of indigenous minorities within the nation-state. I appeal to four contextualizing propositions. In the first place, I argue that all land claims entered by indigenous minorities entail a problem of Hobbesian translation, if members of a claimant grouping are to be recognized at law. The problem concerns the manner by which "Systemes that are Private and Irregular" are to be made "Systemes Political and Regular" and so Persons in Law. In dealings that pertain to the asymmetrical relations (Paine 1985) between nation-state and an autochthonous minority, Leviathan addresses not Aborigines but Aborigines Inc. Thus in Northern Australia there has been a proliferation of Bodies Corporate: to enter a claim the people of Humpty Doo applied to be constituted as the Wairuk Association; the Aboriginal town settlement in Darwin is now the Bogot Community Inc. while the administration of lands ceded to Aborigines under the provisions of the Aboriginal Land Rights (Northern Territory) Act of 1976 will be effected via Lands Trusts. In terms of this act, each Lands Trust is constituted as a body corporate with a common seal, and is defined as a person that can sue and be sued at law. In all of this, Aborigines who would make representations are coerced by a pervasive and perduring imperative of Western political culture: the requirement that to have discourse with the state, an assembly of men must be made over into an entity (Stoljar 1973).

My second proposition has been rendered cryptic by Feit in his discussion of the James Bay Agreement—a unique contract which won for the Cree Indians a special dispensation of complex provisions within the province of Quebec. Feit (1979) writes of the "articulations of hunter-gatherers to the state." Furthermore, he notes that there are many such connections and that the politics of representation can entail the management of situations in which up to a dozen links between applicants and other agencies are all simultaneously relevant. So the Cree (either directly or through fiduciaries) negotiated with welfare agencies, wildlife protection authorities, commercial interests, the province, political lobbies, and other bodies. Representation can thus concern the formation and development of connecting links or, otherwise, be conducted with reference to connections that have already been made. The contrast between simple and complex situations of and for representation can be distinguished with reference both to the number of articulating mechanisms involved and to two distinct orders of activity. These are (1) representation within a given structure, and (2) representation that entails the creation and structuring of a situation by establishing previously unprovided lines of communication and working to gain the appropriate recognition of status that is a precondition of capacity in the business of relating one party in negotiations to another.

Compared with the James Bay negotiations, Land Claims in the Northern Territory of Australia are uncomplicated because the court is specified in advance as the means for articulating claimant group and state. Nonetheless, Australian legislation opens up possibilities for the transformation of simple claims into complex cases in which many interests and parties could be involved. The act in question requires the Land Commissioner to consider detriment—losses that could be sustained or the disadvantage that would accrue to parties with an established interest in the land under claim. Again, Australian legislation contains special provisions in relation to mineral rights. At least one of the mining companies in Australia normally engages a lawyer to keep a watching brief whenever a land claim is to be heard.

Anthropologists come to such structures, or aid in their creation, when they are themselves conceded status. This concession is granted not simply by recognizing an anthroplogists's speciality: command of information and a way with discourse about other cultures. Something more particular is required: the recognition that anthropological skills pertain to a proposed business and that the anthropologists can legitimately take anthropology to a public problem of moment to make a difference either to its definition or to the structure of the situation in which representations of that problem will be made. When recognition is accorded the anthropologist, he or she is granted a concession and comes as an accredited expert to own the definition of a public problem (either wholly or in part). For this view, I am indebted to Gusfield (1981), who argues that both the definition of public problems and the advocacy of approved modalities for their alleviation or resolution are things that are owned. To promote this thesis he points to the ownership of homosexuality in America by the professional associations of American psychiatrists and to the ownership of the problem of drink during prohibition in the United States by Temperance Societies and the churches.

One of the important features of Gusfield's formulations is that they are sensitive to developments over time. Because ownership is alienable, the ownership of specific public problems is apt to change hands. Again, shifts of possession from one defining authority to another are often associated with acts of takeover in which the nature of the problem is itself recast by new owners.

To the ownership of public problems, I add one more item to provide a framework in which to locate anthropological representations that are representations to a purpose. One needs to consider the act of anthropological representation itself. In character this is an act of special translation on the part of a person who is an exponent of a discipline that defines its very business as ''the interpretation of cultures'' (Geertz 1975). Lawyers have a lively appreciation of the aims of the anthropologist who takes the models of academic devising into court. In the language of lawyers, the anthropologist delivers ''terms of art''—definitions of entities, cultural concepts and social process (Gumbert 1981). Because the anthropologist is bidding for recognition as a decisive arbiter of meaning, the success of anthropological attempts to make legal fact can be judged by considering the extent to which proffered ''terms of art'' are accepted into legal discourse and come to be vested in it. By the very nature of anthropological representation, success in the business has the tendency to reduce the anthropological concession by its exercise—so anthropology can be expended (cf. Blau on power, 1964). The point here is that precedental models (which the lawyers consider signally important) are made into law. As Dening (1980) has argued, students of other cultures sometimes provided members of a wider world of discourse with terms to appropriate and then use in their own right and for their own particular purposes. Transposed and appropriated terms then become "artefacts of culture, objects of conversation and instruments of daily understanding" (Dening 1980:87) in a world beyond the academy. This model of transposition and the making over of terms and understandings relate the anthropological arbitration of meaning to Gusfield's notion of the time-bound ownership of problems. Talking to me outside the courtroom, one lawyer put quits to anthropological pretensions thus: "Soon we won't need you anthropologists much as consultants. As the claims go on, we're establishing precedents so that lawyers will be able to argue issues without having to listen to all that technical stuff that you people put into submissions. I'll say this: the judge is very patient with all of you. But he is getting principles if you follow the claims through."

In Australia, anthropologists have had to crave and get judicial indulgence. A problem is that anthropology (out of Maitland and Maine) long ago appropriated terms of law to art. As in the Gove case (noted below), Justice Blackburn had to deal with objections from counsel who protested that anthropologists were bandying words such as "ownership," "right" and "property" in their evidence. These technical terms of law are not for laymen to use with authority in court. As Maddock (1981:100) reports:

> Mr. Justice Blackburn resolved the problem by holding that it was best for experts to express themselves in terms which seem to them to be appropriate, but that it was for the court to decide whether talk 'about' "the land-owning or land-possessing group" . . . is in fact a proper jurisprudential analysis of the relationship (Gove judgment, pp. 164-66).

In Australia, the anthropological concession of recent years has been grounded in the problem of the nature and definition of traditional Aboriginal ownership of land. And applied anthropologists have generally been unprepared for the task and so have had to embark on risky personal ventures into practical ways of doing the job and learning from mistakes. But there has been an even more chastening experience. When Julian Steward was called to address the Indian Claims Commission in the United States in 1944, he had to enter an apology for his discipline. As Feldman

(1980:245-46) explains, "his testimony related to the determination of whether a Native group filing a claim had actually been a 'tribe, band, or identifiable group' and not simply a collection of individuals." The Hobbesian scenario was being re-enacted with reference to *Basin Plateau Socio Political Groups* (Steward 1938). But "Steward also noted the general failure of anthropologists to investigate the notion of 'property' adequately in their Native American research efforts" (Feldman 1980:246). The Australian Land Rights story begins with the revelation of disciplinary inadequacy as two major figures of the Australian wing of the anthropological fraternity enter into the kind of "Formative Travail with Leviathan" that Leach (1977) rules should not be part of an anthropologist's business.

In the Gove case Professors Berndt and Stanner failed to satisfy the court on the perennial Hobbesian issue. Stanner's (1979) wry and retrospective judgment of Gove is that the case showed the inability of the court to recognize the reality of the essential unit of Aboriginal social organization—the "fluctuating group." A lawyer's cold verdict on the matter is that an anthropology designed to academic purpose was found wanting (Gumbert 1981). In Gumbert's estimation, counsel for the Aboriginal plaintiffs was let down because he treated his untested anthropological advisers as if they were expert and already owned the problem of ownership. Neither of them case-hardened, Professors Berndt and Stanner were confident that they could represent the Aboriginal "clan" as a body corporate and so as a person at law. As the hearing proceeded it became clear that although they expressed clannish sentiments, the clan as such was seldom if ever realized as an entity "on the ground"—doing its clan thing in ceremonial performance, setting up camps based on clan membership, forming clan-based work groups and so on. In the judge's view, the produced and clinching fact at law was that a procession of ten Aboriginal witnesses who talked of the place of the clan in their own lives were adamant to a man (no women were called). They could not and would not draw word-pictures that would give the clan more than a principled and nominal existence. An anthropological judgment might read that Aborigines subscribe to norms of kinship that tend toward patrifiliation, but they are not a people of agnation as are, say, the Bedouin (Peters 1960) or Tswana (Schapera 1955). For the last-mentioned peoples, an anthropological case for incorporation of the agnatic descent group could well be made, since local groups are demonstrably made up of fellow-agnates, their wives and unmarried daughters. The judicial finding in the Gove case was that Aborigines could neither be credited with corporate groupings nor granted any culturally entertained notion of proprietory right that could reasonably be translated into any one of the forms of ownership or tenure (e.g., fee simple) that are recognized in Western jurisprudence.

Today, in Australia, anthropologists go to court after Gove and so, to some extent, are prepared to admit that neither anthropology nor ethnographies (though invaluable as sources) will survive in court if rendered in acts of simple citation and appeal to authority. The court has to be led, led to an appreciation of the current state of anthropology and status of the discipline at the time particular versions of Aboriginal social forms were penned. On this score, Maddock (1980) notes the difference between anthropology in Australia and the anthropology of those places (particularly Africa and Indonesia) where ethnographers, conscious of administrative needs, wrote in terms of law and produced Dutch Boeke on *Adat* or Handbooks of Native Law and Custom in English. In the absence of handbooks, the Australianist, as expert witness, has to do a great deal of special pleading. This entails the crafting of special novel and purpose-built models for use in court. The anthropology of Australian land rights is therefore less an applied anthropology of authoritative citation, and more a creative anthropology of inventive interpretation in which one's native wit bows to probity and in which one's interpretive predelictions not only show but are to be declared in anticipation of the inevitable challenge. I think that the Australian courts have shown a judicial receptivity in cases where learning to understand the natives is about as difficult as "learning more anthropology than one thought one would ever need to know" (an aside from the Bench rendered as accurately as I can remember). It is from experience of this Australian scene with its judicial tolerance and anthropological unpreparedness that I issue my main message: processural modelling must be either the stuff of one's representations or the modelling that is behind them. Only this, together with an objectified appreciation of the act and context of representation, will serve if the academic is to turn expert and make professional rather than disciplinary representations.

NORTHERN TERRITORY LAND RIGHTS

After the Gove case, after a referendum in which Australian citizens made the administration of Aboriginal Affairs over to the Australian Commonwealth (1967) and after the election of a Labor government (1972), a commission was set up to consider ways and means of redeeming a Labor election promise—the granting of land rights to Aborigines. The commissioner was Justice Woodward who, before his elevation to the judiciary, had represented Aboriginal interests and appeared as the counsel let down by anthropology in the Gove case. The Second Report of the Aboriginal Land Rights Commission (1974) yielded to anthropologists the ownership of the problem of defining "traditional Aboriginal owners" of land.

The anthropological concession belongs to two periods of official time, which I shall refer to as Phase I and Phase II. Phase I is the period of the Interim Land Rights Commissioner, while Phase II belongs to his successor, the Aboriginal Land Commissioner appointed in terms of the Aboriginal Land Rights Act of 1976. The transition between Phase I and Phase II was marked by the simple deletion of a set of proposed provisions. The act of deletion was devastating in its effects. I briefly explain why.

In his report, Justice Woodward (1974) recommended that Territory Aborigines be ceded rights to land on two separate and distinctive sets of grounds. In the first place, traditional ownership was to be recognized. Aborigines who could refer to tradition to establish the fact and right of claim would be ceded those ancestral lands which could be resumed by the state. In the second place, Woodward provided an account of those Aborigines who would not be served by traditional ownership either because their lands were not resumable or because they were displaced people whose needs might not be satisfied by grants of rights to ancestral tracts. In particular, Justice Woodward drew attention to the urban fringe-dwellers and those Aborigines who had based long-lived communities or encampments on pastoral properties. He thus proposed a second rubric: claims should be entertained on grounds of *de facto* occupancy, long association and need.

Recognition of these grounds would serve the cause of Aborigines who had developed new styles of life in association with particular locations.

Woodward was only proposing that fringe-dwellers and their like be ceded formally what they already used. However, grants on the basis of long association and need would clearly compete with other forms of tenure. The resumption of relevant acres would entail both the variation of pastoral leases and a series of intrusions into the jurisdictions of municipalities, shires and other statutory and local authorities. In the outcome, a craven Commonwealth Parliament dropped the second of the Woodward rubrics. The 1976 Act recognized traditional owners, but gave Aborigines no other priviledged access to title. However, land rights hearings began after the publication of the Woodward Report (1974) and before the enabling legislation had gone through Parliament. An Interim Land Rights Commissioner was appointed, and the hearings that he held in Darwin had, for terms of reference, not an act but the Woodward recommendations.

There is an irony here. In the first instance, the Interim Commissioner addressed claims of need, the type of claim that was destined to be legislated to oblivion. The phrase "needs claim" was quickly established as semi-official shorthand for the genre in quarters that mattered. *De facto* occupancy, long association and need are all creations of Western law. Taken as grounds, each makes immediate legal sense. However, "traditional ownership" is not in Australia a part of the common law; in 1975 its legal status had yet to be established. Claims for traditional rights were held in abeyance while needs claims got under way. Some needs claims were submitted and heard while the Northern Lands Council (on behalf of Aboriginal claimants) set to work on others in train.

At this time I was recruited to prepare a statement of claim on behalf of Aborigines associated with Humpty Doo. I made my report, but the Humpty Doo claim never got to court, for the whole category of "claims of need" was (in the literal sense of a cliché) rendered a dead letter. On 20 May 1981, however, the House of Representatives Standing Committee on Aboriginal Affairs took "Fringe-Dwelling Aboriginal Communities" as its reference. It can be argued that the location of Humpty Doo station outside a small settlement south of Darwin makes its inhabitants members of a

fringe-dwelling community. But, more broadly, the Standing Committee was charged to establish a new rubric, and the probability
is that fringe-dwelling ''communities'' will be granted not land
rights, but qualified tenure of designated camps that recognized
communities (as bodies corporate) will acquire on leasehold terms
that will be heavily qualified as to use, management, circumstance,
and permission. For the anthropological concessionaire, new
possiblities are implicit in current developments. People of outlying camps will probably need representation under terms of
reference yet to be provided. Predictably, these terms will deal with
both ''need'' and the Aboriginal body corporate, that is, the nature
of ''community.'' In its very inference to the Standing Committee, Parliament assumes that fringe-dwelling Aborigines constitute
communities. Twists of time have meant that the significance of
submissions with respect to Humpty Doo belong to the future. In
contrast, the Finniss River story is not only history but part of the
story of an anthropological concession all but finished up and so
I deal with it (a Phase II hearing) before I turn to Humpty Doo.

Finniss River: A People's Sense of Time

A passage from Evans-Pritchard's (1961:7) lecture on ''Anthropology and History'' can be read as a declaration of an anthropological unpreparedness to deal with the central issue in the
Finniss River case:

> Anthropologists of today and yesterday, owing to lack of interest
> in history, have not in this matter asked themselves some im-
> portant questions. Why among some peoples are historical tradi-
> tions rich and among others poor? Almost 70 years ago Codr-
> ington noted that 'A point of difference between the Polynesian
> and Melanesian sections of the Pacific peoples is the conspicuous
> presence in the former, and the no less conspicuous absence in
> the latter, of native history and tradition' but he gives no reason
> for this. Again, Dr. Southall has recently remarked that
> knowledge and interest in past events among the Alur is much
> greater than among neighbouring peoples to the west of the Nile
> and Lake Albert, but he likewise does not suggest why this should
> be so. Another question concerns the content of tradition. What
> sort of events are remembered and to what social attachments
> and rights to they relate (e.g., the rights of a family or clan to
> lands or the rights of a line of descent to office)? Malinowski has

paid some attention to this matter, but not systematically, and to 'myth' rather than to history. Then, what mnemonics are employed as points of reference in tradition—features of landscape (history is often attached to places rather than to peoples, as de Calonne has pointed out, or, as Frederica de Laguna has remarked, speaking of the Tlingit of Alaska, peoples conceptualize their geography in history); features of the social structure (genealogies, age-sets, royal successions); and artifacts (heirlooms)? Then again, to what extent do environmental conditions affect tradition and a people's sense of time?

Anthropologically speaking, the Finniss River hearing ended up as a demand for a partial answer to the set of questions raised in Evans-Pritchard's Manchester lecture. One had to explain how (rather than why) Aborigines join with Melanesians as a people of little legend, a hesitant oral history and a truncated sense of time.

The 1976 Act provided a definition of traditional Aboriginal owners, and, together with provisions for the creation of Lands Trusts, put an end to the problem of determining whether members of hunter-gatherer groupings could ever be given corporate identity in law. The definition in the Northern Territory Act gives statutory recognition to a "local descent group." The problem is, then, to determine whether a group of claimants qualify as such. According to the act,

"Traditional Aboriginal owners," in relation to land, means a local descent group of Aboriginals who

(a) have common spiritual affiliations to a site on the land, being affiliations that place the group under a primary spiritual responsibility for that site and for the land; and

(b) are entitled by Aboriginal tradition to forage as of right over that land.

Once this definition of traditional Aboriginal owners was supplied, the second phase in Territory Land Rights hearings could begin. The definition provides terms of reference for each hearing and also specifies the terms of a curtailed anthropological concession. As a result, there is an anthropological community in Australia that is united by the ability of its members to recite the definition and other portions of the act to one another.

In the Finniss River claim, there were two opposed Aboriginal groupings, the Maranunggu and the Kungarakany/Warai, each claiming exclusive traditional ownership of a defined area of land. The two groupings were distinguished by different lifestyles. The Maranunggu identify themselves as "countrymen" of the Darwin Hinterland. They had a base camp near the contested area, and used other camps, moving between pastoral stations and the urban-fringe camps of Darwin and Adelaide River. They claimed to be the "traditional owners" of the contested area, asserting that it is dotted with sites which are embraced in Maranunggu mythology and for which the Maranunggu therefore have "primary spiritual responsibility."

On the other side, the Kungarakany claimants are part-Aboriginal people, and most of them live in urban housing. Little of the Kungarakany language survives, whereas Maranunggu remains a language of everyday interaction. The association of Kungarakany and Warai as co-claimants was an alliance based on traditional precedent, of which the Warai claimants were, in general, more of the country than of town. In the course of evidence two pictures of the contesting claimant groupings were constructed, with anthropologists advising each group. These pictures were detailed and exhaustive. In the end, the case was to hinge on a single major question: is the takeover of land by an incoming group possible in Aboriginal tradition? On the one hand, there was documentary evidence to show that the Maranunggu were interlopers who hailed from the region of the Daly River hundreds of miles to the south. The Kungarakany, on the other hand, were indisputably descendents of a group who had held the contested area in traditional ownership from the time of first contact and for whom there was no documented history of desertion of homeland. A further and important fact of evidence was that only the older members of the Maranunggu claimant group were aware of the Maranunggu removal. The youngsters had been starved of knowledge. At this juncture the case began to appear to some as a case tainted by gerontocratic deceit. The requirement was to model the active creation of *time immemorial* in native ideology. I argued as follows (Sansom 1980:2-4).

The essential issue in the takeover of land in Aboriginal Australia is the process by which *de facto* use and occupancy by an incoming group are converted into ownership as of right and by which *de facto* use and occupancy can be converted into ownership as of right from time immemorial. In his early investigations of the Murngin, Warner was well aware of the process in question. He wrote (Warner 1937:18-19):

> No land can be taken from a clan by an act of war. A clan does not possess its land by strength of arms but by immemorial tradition and as an integral part of the culture. Murngin myth dies hard, and ownership of land is in Murngin myth even after the final destruction of a particular clan. It would never occur to a victorious group to annex another's territory, even though the entire male population were destroyed and the dead men's women and children taken by the victors. In the passage of time the clan using it would absorb it into their own territory and the myth would unconsciously change to express this. In the thought of the Murngin, land and water, people and clan are an act of the creator totem and the mythological ancestors, who always announce in myth and ceremony that this is the country of such and such a clan; to expropriate this land as a conscious act would be impossible.

So, Murngin rights to land are inextinguishable; yet one Murngin clan can absorb the territory of another and incorporate the sites of the absorbed country into its clan mythology.

Writing of desert Aborigines who ranged widely over the estates of various owners in traditional times, Stanner (1965:2) points out that in an environment of the utmost stringency, "consideration of range (especially in protracted drought conditions) might dominate those of estate for as much as a decade. But wandering desert-steppe groups could always identify their 'country' even if they had not been able to visit it for years. Nothing could extinguish the fact and claim of estate." When these citations are considered together, the following principle is clear: for as long as there is living memory of traditional ownership of land, the "fact and claim of estate" are not extinguished. For claims to be wholly extinguished, consciousness of them must die. And the death of memory in an oral culture is closely associated with particular clan affiliations. With the dying of predecessors, aspects of historical dispositions can be relegated to what Dr. Sutton (another anthropologist) aptly designates (in a written submission) the realm of "time out of mind." Furthermore, for any culture, there is a structure that determines the depth of group memory and the point of onset of what one anthropologist has called "structural

amnesia'' (Cunnison 1959). In Aboriginal Australia, shallow
genealogies, groups of small-scale and cultural injunctions that
positively discourage the reawakening of historical disputation all
combine. The result is that the structurally determined timespan
for Aboriginal historical memory is notoriously short. This, in turn,
means that events of the order of Warner's unconscious absorption of one clan's territory by another can occur quite soon after
the actual depossession of the original owning groups. What is required is a lapse of about two generations, together with the
absence of surviving counter-claimants. With the efflux of time,
uncomfortable facts concerning the prior and original rights of
now-defunct groups can finally become irretrievable.

Appreciating processes of this order, Dr. Sutton states that the
present land claim has caused younger Maranunggu people resident on the Wagait Reserve to be confronted for the first time with
the assertion that as Maranunggu they are members of an ''immigrant group.'' ''This,'' he argues, ''represents an interruption
to the normal process by which their ultimate genealogical connection to the Daly River would have eventually been obscured
and forgotten by *all* Aboriginal people in the region'' (Sutton
1980:8). While going along with the gist of Dr. Sutton's analysis
at this point, I would put the matter more strongly. The ''normal
process'' to which Dr. Sutton refers has not so much been interrupted as wholly subverted by this hearing and the investigations
that preceded it. The ''normal process'' involves the nontransmis-
sion of items of historical information between Aboriginal elders
and their juniors. Successors are not heir to the full quantity of
knowledge that their predecessors command, for there is no obligation on elders to tell all. Within the jurisdiction of the local groupings they command, elders in their political wisdom should pass
on knowledge to advantage, and not disadvantage, the young. In
this instance, the consciousness of young Maranunggu has been
inappropriately raised to match that of older people, and the very
mechanisms that promote structural amnesia (involving the cen-
sorship and selection of information transmitted by older people
to their successors) have been overridden. For the younger
Maranunggu people concerned, the consequence is an irretrievable
resurrection of the past. They can never return to an innocent
unawareness of the alleged immigrant status of their group. Dr.

Sutton's notion of a normal process has much in common with Warner's statement concerning "unconscious absorption." The accommodation of the takeover by one clan of another's land is finally accomplished only when there is no one either able or sufficiently interested to assert unforgotten claims to prior ownership or identity.

Anthropologically speaking, there is an intimate connection between a truncated sense of time and the social organization of the "fluctuating group" in Aboriginal Australia. In a world of movement between camps and groups in which a propertyless people have intermittent but momentarily absorbing and significant experience of one another, the relegation of the past to a limbo that is the space between real time and the Dreaming is a social necessity.

The mobs in which Northern Aborigines 'run' are labile groupings. Each is made up of people in current association, and the composition of each mob is prone to variation and alteration over time. Mobs are brought into being by acts of recruitment of people to place, and, as I have shown elsewhere (Sansom 1980a, 1981), Aborigines command a refined conceptual apparatus for the modelling of association in unlasting and fluctuating groups. Expected fluctuation of group membership and individual expectation of mob-to-mob movement gives personal identity its meaning. In a world of unlasting mobs, long-term identity is, for the individual, his or her shared membership in the hinterland collectivity made up of all those Aboriginal others who over the years have, on and off, shared together in times and places.

HUMPTY DOO: A SENSE OF PLACE

In July 1976, when I was presenting a "needs claim" for Humpty Doo, my problem also concerned time; time and the nature of a "fluctuating group" that had to be established as a needy subject. The Humpty Doo people could not, without special pleading, advance their cause as members of a stable, residential community. A static definition of their form of association would inevitably fall apart in the face of questions such as: "How often do you sit down in that camp?" In this and a previous needs claim I decided to take the risk that had to be taken and present a detailed representation of the realities of movement and so argue the reality of the "fluctuating group" into legal recognition. The terms of reference under which I worked were those of the Woodward report (1974). Its criteria—long association, need and *de facto* occupancy—were, I reasoned, permissive enough to accommodate the realities—provided that the court was prepared to listen.

Let me turn to what I see as the anthropological 'facts' on which I grounded representation by citing a summary representation of the Aboriginal view of the kind of "long association" that generates a sense of ownership of place:

> Members of mobs in their domination of scenes protest exclusive possession and hold potential usurpers off. But recognizable mobs do not historically belong to scenes at all. Rather a set of scenes belongs to the wider population of Countrymen taken entire. Only the collectivity of all Countrymen can claim that there was continuous representation of their number on the historical scenes they claim. Thus in a court-hearing in Darwin where supplication was made to gain tenured right to land for fringe dwellers, I could argue in evidence that Aboriginal Countrymen of the hinterland had maintained a representative presence on the urban fringes for at least forty years—the period for which I could elicit reliable memories of Darwin experiences from the people I questioned. Seen as Countrymen, a grouping of people has been represented on the city fringes for as long as its members can credibly remember. But this sort of continuity cannot be ascribed to a mob presence. Project time and, on the basis of past experience, the scenes and sites of the Darwin hinterland belong not to particular aggregations which, in any case, belong to their own brief periods of realization, but to the general category of those who share generally in time with one another. Think in terms of scale and this treatment of the association between people and place makes further sense: today the Countrymen number about 500 and the sites they claim within their territory are many and well distributed. The capacity to hold such a range of places in more than notional possession belongs to 500 and not to a mob even when as at Wallaby Cross it can boast 80 members (Sansom 1981b:266-67).

My purpose in writing about the Humpty Doo needs claim is twofold: first, in citing parts of my report, I seek to deliver up my concessionary artifact—a model of Aboriginal social organization, to which I repeatedly return in order to back public representations; secondly, when making representations on behalf of the people of Humpty Doo, I was doing something else as well. I sought to establish precedent. The Humpty Doo report is a bid to gain official recognition for an anthropologically derived definition of a type of organized population. Given this, an anthropological concession was at stake. In routine representation, when concessionary precedent has been established, this is of no major concern. Routine representation is thus to be distinguished from instances of special representation in which claimants and concessionaire stand similarly in their respective ways to win or lose futures. In this, I emphasize professional and disciplinary rather than individual futures. The Humpty Doo claim was as much about the anthropological ownership of needs claims as it was about the pastoral lease in question.

In the following excerpt from my report, I have isolated that part of the submission (pp. 3-6) that could have further concessionary implications.

> [Here] I provide the necessary background that makes sense of a definition of a type of grouping wholly characteristic of the Western side of the Top End.
>
> (1) This type of grouping is made up of Aboriginal people who regard a particular locational centre, often an Aboriginal camp on a cattle station, as their home-place.
>
> (2) Despite the fact that this home-place is not necessarily a part of their home-territory as defined in traditional terms.
>
> (3) These groupings of people are, furthermore, usually of mixed tribal origin and, in consequence, their various members speak a number of different languages or dialects. In such mixed groups, the general use of such a form of non-standard English (usually called "pidgin") facilitates communication between those members of the group who do not have an Aboriginal language in common.
>
> (4) Vital social links between members of such tribally mixed groups are based on years of joint experience of work not merely on one, but on a number of cattle stations as well as in other forms of European-controlled employment. As the people themselves are apt to put the matter: "We bin work together for years n years."
>
> (5) Links forged by years of association in cattle-station employment or in other work, are reinforced by ties of marriage, of "in-

lawship'' or affinity. Men who have worked together often take
each others' kinswomen as wives. The result is that second and
subsequent generations are produced whose members, while still
''mixed'' in terms of patrilineally reckoned tribal origins, are
closely linked both to their contempories and to their
predecessors in the local group by ties of kinship and affinity.
(6) It should be noted that adult members of this type of grouping have not necessarily all worked together at one place or for
the same employer for their entire careers. Rather than sharing
a single station of employment, the people of the group have
shared what may be called a ''work beat.'' Such work beats are
made up, for example, of several cattle-stations, a couple of
buffalo-shooting camps and, perhaps, a farm, the owner of which
offers seasonal employment. It is characteristic of such work beats
that they expand or contract over the years, often because of
either the success or the failure of Top End enterprises.
(7) Certain places that are part of a work beat gain particular
significance. These are places that those persons who claim to
be members of ''one mob'' come to regard as their base or home-
place. Given the seasonality of employment in Northern
Australia, the home-place or base may often be defined as the
place at which a person establishes his residence during the Wet
Season. For many years, Humpty Doo has served this last-
mentioned purpose for a locally recognized Wet Season
population.
(8) For convenience, the type of grouping that is characterized
by the seven attributes listed above will be referred to as a
Hinterland Aboriginal Community. A summary definition of a
Hinterland Aboriginal Community can now be supplied: A
Hinterland Aboriginal Community in the north-west of the Territory is a group of people of mixed tribal origins who are now
based on a particular home-place, who are united by ties of shared
work-experience, by ties of kinship and affinity and who are
generally to be found living together in the Wet Season while,
at other times of the year, some of the members of the group
will be absent from their home camp for extended periods
because occupied elsewhere. The population of Humpty Doo con-
forms with this definition to constitute a Hinterland Aboriginal
Community. It is further submitted that the Hinterland
Aboriginal Community is a major type of social grouping and
that the emergence of this type of grouping has, for many north-
western people, superceded and, in certain respects, functioned

as a substitute for association based on more narrow and exclusive tribal membership and the continued occupancy of an original tribal territory. For a section of the Aboriginal population, the Hinterland Aboriginal Community made up of a group or ''mob'' is the primary and existent social group that supplies each person with a social identity. It is further to be emphasized that the designation of ''Hinterland Aboriginal Community'' has here been applied to a type of local grouping that, while emergent, is not new. Communities of this sort originated in the Aboriginal response to the initiation of the demand for Aboriginal labour. Where a claim for land is made by people who constitute a Hinterland Aboriginal Community, their claim is made by an already existing group whose members have elected to live and work together and who acknowledge a joint identity in asserting that, taken together, they form ''one mob.''

The people of Humpty Doo, in seeking to constitute themselves as the AWIRUK Association and in initiating a Land Claim, are attempting to gain greater security to procure the advancement of the Aboriginal grouping that is, for them, in terms of their daily lives, the functional equivalent of the traditionally constituted tribal group of former times.

Once the type of grouping was delineated in general terms, a further essential step was to elaborate on the way in which Humpty Doo people themselves spoke in terms of the model, working to supply officers of the court with a vocabulary of locally recognized concepts, used when claimants themselves were called to attest in court. Anthropologically supplied data on general trends will be tested and one does not want either judge or lawyer to ask a witness whether he or she is an accredited member of a constituted Hinterland Aboriginal Community. As land claims are conducted in the Northern Territory, anthropological models stand and become established if claimants themselve yield up the components and confirm the reality of the general trends defined by the anthropologist in the language they use about themselves.

A section of the Humpty Doo report was therefore devoted to the business of glossing terms that Aborigines employ when describing the formation of mobs and the criteria for recognizing valid attachment to place and other people. Having thus cited Humpty Doo as a case in which the anthropologist attempted to establish concessionary competence, I now turn to consider the context for the creation of anthropological concessions in Fourth World politics in more general terms.

CONCESSIONAIRES AND FOURTH WORLD CONCESSIONS

Whenever Third and Fourth World peoples are most thoroughly colonized and oppressed, their affairs—and I mean all their affairs—are appropriated to a single government department. Designated a Department of Indian, Native, Aboriginal, Bantu or whatever Affairs, such departments of commodious implementation provide an apparatus for total control that makes Barthian imperative status (Barth 1969) a reality. The supreme contemporary realization is, no doubt, the Bantu Affairs Department (B.A.D.) in South Africa. This department is constituted as an *imperium in imperio* (Brookes and Macaulay 1958). Its subdivisions match those of the parallel departments of health, welfare, employment, and so on that cater to the population of white South Africans. Concentrated administration of the affairs of indigenous people is, I suggest, associated with the state-sponsored perpetuation of oppression.

When, in any country, an era of special rather than stigmatized status for autochthones is ushered in, there are two alternative destinies for any established Department of Indigenous Affairs. On the one hand, it can be dismantled; on the other, it may be charged to implement the provisions of special status. When the latter course is adopted, surviving departments are charged to modulate the business of positive discrimination. My distinction between departments for oppression and departments for special provision is clearly drawn, but mixed types can exist. In Australia, the Commonwealth Department of Aboriginal Affairs currently remains an example of the mixed type, mainly because the Commonwealth government has yet to exercise fully the powers mandated to it in the referendum of 1967. This referendum gave Aboriginal Affairs over to Commonwealth control. However, the Commonwealth has been dilatory, and successive Commonwealth governments have yet to invade wholly the administration of Aboriginal affairs in the two most racist Australian states—Queensland and Western Australia. In these two states there is an uneasily negotiated division of the labour concerning Aboriginal administration, which, in turn, belongs to both state and Commonwealth agencies.

I have adduced these few facts about Aboriginal affairs in Australia to make a more general point. It seems to me that one can be more optimistic about the official provisioning that affects the destiny of Fourth World peoples when there is a pluralistic administration: when; in short, the state's responses to the special problems of indigenous populations are no longer in control of a bureaucratic monopoly but have instead become aspects of diversified administrations as adjunct to the activities of the departments of Health, Welfare, Lands, Culture, and so on. The needs of Fourth World peoples can also be recognized and served by the creation of special statutory bodies. Thus, in Australia, there are allocations and organizations for Aboriginal legal aid, Aboriginal housing, land rights, and special programs for the promotion of Aboriginal health. I remark on such developments to note a consequence. In the pluralistic administration of special provisions for indigenous peoples, there is a proliferation of concessions.

The struggle for recognition of special status is, then, a single struggle fought on many fronts, and its history becomes a saga of gains here, offset by losses there. In such circumstances, Aboriginal representation can potentially gain integrity. Representative bodies can take *the* Aboriginal interest to various departments, participate in inquiries and in the total context of political lobbying, and gain recognition as one of the relevant interests to be taken into account in the range of investigations that lead to legislation.

Paine (1985) emphasizes structured asymmetry as a problematic aspect of Fourth World representation. The asymmetry is, for me, a given. Perhaps seduced by Hobbes, I accept that in the nation-state anything less than the state itself is a subordinate "Systeme." Hobbes' (1914:118) principled statement on the "errour and misreckoning" entailed in the creation of *imperium in imperio* is this: "To give leave to a body Politique of Subjects, to have an Absolute Representation to all intents and purposes, were to abandon the government of so much of the Commonwealth, and divide their Dominion." Far more problematic and sociologically interesting than asymmetry are the various and temporally particular issues that can be entailed in the articulation of national and minority interests. To elaborate this contention, I am well served by Beckett's (1977) analysis of the Torres Strait Islanders and the pearling industry.

Beckett deals with a phase in the relationship between Islanders of the Torres Strait and Australia that, he argues, is susceptible to an analysis in terms of a model of internal colonialism. Beckett describes labour relations, the emergence of islander elites and the way in which Queensland's segregation policy tied Islanders to the isolated and distant communities in which they could support themselves with little money, but still be induced to work for wages in pearling, the only locally available industry. Beckett's (1977:100-01) conclusion to his essay begins thus:

> In this paper I have analysed Torres Strait's relationship with Australia in terms of a model of internal colonialism, focussing on the articulation of subsistence and capitalistic modes of production. I have taken the marine industry as the dominant mode, supported by the subsistence sector, and I have represented the Queensland government as regulating the articulation. This is not to suggest that they were under unified control: each had its own institutional autonomy, but in the local setting the two meshed into one another. Government policy may not have been designed with the needs of the masters directly in view, but it tended to their advantage in the long run. And when the government itself became an entrepreneur, with the aim of making the communities self-supporting, their immediate interests converged.

It is no accident that for the duration of the period in question, administration of the Torres Straits Islands and their people was in the monopolistic and less-than-beneficient control of the Queensland Department of Aboriginal and Islander Affairs. The phase of Torres Strait history to which the model of internal colonialism applies has (if I understand Beckett) now been superceded. And the change begins with the end of the Second World War. "As in other parts of Australia, there was an increasing post war inflow of special aid for indigenous people, in the form of housing, health and education facilities, and development projects. With the decline of the marine industry Torres Strait politics has increasingly focussed on the distribution of government funds . . ." (p. 102). Today, government funds are to be gained by plural representation.

In Australia, at least, the practical politics of the representation of indigenous peoples is presently not only the politics of special status, but is also the politics of special issues. The struggle on many fronts is defined in terms of both (1) indigenous (Fourth World) status and (2) public problems of moment. This is a recent (and, I think, more optimistic) formula for the practical politics of the representation of the interests of indigenous Australians. A product of the emergent pluralistic structure for articulations between indigenous constituencies and state agencies is the proliferation of concessions and concessionaires. In the emerging and pluralistic structure, the representation of indigenous peoples is assimilated to what Gusfield (1981) defines as "the culture of public problems." So in Australia there is the problem of alcoholism, but there is especially the problem of Aborigines and Alcohol (an application of the formula). There are Australian problems of law reform and, in particular, the issue of the possible recognition of Aboriginal customary law. The pairing of these two examples is piquant because the first is a reference to the House of Representatives Standing Committee on Aboriginal Affairs, the second a subsidiary reference in the brief of the Australian Law Reform Commission. Ethnicity thus enters into the definitions of issues in two distinct ways: terms sometimes function to give the form of a problem to the constitution of a commission or committee, or otherwise to give the problem as content to a constituted committee on Aboriginal affairs.

WHY PROCESSURAL MODELLING?

Processural modelling is the business of treating produced social structures in terms of the processes for their creation, maintenance and transformation. More particularly, the business is to relate social mechanism to produced form and structure to event. The challenge is thus to describe not only discovered forms but activity— the social construction of reality. I argue that nowadays, anthropological concessions can only be won and confidently held if the anthropologist proffers arguments that are themselves structured in terms of production and reproduction. There must be an anthropology of processural modelling *behind* each of the abbreviated, edited and terminologically simplified models that are rendered over to the world of practical purpose and pointed decisions. So much for reassertion. However, let me now finish my argument by listing four reasons to explain why the anthropologist who deals with indigenous minorities must rely on models of process.

First, I refer to the social constitution of the traditions of Fourth World groupings. The people concerned often tend to be the descendents of ancestral precontact peoples who exploited the land as hunter-gatherers, snatch farmers, fishers, pastoralists, or long-cycle swiddeners (cf. Geertz 1966), or otherwise as a people in whose economy two or more of these five modes were combined in a complex patterning. The hunters, gatherers, fishers, pastoralists, and long-cycle swiddeners of this world are peoples of labile groupings, flexible social arrangements and a set of tenurial provisions that require a developed sense of the spatio-temporal use of space (Barth 1969) for their appreciation. Such peoples are normally neither closely settled on the land nor stabilized in local groups that announce possession of vicinage or neighbourhood either by the fact of occupancy or a history of permanent residential association with a narrow and unranging definition of place. Historically, these were people highly susceptible to displacement and dispossession by incursive Europeans who, with guns, clearances, guard dogs, punishment commandos, and all the other instrumentalities of settler appropriation, could usurp the original inhabitants, undo their system of spatio-temporal tenure (which was less than 'holding' land), and either drive autochthones deep into further hinterlands beyond the settler frontier or concede remnant tribes' or groupings' islanded 'reserve lands' to a sea of settler expropriation.

The economic traditions that made the ancestral autochthones of many present-day Fourth World people easy prey in the era of settler expansion are traditions yielding social forms that are consistent with an order of shifting exploitation. European successors of the early settlers still fail to comprehend such social forms precisely because those forms are characterized by their lability and the impermanence of their realizations. Hence the problem of the "fluctuating group." People who still know labile social groupings continue the struggle to gain credence when they try to constitute groupings that are to be representative bands or representative band councils (cf. Weaver, this volume). As Preston

(1975:138) has recently remarked of the Cree (of James Bay), these are people who in their social lives are concerned with particular meanings and precise understandings in context, and who emphasize meaning more than form (pp. 11-14). Elsewhere I have provided a similar characterization of trends among Aborigines in Northern Australia (Sansom 1981a, 1981b). There is again an irony. Peoples who still order their affairs in terms of received tradition and whose traditions derive from a mobile, shifting past are today fighting the battle their ancestors fought in the early days of contact. They fight from changeable lines drawn in terms of the "fluctuating group," and have to translate traditions that emphasize particular meaning over form into representations for authorities who belong to a world of perduring institutions based on the fictions of corporate personality and perpetual succession. Noting this, one identifies a true clash of cultures; that is, a contraposition of all-but-irreconcilable inherited principles that are brought to the constitution of enduring corporations of ownership, on the one hand, and to labile "mobs" of "Countrymen" who have "gotta lotta place altogether," on the other. Because peoples of the Fourth World are often people who emphasize process rather than produced structure, the social forms of such Fourth World peoples themselves require processural modelling if representations of them are to be neither denatured caricatures nor misplaced notional consolidations (cf. the Gove case in which the nominal clan was concretized in anthropological representation).

To one good reason, I add a second. Fourth World claims for recognition of special status (rather than the need for special provision) entail assertion of historical ethnic identity, and at the same time are appeals for the statutory or formal recognition of rights or immunities that derive from native tradition. In the case of Finniss River, the Aboriginal Land Commissioner, when submitting his report on the claim, rejected an unchanging vision of tradition in favour of one that entertained time. He wrote: "This view may not appeal, especially to those who think of traditional Aboriginal society as something static. But should one assume that Aboriginal society is unique in this respect?" (Aboriginal Land Commissioner 1981:22). To reconcile active tradition with a history of post-contact vicissitudes, Fourth World populations that have kept tradition have maintained it by exploiting the capacity of tradition to accommodate shifts and changes and to be reworked as tradition itself was brought to novelty to embrace it. Either to explain current traditional dispensations that are agreed upon, or to elucidate native disputation about the application of traditional norms to instances, models of process are again required. As in the Finniss case, the anthropologist has to be able to explain how rival parties can each aver that tradition supports their conflicting assertions. In that case, sketched models of the systematic "editing" (Sutton 1980) of historical accounts and the generation of a "people's sense of time" were both needed. Such models are distinguished because they invoke mechanisms to explain the coexistence of two contradictory but independently asserted charters for ownership.

To enter a claim that purports to represent need, one again requires models of perduring trends of being and becoming. As in the case of Humpty Doo, a conception not merely of resultant forms, but of their dynamic reproduction must be inherent in representation. This is to emphasize not what people are, but what they do in order to become members of an anthropologically labelled Hinterland Aboriginal Community.

My fourth reason is simply put and is of a different order. Anthropology has itself grown beyond the stage of positivistic and functional representations that deal with a given world of stable systems that are held to their repetitive expression by Parsonian (1951) mechanisms of "pattern maintenance." The best that anthropology can do is not to produce any longer "as if" analyses posited on social stasis and the synchronic consideration of social entities. In various ways, anthropology today entertains change. To present versions of Fourth World realities in terms that require any arbitrary arrest of time is to deny current anthropology itself. The modelling of process is now an anthropological requirement and the challenge is to contrive improved means for advancing it.

"Knowing How to Talk to White People": Torres Strait Islanders and the Politics of Representation

4

JEREMY BECKETT

Australia has two indigenous minorities. As well as 145,000 Aborigines, there are some 16,000 Melanesians whose ancestral homes are a score of islands in the Torres Strait, between the tip of Queensland's Cape York and the southern coast of Papua - New Guinea. Drawing on a distinctive cultural heritage, with a more benign experience of colonialism than the Aborigines', this other minority invites some instructive comparisons, not least with respect to representation.

Colonialization, which began in the 1860s, was not the catastrophe for the Islanders that it was for so many Aborigines on the mainland. It did not involve displacement from ancestral lands or the usurpation of the resources from which they had traditionally drawn their livelihood. Thus they were able to adjust to the new order at a leisurely pace, alternating between subsistence production and wage labour for white employers.

In this adaptation the Islanders were guided by missionaries who reconstructed their communities along congregational lines. When the Queensland government took the Islanders under its care, it adapted this community structure to its own administrative needs, establishing elected councils as early as 1899—well ahead of any other colonial authority in the South Pacific. Initially, councillors played only an advisory role in local affairs; but as government activity increased, they became important as channels of communication with the communities, and as agents for containing discontent. As government policy came under public scrutiny, councillors also became a device for legitimating its activities.

With the explosion of welfare capitalism in the 1970s, the conditions of Aborigines and Islanders became a national issue, giving rise to a new kind of indigenous politics. In the process, both the strengths and the weaknesses of the Islanders' representatives became apparent; they knew better than Aborigines ''how to talk to white people,'' specifically bureaucrats, but they were inexperienced when it came to mobilizing public opinion.

THE STRUCTURE OF REPRESENTATION AND ITS SIGNIFICANCE IN A FOURTH WORLD SETTING

The essence of representation is that someone stands for some others in dealing with a third party. For this to occur there must be a discontinuity between the two parties, which is not negated but rather reinforced by the act of representation. One major set of problems clusters around the relationship between the representative and his constituency. His existence amounts to the assertion that there is a group that is representable in terms of a collective will or set of interests. However, it is important to recognize that this is a form of alienation that is in no sense natural or automatic. No individual can *be* another, and the ways by which one comes to represent others are devious and obscure. Representation is mediated by the alienation of an individual (Simmel) by the society of which one is a part.[1] For an individual to *be* that society seems only to compound the condition. But there are both political and cultural processes for overcoming it: on the one hand, the group tries to control the actions of its representative; on the other, it tries to legitimate them, or the person who performs them, through symbolic processes ranging from election to the installation of an hereditary ruler. Legitimacy and political control are, to some degree, alternatives—and liable to conflict.

Legitimacy is important to both parties because the representative is rarely just an agent adhering to a precise mandate; processes of any complexity require a measure of discretion, in which he is trusted by his constituency and accredited by the others. In an extreme case he is deemed to know better than his constituency what their ''true interests'' are and how these are best served, either because he has access to information that they lack, or because he is in some sense forming those interests. One might call this quasi-representation. However, not everything that a representative does need be legitimate in this sense: in clientistic politics, for example, it is understood that he has a free hand to pursue his own or anyone else's interests, once he has acquitted himself of particular promises. Here the constituency is no more than an aggregate of private interests, brought together by an accident of geography. At the other end of the scale, where group consciousness is highly developed, he represents them totally even in his private life.

A second set of problems clusters around the functions of representation in the overall political process. Communicating the needs and aspirations of the constituency is always the ostensible purpose, but this may take second place to the function of legitimizing the decisions of some superordinate body. In the Western democratic tradition, committees, councils, legislatures, and assemblies must be representative, often in specified ways, in order to be legitimate. In consequence, representation is a political resource, to be controlled and manipulated, even through electoral fraud. We are all familiar, not least in the Fourth World, with pseudo-representatives answerable to, and appointed by, governments rather than to the constituency with which they are associated. However, to the extent that the representative body is important and the discontinuities between it and the constituents are great, there will be some tendency for cooptation. Aside from direct pressures, the forms of consultation and decision-making can subtly blunt intentions and divert them into harmless channels. Moreover, effective performance in such arenas may require the kind of expertise which can be acquired only outside the constituency, and which then distances the representative from his people. This leaves them alienated from, yet still dependent on him. If one is to cope with these contradictions it must be by exploiting the discontinuity with Janus-faced shifts in style and rhetoric.

Such problems are particularly characteristic of the Fourth World where an indigenous minority confronts not just other ethnic groups but also the state, from a position of cultural inferiority and powerlessness. Representation, where it occurs, is part of the apparatus of government and sometimes little more than window-dressing.

The term ''Fourth World'' comes to us out of practical politics rather than social science, but it is a useful way of characterizing an historical phenomenon than can be precisely defined. One is not part of the Fourth World simply by belonging to what could be objectively defined as an indigenous minority. There must be a consciousness of this status as an entitlement to particular rights, and a recognition in the wider society that such entitlement exists. Some of these conditions are met when expatriate colonies try to forge a nationalism that separates them from the mother country, as in, for example, the *indigenismo* of postrevolutionary Mexico. However, the Fourth World phenomenon seems rather to have come out of the welfare-capitalist phase of liberal democracy in the 'First' World. Under welfare capitalism the state redistributes wealth in the form of pensions, grants, the dole, scholarships, and a variety of public services and programs. Whatever the ultimate motive of this expenditure, the rhetoric with which it is justified and which various groups use to bid for it is moralistic. Potential recipients are designated as "disadvantaged," "deprived," or in some other way "deserving." This kind of political culture offers indigenous minorities the possibility of transcending their small numbers and powerlessness, while giving governments the opportunity of demonstrating their humanity at what may be relatively small cost.[2] Thus in Australia, Aborigines as well as various immigrant groups have judged it more advantageous to follow this strategy rather than play class or party politics.

The politics of morality has not remained within the bounds of individual nation-states, but has spread into international arenas such as the United Nations and meetings of British Commonwealth heads of state. Perceiving the sensitivities of their governments to criticism from former colonial Third World states, indigenous minorities have cultivated the politics of embarrassment. Thus, recently the prime ministers of Zimbabwe and Vanuatu, both newly independent states, found themselves petitioned by Aborigines when they visited Australia. Similarly, Third World countries, which are commonly neither liberal-democratic nor welfare-capitalist, find themselves under attack for mistreating indigenous minorities. The United States' recent attack on Nicaragua for alleged massacres of Indians is a case in point. However, the final act of the Fourth World drama must be played out between the indigenous minority and its national government. It is my assumption that the prospects of the minority are most favourable when liberal democracy is combined with welfare capitalism. Governments that rule in terms of a national emergency, or are committed to a 'develop or die' strategy are inevitably less responsive to external or internal appeals in terms of human rights.

It is not an easy task to achieve the cohesion necessary to be an effective Fourth World minority, even in favourable settings. The societies that make up the Fourth World were originally either acephalous or segmentary states whose boundaries broke up at conquest. In the years that followed, they suffered further fragmentation and the blurring of boundaries. And although, overall, the distinctions between native and settler, savage and civilized persisted, the individual was not always inexorably assigned to one or other. Policies of uplift and assimilation promised—if they did not always provide—escape from subordination and inferiority; legislative loopholes and administrative quirks permitted passing and gave rise to ethnological enigmas such as the Lumbee (Blu 1980). Confusions of culture and genetics gave rise to anomalous half-caste populations. Under such conditions, representation occurred only at the village level, if at all, while officials and missionaries interposed themselves between their native wards and the higher levels of government. Even locally, the levelling characteristic of the poor and the dispossessed inhibited the development of legitimating processes and cut down anyone who stood out from the crowd.[3] Often, as in the case of the Torres Strait, representative institutions were initially imposed from above, before the people were able to control or legitimate them.

THE COLONIZATION OF TORRES STRAIT

The traditional ethnography of Torres Strait need not detain us for long.[4] We can view it as a culture area that included coastal Papua and parts of Cape York, integrated through regular canoe traffic and trade. The economic adaptations that particular communities made to local conditions, be it hunting, fishing, gathering, and/or gardening activities, were influenced by the possibility of trading surpluses and making up deficiencies. The social organization was broadly characteristic of coastal Melanesia in that it consisted of local groupings and cult activity. Leadership seems to have been manifested mainly in warfare and ritual, both of which ceased soon after contact. What survived was a tendency to utilize kinship connections in the formation of groups and action sets.

Although the first Europeans came to Torres Strait at the beginning of the seventeenth century, it did not become a regular waterway until the founding of the Australian colony in 1788, and there was no permanent European presence until the 1860s. This began with the arrival of small boats to work the rich deposits of pearl shell and trepang *(bêche-de-mer)*. The marine industry, unlike the pastoral industry on the mainland, did not encroach on the indigenous economy, since the resources it exploited did not form part of the native diet (Beckett 1977). Indeed, though it was slow to recognize the fact, the marine industry had an interest in keeping the island communities intact, since they could support a labour reserve without needing a cash economy. For the moment, however, the native population was suffering the impact of exotic disease, so that the bulk of the industry's labour needs were being met by importations from Asia and the Pacific.

The Queensland government established its jurisdiction in the wake of this economic development, initially to protect shipping and to secure its northern marches from the encroachments of foreign colonialism, but also to bring some order to an industry that was proving increasingly profitable. It had little interest in the Islanders themselves, leaving them to the care of the London Missionary Society (LMS), which made its appearance in 1871 (Beckett 1978).

The LMS quickly won the adherence of the Islanders and set about reconstructing their shattered societies and unifying the dispersed village populations around the church. The aim of the Society was to establish model Christian communities, and the congregational form of government it brought with them allowed it to enlist the help of native deacons. Offenders such as fornicators and adulterers were brought to trial before local courts, and then delivered over for punishment to a 'chief' who had been appointed by the government on the missionaries' recommendation. During the early years, white missionaries exerted considerable control over the communities, but by the 1890s they were leaving the work to Polynesian pastors. This proved unacceptable to the

Queensland government, which was by this time better able, and more inclined to, intervene. Its first move was to post white teacher/ magistrates to the main communities, and the conflict that followed resulted in the LMS handing its flocks over to the Church of England, which had no pretensions to secular authority.

Until the early years of the twentieth century, Islanders had been regarded as superior to Aborigines and not in need of special controls. In 1907, however, they were made subject to the authority of the newly appointed Protector of Aborigines and to the grow-ing body of legislation regulating Aboriginal life (Bleakely 1961; Evans *et al.* 1975).[5] Like the other governments of Australia, Queensland pursued a policy of, first, segregating its native population—ostensibly for their own good but usually in response to European pressure—and secondly, controlling their labour power. Where the Queensland government differed from the others was in the comprehensiveness and effectiveness of its regime, par-ticularly in the large, supervised settlements to which much of the population was soon relocated. In Torres Strait, however, there was no need for relocation: the island communities were already isolated and had already made their adaptation to the new order; moreover there was a market for their labour which, combined with subsistence production, could make them self-supporting.

The inclusion of Islanders under the Protector's care seems to have been prompted by their growing importance as a reserve of labour for the marine industry (Beckett 1977). The white Australia agitation was then at its height, and bidding to cut off the in-dustry's supply of cheap foreign labour. Meanwhile, the Islanders were acquiring a measure of immunity to new diseases and begin-ning to increase in number. Moreover, their intact subsistence economies could support the workers and their families during the periodic downturns in production. The problem was that whereas some communities were reluctant to get too deeply involved in the cash economy, others were too eager, developing needs for goods beyond what the industry was willing to support. The government undertook the difficult task of conserving the labour force: on the one hand it ensured that subsistence production was not allowed to die; on the other it kept a brake on the consump-tion of commodities by holding workers' earnings on their behalf and limiting their access to retail outlets. These controls were

justified on the ground that Islanders were incapable of managing
their own affairs and must be taught thrift.

The result was a regime that was no less restrictive than that
of the LMS, though with different priorities. It included a European teacher/magistrate in residence, assisted by Islanders—just
as the missionaries had been assisted by their deacons. At first these
were the old appointed chiefs, but from 1899 there were two or
three elected councillors. This was a surprising innovation, without
precedent or parallel in the Australian administration of Papuans
or Aborigines, but probably devised to counter the congregational
forms of the LMS (Haddon 1935:326). One of the functions of the
councillors, in fact, was to enforce the old LMS code of conduct,
which became local by-laws. The cooptation of native councillors
into the administrative structure, however, did not ensure the
smooth implementation of government policy. There was periodic
resistance, particularly during economic downturns, and in 1936
there was a Strait-wide strike against the regime (Beckett 1977).

The Queensland government took this demonstration seriously
and set about a restructuring. It retained its controls over Islanders'
employment, earnings and consumption, but exercised them from
the commercial and administrative centre on Thursday Island, leaving the communities to run their own affairs. The councils proved
more than equal to this task, satisfying the government in their
maintenance of law, order and public health, and satisfying the
people in their exercise of a degree of autonomy. Under this new
regime, the Islanders, having only restricted contact with the outside world, were able to develop a rich creole culture around the
church and council.

The councillor's role entailed a number of contradictions,
however. He was simultaneously a representative of the government to the people and of the people to the government. This
might mean having to implement programs such as compulsory
medical treatment, which were unpopular. Fortunately, the
distance to Thursday Island permitted a good deal of equivoca-
tion and procrastination. But if the authorities exerted pressure,
he had to give way or lose his job and the tiny stipend that went
with it. There were also internal contradictions relating to the im-
partiality required of the councillor and the partiality required of
the incumbent as kinsman, so that a few years in office tended

to alienate much of his support: non-kin through actual or supposed favours to kin, and kin through failure to meet their demands. The result was a fairly steady turnover in councillors. In other words, the Islanders dealt with the contradiction on a contingent basis rather than coming to a decision about principles. This was possible because the demands of office were not very great, and the qualities required were widely distributed so that a regular turnover caused little dislocation. And if no particular individual represented the community to itself, there was, nevertheless, a close correspondence between any given councillor and the ordinary citizen.

Impressed by the momentary unity of the 13 communities during the 1936 strike, the government set about institutionalizing and controlling it. In 1938 it called the first conference of Torres Strait councillors, acceding to their request to be differentiated from Aborigines. In the following year the Queensland Parliament passed legislation that established the Torres Strait Islanders as a distinct indigenous minority. Islanders, however, now had to learn the arts of external representation.

THE DEVELOPMENT AND CONTROL OF REPRESENTATION

Although the councillors' work would lie mainly in the community for some years to come, the 1937 conference established the machinery for an increasingly active external representation in the postwar period.

It was the ex-servicemen who had served in the Second World War who began clamouring for rights. Their experience of military service articulated and legitimated a claim for citizenship and economic equality. The Queensland government, for its part, declined to relinquish its special powers over them, or to put wages in the marine industry on a par with those in the mainland economy; but with Australia now entering a phase of welfare capitalism, it had a licence to upgrade facilities in the communities, effectively subsidizing the low wages. Even so, the government faced the task of transforming the radical aspirations of the ex-servicemen into piecemeal reforms.[6] The representational structure provided the instrument.

The conference of councillors became a biennial event, presided over by a senior official and occasionally graced by the presence of the minister. Overawed by these august presences, and hampered by a previously fixed agenda, radical representatives found it difficult to raise the broad issues that concerned their supporters, still less to demand the abolition of the administrative structure through which they had to work. They were likely to come from home empty-handed, inviting unfavourable comparison with representatives—usually not ex-servicemen—who were prepared to settle for limited but tangible benefits which the government was ready to concede. After the first few years they became a small and largely ineffective minority.

The new representation, which had to operate in what might be called welfare politics, required a new set of skills. As one individual who had failed in the task remarked to me, "You've got to be a smart man to be a councillor these days; not like before." To compete with other communities for such amenities as piped water, housing, a new school, an emergency air strip and so on, required a grasp of English, an understanding of how government worked, and an ability to negotiate the personalistic regime maintained by long-established officials. One had to "know how to talk to white people." Such skills were mainly to be found among the store managers, school teachers and boat skippers who had dealt with white officials for some years. However, such individuals were, to some degree, dependent on the government for their livelihood and had accommodated themselves to it in the course of advancing in their occupations. As one man, himself a long-time government employee, observed: "The councillors used to take off their coats to the government before. Not this time. They are all government men!"

The extent of the shift is well illustrated in the case of voting rights. In 1949 the Councillors' Conference had requested the franchise, without result. In 1958, the councillors declared themselves to be unready for such a responsibility and so, by implication, content to be represented in Parliament by the minister. Then, only three years later, when the federal government sent round a committee of enquiry into Aboriginal voting rights, every Torres Strait councillor was in favour. According to the report, the Queensland government had decided to drop its initial opposition and advised its trusted men accordingly.

As external representation increased and became more demanding, three elected delegates, representing the councillors of the three island groups (Eastern, Central and Western), took over the responsibility of dealing with the state government while the councillors retained their local government functions. Nominally the delegates were elected by the councillors immediately after the latter had been elected by the people. But since they acted as returning officers at the elections, they were in a position to influence the outome, and it was well known that at least one of them did. In fact, two of the three who held office during the 1950s and '60s had somehow been elected "for life"; as it happened, they were also well known to be friends of the government. However, the Eastern Island delegate who took office in 1956—and who still holds it today—submitted himself to re-election every three years and was regularly returned. Each of them, and those who succeeded in later years, developed a highly individual and personalistic style in dealing with officials, much of the time *in camera*. As far as their constituencies were concerned, their effectiveness was indicated by the benefits they wrought for them, combined with their own account of their role in getting it. If they sometimes claimed more credit than was strictly their due, it was probably in the government's interest that they should do so, since it strengthened their position. Certainly, over the years, both government and people became heavily dependent on the same delegates, so that the prospect of replacing them seemed increasingly difficult. Ordinary councillors could be turned over at regular intervals, as previously, but not the delegates. Murray Island, which has been noted for its turbulent politics, twice voted out a delegate only to vote him back in again, presumably as a rebuke and a way of reminding him of his dependence on their support.[7]

As expertise built up, as well as the need for it on the part of both the state government and the Islanders, representivity became increasingly problematical. The cohort of ex-servicemen were inclined to reject those who worked with the government out of hand, and many more wondered to what extent representatives looked after their private interests rather than those of their constituencies, since the benefits they brought were few and far between. No one knew what went on when a delegate went into the office and closed the door, with the result that rumour ran riot. Delegates were becoming increasingly withdrawn from their com-

munities, as official business took up more of their time. By the
end of the 1960s, two of the three delegates maintained a residence
on Thursday Island. They still recognized ties to kin and were
usually addressed by first names or kin terms, but the idiom was
increasingly out of keeping with the power they wielded and their
involvement with government.

UNOFFICIAL REPRESENTATION AND POLITICAL ALTERNATIVES

By 1970 Islanders received most of the things for which the ex-
servicemen had clamoured in 1946. Queensland had effected
substantial material improvements in the communities, and with
the collapse of the marine industry, it had relaxed its control over
employment and movement. Some Islanders began working for
regular wages on the mainland. But these changes had been a long
time coming, and in the meantime many had lost faith in the
government and its representative system. Radicals had long looked for white sympathizers outside the official framework: in 1946
the Communist party looked to be a possible ally;[8] a little later,
an Australian war veterans' organization seemed to promise
help;[9] some individuals took their problems to visiting members
of Parliament. In the 1960s radicals looked to the Aborigines and
Torres Strait Islanders Advancement League, a civil rights organization based mainly in the southern states.

However, there had been a growing recognition that only the
federal government could overrule the state. Hitherto it had remained aloof from Torres Strait affairs, but Islanders remembered
that the army, which had given them their first sense of citizenship, was a federal body. Moreover, its 1960 intervention in the
matter of voting rights suggested a more liberal attitude. When,
in 1972, the newly elected Labour administration opened an office on Thursday Island, it looked as though a new era were dawn-
ing. This intervention was all the more timely because, with local
industry at a standstill, government was the only source of funds.

The two governments quickly fell into an adversary relationship, partly because they were of opposing camps, partly because
of the issue of state versus federal powers, and partly perhaps
because of the possibility of oil in the Strait. With Australian welfare
capitalism at its height, the two were virtually competing in the
allocation of funds and for the support of Islander representatives.

Concerning the latter, the federal government came off second best in the first encounter. With the independence of Papua - New Guinea imminent, it announced prematurely that three offshore islands, presently in the Torres Strait group, would be ceded as part of an adjustment to the old border, which ran to within two miles of the Papuan coast. Taking advantage of the alarm this caused throughout the islands, the Queensland premier convened a Border Defence Committee, consisting mainly of councillors and the three delegates. Eager to make good its mistake, the federal government called the committee to Canberra for consultation. The committee went but publicly snubbed the minister for Aboriginal Affairs, and refused to recognize the delegation of Islanders that had arrived independently, at his invitation. Obviously well drilled, the committee kept a predetermined position of no compromise, and refused to be drawn into a number of issues which were known to be a cause of contention between it and Queensland.[10]

In the event, no islands were ceded, though the committee and the Queensland government continued to protest the agreement on seabed rights.[11] By this time, the Labour government had been replaced by one of the same complexion as that of Queensland; but the rivalry did not abate, and the incoming prime minister personally visited the Strait to win over island leaders. The federal Department of Aboriginal Affairs maintained its office on Thursday Island, and the Strait's two members of the National Aboriginal Council continued to represent their people in Canberra. With the border virtually a dead issue, some leaders began to transfer their loyalties to the federal government, though the Queensland director of Aboriginal and Islander Advancement continued to exert a powerful personal influence.

The old loyalties became strained, however, when the question of land rights erupted in 1981. The federal government had for some time been facilitating Aboriginal land claims in the Northern Territory, which was under its direct administration. Queensland, however, resisted the idea of land rights, despite widespread criticism from politicians and Aborigines. The Islanders, for their part, took little interest in what they supposed to be an Aboriginal problem: having enjoyed uninterrupted occupation of their ancestral lands, they did not realize that they too belonged to the Crown, reserved for their use at the pleasure of the state. Islanders suffered a rude awakening when, in 1981, the Queensland premier announced that all Aboriginal and Islander reserves would be turned into 50-year leases. Immediately the three delegates flew to Brisbane and, adroitly sidestepping the officials who usually mediated such contacts, secured an audience with the premier. Given an undertaking that he would delay action until they had a chance to consult their people, they conducted a series of meetings at which all voted overwhelmingly for Perpetual Freehold Title. This information, together with a request for increased local autonomy, was submitted to the premier by the Torres Strait Area Advisory Council, a group of councillors and representatives convened by the federal Department of Aboriginal Affairs.[12]

The local elections, which were due at the beginning of 1982, were hotly contested, with Queensland obviously anxious to secure the election of its friends. One critical result remained undeclared for some weeks, arousing widespread speculation; another was the subject of an appeal to the Supreme Court, lodged with the assistance of the federally funded Aboriginal Legal Service.

Soon after, the premier proposed a Deed of Grant in Trust by way of compromise, but this too proved unacceptable. There followed a battle through the media over whether Islander and Aboriginal representatives were or were not in favour of the proposal.[13] In their campaign to oppose implementation of the proposal, Aboriginal and Islander collaborated for the first time, through the Queensland section of the National Aboriginal Council. The campaign reached a climax during the Commonwealth Games in Brisbane.[14] Nevertheless, the proposal received the approval of the state legislature.

Meanwhile, further debate had arisen over the revision of the Torres Strait Islanders Act. At the biennial meeting of Island representatives held in mid-1982 and at a subsequent meeting held in November, there was considerable support for a proposal to transfer administration of the islands to an island-controlled Torres Strait Affairs Commission. Queensland's Department of Aboriginal and Islander Advancement would be phased out, though the incumbent director would be asked to carry on in an advisory capacity.

TORRES STRAIT REPRESENTATION AND FOURTH WORLD
POLITICS

The Torres Strait Islanders were quick to emerge as a clearly defined, internally structured minority. Unlike most Aborigines, they
came into the colonial world with their traditional communities
intact, and these became the building blocks both of European administrative structures and of an emergent identity. Various
historical circumstances combined to weld the communities, 14
in all, into a single entity. The decision of the LMS to work with
Islanders and Papuans, to the exclusion of Aborigines, established one boundary during the critical period of conversion. The
drawing of the border between Queensland and the new colony
of Papua, divorced them from their northern cousins. Even when
Queensland made Islanders subject to its Aboriginal legislation,
between 1904 and 1939, there was always some notion that the
Islanders were superior. By 1936, if not before, a shared experience
of colonial conditions, combined with intercommunity contacts
through the marine industry, had imbued the Islanders with a sense
of a distinct identity, and of the advantages of asserting it vis-à-
vis Aborigines. Even today, Islanders relate much more readily to
Pacific Islanders.

Representation had its beginnings in the needs of external
church and government, rather than in the needs of indigenous
peoples. And though these needs have changed and become more
complex with the years, representation must still be understood
as part of the structure of European domination. Once representation was instituted, however, Islanders learned to use it for ends
that were not always consonant with those of the regime, which
then had to control what it had created. Islanders have often
challenged the legitimacy of particular individuals, and some have
felt alienated from the representative system itself; but its groun-
ding in the exercise of local autonomy enabled it to take root during the early years. With the growth of welfare capitalism, representatives had to develop an expertise and a degree of collaboration
with the authorities, who tended to distance them from their constituencies. This gave rise to intermittent conflict, but the underlying tension was, to some degree, offset by the increasing
dependence on government and the consequent relaxation of community cohesion. If the delegates and councillors are today less

representative of Islanders than their predecessors, they get more for them. Today's representatives no longer 'represent' their people in any total Durkheimian sense; at the same time, their upbringing and their situation within the web of kinship has saved them from becoming mere pork-barrel politicians.

Representation evolved in Torres Strait independently of political developments on the mainland. When the first conference of councillors was held in 1937, Aborigines were still politically inert, and white opinion uninterested. For this reason, however, Islander representation was normally contained within the Queensland administrative structure, if not actually coopted. With the collapse of the marine industry, the government became all important in economic affairs. Consequently, the successful representative was one skilled in negotiating the personalistic labyrinths of the bureaucracy, and in making diplomatic approaches to senior officials and politicians. Such persons had little understanding of, or sympathy for, the kind of activism that overtook mainland Aborigines in the early 1970s. Long believing themselves to be different from, and superior to, Aborigines, they remained aloof from the struggle. Only with the intervention of the federal government and the eruption of the border issue did Islanders gain some sense of the national and international pressures to which the governments were responding. Even then the representatives preferred the discrete official approach to the rhetoric of the open arena.

The problem with such a strategy is that the necessary skills and connections can be acquired only over a long period; and being exercised *in camera,* they are not communicable by example. They are thus confined to a small clique of long standing. The Eastern Islands delegate, who is also one of the NAC members, has held his office for 26 years. The Western Islands were likewise represented by the same man for 30 years, and are now represented by his son; his brother holds the other NAC seat.[15] There have been only three incumbents of the Central Islands delegacy, the present incumbent being the son of the second. Similarly, among the island councillors, almost half have been in office for more than 20 years, whereas emigrants returning from the mainland find it hard to get elected.

With more than half the population settled on the mainland

today, there are also grave doubts about the representativity of the old Queensland, community-based structure. According to one interpretation of state policy, the 8,000 Islanders who live in the cities and towns of northern Australia are ex-Islanders who have forfeited all rights to their ancestral communities. They cannot vote in council elections and may visit only with council permission. Islander representatives who have little or no experience of life on the mainland seem unwilling to include ex-Islanders in their constituency, even in voting on major issues such as the border or land rights. As a result, their base is dwindling, and they are creating a large body of dispossessed Islanders who may one day challenge their legitimacy.

For the moment, however, the expatriates are politically weak. Community loyalties are divisive in the urban situation, and the only overarching organizations are the Islander churches, which compete for members. Although Islanders outnumber Aborigines in Townsville, the main centre, they have never succeeded in agreeing upon a candidate for the NAC. Nor have they succeeded in uniting with the Aborigines. In the organizations, such as medical and housing services, which the federal government has established for the two groups, Islanders find themselves in conflict with Aborigines and at a disadvantage because of their defective English and inexperience of arena politics.

Political frustration resulted in the formation of a Torres Strait United party in 1979, which sought independence for Torres Strait by challenging the original Act of Annexation and by appealing to the United Nations.[16] According to some, this was really a strategy to get the Commonwealth government to re-annex the islands, while releasing them from the control of Queensland. Either way, it would mean an end to the old system of representation and open the door to the returning migrants. In the event, the High Court upheld the Act of Annexation,[17] but there can be little doubt that these urban Islanders will be making further forays into the realm of Fourth World politics.

So far the official Torres Strait representatives have made sparing use of the tactic of appealing to higher authorities. Only during the border dispute did they make a broad appeal to the public, and this with the discreet support of the Queensland government. Yet it is obvious that the attentiveness of the state and federal governments to them, and their ability to attract substantial funds for their tiny communities are consequences of worldwide concern for indigenous minorities, and—indirectly—of the freewheeling agitation of Aboriginal activists farther south. In this sense, then, if in no other, the Torres Strait Islanders are part of the Fourth World.

Notes

1. For an insightful exploration of these themes, see Robert Murphy 1971:129-47.
2. Paine refers to welfare activities among minorities such as the Canadian Inuit as "welfare colonialism" (Paine 1977:3-52).
3. The authoritative work on this theme is Jayawardena 1968. For an exploration of the problem in a Torres Strait community, see Beckett 1971.
4. The principal sources for Torres Strait ethnography are the six volumes of *Reports* by Haddon 1904-35.
5. Much can also be gleaned from various reports in the annual *Votes and Proceedings of the Queensland Legislative Assembly.*
6. See the report of the Sub-Department of Native Affairs for the year ending 1947, *Votes and Proceedings of the Queensland Legislative Assembly.*
7. For a detailed account of one community's politics, see Beckett 1967.
8. Communist journalists visited Thursday Island soon after the war and published a series of articles in the party newspaper *Tribune.*
9. The *Australian Legion of Ex-Servicemen and Women,* under left-wing influence after the war, at one point took up the cause of Torres Strait veterans.
10. *The Australian* 13.6.73.
11. *Sydney Morning Herald* 15.6.78.
12. Submission of the Torres Strait Advisory Council to the premier of Queensland.
13. *National Times,* 11-17.4.82.
14. *Sydney Morning Herald,* 25.5.82; *Sydney Morning Herald,* 13.7.82.
15. Torres Strait has two National Aboriginal Council members: one representing the old Islander communities and one representing Islanders living in the Thursday Island township and in government settlements on Cape York. See Weaver, this volume.
16. *Australian Financial Review* 7.5.81.
17. *Sydney Morning Herald* 13.11.81.

Political Representivity and Indigenous Minorities in Canada and Australia[1]

5

SALLY M. WEAVER

It is commonly held that without representivity, native organizations would not be able to persuade governments to adopt the policies they prefer. Implicit in this belief is the assumption that representivity is an objectively demonstrable and attainable condition, even for governments in democratic systems where representation is basic, and that representivity poses problems for the native organizations rather than for governments. This perspective, however, disregards the fact that for policy-making governments need advice that reflects native views. Moreover, this view underestimates the difficulties governments experience in dealing with politically unorganized sectors of the public that, like Indians and Aborigines in the 1960s, are unable to define their interests and articulate them clearly and coherently.

This paper argues that (1) political representivity of native organizations at the national level is as much a problem for governments in Canada and Australia as it is for Indian and Aboriginal groups; (2) representivity of native organizations is a political *resource* which governments can award or withdraw—in other words, that representivity can be an *assigned* political status rather than an achieved political status; (3) from the Indian and Aboriginal perspectives, representivity may, in certain situations, be neither possible nor desirable; and (4) native leaders, like government personnel, can use representivity as a political resource to protect and to promote their own interests.

CONCEPTS AND CONTEXT

The concept of political representivity can be understood to have three somewhat interdependent meanings (Kornberg et al. 1980). In the first meaning a (native) organization is considered to be representative if it is seen to represent the views, needs and aspirations of its constituency to the government and the public. Thus a (native) organization would be expected to convey the feelings and demands of its membership to the government in a fairly accurate way: to be a reliable vehicle of communication. But in a more formal sense this meaning is often extended and it is understood that the organization is *authorized* to convey views and is held *accountable to* its constituents for this conveyance, through elections or delegations for example. According to this meaning the structure and procedures of the organizations are stressed because it is through them that the organizations maintain their contact with, and secure their legitimacy from, their constituencies.

In the second meaning, a (native) organization is seen to be politically representative if it is *representative of* its constituency. In other words, the members of the organization are expected to be a social microcosm of its constituency, particularly its "politically important social characteristics" (ibid.:1). Underlying the notion of "social" representativity is the belief that if the organization's members replicate their constituents, the organization will be more sensitive to their needs and goals and therefore able to convey them accurately to the government and the public.

The third meaning stresses representativeness by *responsiveness*: whether the organization actually responds to the needs and demands of its constituency by providing services needed or expected by the constituency. As such, it involves more than formal accountability.

Although the three meanings of representivity rarely take form in the practices of governments, collectively they comprise an ideal principle in the political culture of Canada and Australia, where the conventional first meaning of the concept—to represent—has been a major principle of the parliamentary system. The second and third meanings have received attention since the 1960s. For example, studies in both countries show that neither the elected politicians nor the officials (public servants) are social microcosms of society, but rather members of the upper socioeconomic strata (e.g., Porter 1965; Boreham *et al.* 1979). The third meaning came to the fore most forcefully as public attitudes became increasingly critical of government, which was perceived as insensitive and unresponsive to societal needs, particularly to those of the disadvantaged and politically unorganized groups (e.g., the poor, natives, aged, and chronically ill). All three notions are applied by government personnel, and on occasion by native groups, to national native organizations in both countries in their judgment of whether Indian and Aboriginal political organizations are "representative."

In order to identify some of the difficulties experienced by both native groups and governments over representivity, I shall examine, in broad overview, the development of native/government relations at the national level in Ottawa and Canberra from the 1960s to the early '80s. Although not denying the variability of native criteria of representivity (nor assuming that native cultures have an equivalent concept), I am concerned with the dynamic, adaptive behaviour between national native organizations and the federal governments as a result of the application of the nation-states' criteria of political representivity. Because judgments of representivity tend to be situational, I shall identify contexts in which these judgments are made by government personnel (political and bureaucratic) and the native responses to these evaluations.

National native organizations, of recent (1970s) origin in both countries, are very real components of the political systems in Canada and Australia. Much attention and some support have been given to their development by governments, and some native activists have struggled against incredible odds to create national organizations in the hope of influencing the central policy-making processes. These activists are aware that policy changes of the magnitude they seek must ultimately occur at the federal level for jurisdictional reasons, irrespective of the leverage they use on this system (e.g., protest, reason, international opinion, petitions, and so on). And, in time, they have become equally aware that national organizations are particularly vulnerable to criticisms of distance from grassroots people and opinions. In structure and behaviour, national native organizations have been shaped by government as much as by native politics, partly because of government funding and intervention, but partly because interest groups generally tend to adapt their organizational arrangements and procedures to those of government in their efforts to influence its decisions (Loveday 1970:377; Pross 1981:232). Thus political representivity, with regard to native organizations, is as much a product of government behaviour toward them and expectations of them as it is of factors internal to the native organization and their relations with their constituents. Consequently, any serious effort by anthropologists to understand national native organizations and their representivity must entail an examination of government behaviour.

Finally, I wish to stress that I am not discounting the existence of, or at times the need for, empirical representivity in native groups; that is, instances when native organizations can demonstrate they meet all three notions of representivity to a reasonable degree. Rather, I am arguing that particularly at the *national* level of native organizations, representivity can be a government-assigned status rather than a native-achieved status. I consider native organizations to be pressure groups, one of whose aims is to persuade governments to adopt their preferred policies. I emphasize, however, that I do not expect native pressure groups to be any more politically representative than their non-native counterparts. As Matthews argues for Australia, "There are no systematic studies on how far groups represent the views of their members. But we should be very cautious about claims that they do" (1977:231).

NATIVE POLITICAL MOBILIZATION

Historically, in Canada and Australia indigenous minorities were excluded from the making of policies that influenced their lives. Indian and Aboriginal views were rarely sought by governments, and native efforts to develop associations to promote their interests faced almost insurmountable problems, among them localized native identities, cultural and linguistic heterogeneity, intertribal animosities, political apathy, and poverty. Because natives were politically unorganized as pressure groups (Hawthorn 1966:363-65; Rowley 1972b:384-85), they were unable to define their interests and articulate them to governments effectively. As a result, native needs did not receive government priority except when they were defined and promoted by white advocate groups — initially by the churches but most prominently in the 1960s by the Indian-Eskimo Association (IEA) in Canada, and the Federal Council for the Advancement of Aborigines and Torres Strait Islanders (FCAATSI) in Australia. FCAATSI, for example, was almost solely responsible for persuading the federal government to hold the 1967 constitutional referendum, which gave the federal government shared jurisdiction over Aborigines with the state governments.

This condition of white advocacy changed dramatically in the late 1960s as native minorities began to organize politically (initially in local-level protests which expanded nationally), demanding a fair share of their country's resources and societal recognition of their unique ethnicity as aboriginal people (Cardinal 1969; Manuel and Posluns 1974; Perkins 1975; Berndt 1971; Duncan 1974). Native political organization took the form of a social movement, a collection of diffuse and initially unfocused pressures for change in the political and social systems. Native spokesmen emerged, whose tasks were to mobilize their potential constituents around common causes and shared experiences, and to promote a collective self-awareness. To achieve some degree of mobilization, the leaders had to define the goals and aspirations of the movement; in short to change apathy or reluctance to activism by creating a vision and an ideology around which the native public(s) could identify and organize politically. Some native activists endured, learning leadership skills quickly, while others failed and were replaced often by younger, more educated men who were better able to articulate the new demands in a forceful and rhetorical fashion.

The emergent native leaders, who were the architects of the social movements, sought to establish native organizations, which soon discredited the white advocacy groups (IEA and FCAATSI) on the ground that these groups were not socially representative of natives, given their largely white leadership. Although white advocate groups had been useful in raising the public consciousness about the plight of native peoples and in fostering political networks among them, it was predictable that they would be supplanted by native leaders who sought to destroy patterns of white paternalism and advocacy.

Inevitably, however, the representivity of native spokesmen

was questioned by government and the public (press). Thus, for example, there were questions in Ottawa as to whether Harold Cardinal, a prominent Indian spokesman in the late 1960s, "really represented" the views of Canadian Indians. And in Australia, as late as 1973, officials of the Department of Aboriginal Affairs felt that Charles Perkins, who in 1965 led the highly publicized Freedom Rides in New South Wales against discriminatory treatment of Aborigines, should not be considered an Aborigine, given his university education (Tatz 1979:10). Indeed, as Tatz has noted, as soon as Aboriginal leadership began to emerge and demand changes,

> . . . the first reaction is to demand of each: 'how representative are *you* of Aborigines?' (as *we* define them). Unless they can show—and clearly they cannot—that each has been given a unanimous mandate, that each has been authorised, is accountable for his actions, is truly symbolic of and each is acting for the total 'grassroots' community, then they are written off as non-leaders, non-spokesmen (*ibid.*).

This questioning of native leaders' representivity placed them in a no-win situation for various reasons. First, because they lacked organizational bases through which to obtain grassroots opinions and communicate them to governments, spokesmen were unable to demonstrate that their demands reflected the views of native peoples in general or those beyond their own grassroots contacts. Second, without the ability to research and rationalize their demands, these spokesmen could not substantiate the 'needs' they claimed the native populations had; for example, the Aboriginal need for better housing, or the Indian need to control their own educational system. Third, *if* these spokesmen had communicated the feelings and attitudes of the native minorities in the 1960s, they would have conveyed apathy, alienation and defeat in many instances, the very conditions they were trying to change. Fourth, and most significant, the native leaders were themselves engaged in the activity of shaping and defining the interests of their minorities. In short, they were in the process of *creating* commonly held goals and of *creating* a constituency. For these reasons, the demands of the new leaders could not reflect solely the views of their constituents.

Early organizing efforts of native peoples in both countries resemble Pross's *issue-oriented* pressure-group model, which features an unstable membership, a weak organizational base, the absence of a secretariat to research and rationalize their demands, a limited knowledge of government, limited access to government, and a preference for confrontation and protest as means for gaining public support and dealing with government (Pross 1975:10). Indian and Aboriginal demands were often symbolic and ideological rather than pragmatic and substantive as governments prefer, and their use of protest in dealing with governments often inspired hostility among ministers and officials. However, issue-oriented groups have the advantage of flexibility over more institutionalized pressure groups whose personnel are frequently locked into private and carefully nurtured interpersonal relations with government officials. Hence Indians and Aborigines could "go public" with their demands. In both countries the aboriginal land rights campaigns, which heavily involved white support groups, graphically illustrate the effectiveness of such pressure-group behaviour in influencing governments to adopt the preferred native goals.

But issue-oriented pressure groups, although effective in the short term, lack the capacity to *sustain* pressure on governments and to monitor long-term government policies and programs. Aware of these limitations, and of governments' questioning of their representivity, some Indian and Aboriginal leaders sought to develop, at the national level, a more stable organizational base for their movements. But native leaders encountered problems in this process because they lacked many of the requisite political resources, namely, leadership skills, organizational experience, finances, an identifiable constituency, knowledge of government, access to government, interpersonal and media communications skills, and recognized 'expertise' in the fields of interest to them. Furthermore, the perceived need for these resources varied extensively among native leaders, as did their ability to use the resources they commanded. However, many native organizers felt that the only realistic source of funding for more permanent native organizations was the government. Although governments could by no means provide all of the requirements for building effective organizations, they could (theoretically) provide the funding, as well as provide access to government decision-makers and the policy process. The central question, however, was whether governments would provide these resources.

GOVERNMENT RESPONSE TO NATIVE MOBILIZATION

Governments need advice from specific sectors of the public, which is often provided by pressure groups (e.g., Loveday 1970; Pross 1975) The need for pressure groups stems from the need for information, advice, for testing public reaction to new policies, and securing compliance with, and legitimacy for, policies and programs. Although the perceived need for advice will vary over time, and between issues and government personnel, advice which is felt to be representative of public views is a vital source of intelligence for governments.

In Canada and Australia the governments' need for public advice in shaping policies was sharply reinforced in the late 1960s and early 1970s. During this period the public brought pressure to bear on governments to be more sensitive to minority needs, including those of native minorities, and to be more responsive to their demands (evoking the third meaning of representivity).[2] Governments in both countries were heavily criticized for being excessively paternalistic toward native minorities, and for devising policies which ignored the special needs and rights of native groups. Governments, however, were not as experienced in dealing directly with native minorities as they were with other sectors in society. Furthermore, under the barrage of public criticism and native protests, governments were often disinclined to open up the policy process, even if they felt native advice had some value, and even though they espoused some form of participatory democracy. In their initial responses to these pressures, governments could, and did, use the perceived lack of political representivity of native leaders as justification for ignoring or discrediting their demands, or for not consulting them. But under continued public pressure, governments were forced to respond to the demands that natives be consulted and their views be considered in the policy process.

MECHANISMS FOR OBTAINING POLICY ADVICE FROM NATIVE MINORITIES

When governments need short-term advice on specific issues from unorganized minorities such as native peoples, the standard procedure is to conduct a public inquiry whereby a team or a commissioner collects public views and organizes them in a "usable" form for governments. This mechanism was adopted in the land rights issue in both Canada and Australia (Woodward 1974; Berger 1977). Parliamentary committees that invite public "representations" can also fulfil this same function.

For long-range policies, however, the need for reliable information in which both governments and natives have confidence inevitably involved the governments in fostering more permanent mechanisms for obtaining native advice. The evolution of this process has occurred in three stages to date: (1) governments promoted their own national advisory committees; (2) governments funded native groups to form their own national organizations (pressure groups); and (3) government (e.g., Australia) or native groups (e.g., Canada) restructured the national organizations.

Although there were important differences between the two countries in the way each of these steps was conceived and implemented, the three stages constituted an unfolding dynamic between the native movements and the governments at the national level as each sought, in its own way and for its own purposes, to establish more effective links of communication with, and influence over, the other. This was a new experience for both native minorities and governments, and until the mid-1970s it was played out in the political context of increasing native unrest and unprecedented government expansion of services to the native populations. Relations between the native political groups and governments were generally characterized by confrontation and mutual distrust, and political representivity was used as a political resource by both parties in their attempts to influence, if not control, the behaviour of the other.

In the first stage of developing national advisory mechanisms, before native national organizations emerged, the federal governments in both countries promoted their own advisory committees, a standard method for obtaining policy advice from sectors of the public.[3]

Canada

The federal government's Indian Affairs Branch established a National Indian Advisory Board in 1966, composed of Indian-appointed delegates from regional advisory councils. In turn, the regional councils were composed of delegates appointed from the band councils on Indian reserves (Weaver 1981:29-30). However, the Indian delegates were unclear whether the government expected them to present their personal opinions on issues, or to convey (represent) the views of their regions. If it were the latter, they felt they should be given funds to travel to reserves to discern public opinion, but funds were not provided. In addition, Indian delegates were expected to work with an agenda that reflected government priorities and timetables (e.g., revising the Indian Act). Indian members quickly became disenchanted with the government's approach, and it became clear that they lacked the expertise to deal with the government's new budget program, which they were expected to address. Then, because of the Prairie Indians' disaffection with the government's lack of response to their advice, they boycotted the meetings in 1967, which effectively terminated the advisory committee experiment.

By this time, Indian political organizations were emerging or being revitalized at the provincial level, particularly in the Prairie provinces, where Indian leaders were securing their first meagre government funding (Cardinal 1977:169-74), and where the impetus for Indians' organizing on a national scale originated. These leaders had viewed advisory committees as unrepresentative of Indians in all three senses of the term. Equally important, they regarded advisory bodies as agents of government interests and as powerless instruments in influencing government decisions.

Indian Affairs officials, on their part, also found the advisory committee mechanism unsatisfactory, partly because the delegates' views were individual opinions, and partly because the delegates did not have the same priorities as government. This experience, together with pressures from the Privy Council Office (the central agency advising cabinet) and the public to seek broadly based Indian opinions on issues, eventually led the department to devise a series of regional consultation meetings with Indians with the aim of revising the Indian Act (DIAND 1968). But during the meetings, the newly-elected Liberal government privately changed the policy direction from one of revising the Indian Act to one of terminating all special treatment of Indians (including Indian reserves, the Indian Act, treaties, and the Department of Indian Affairs bureaucracy) (Weaver 1981). The new White Paper policy (DIAND 1969) became the major catalyst to Indian political mobilization. Angered at the duplicity of the consultations, Indians repudiated the White Paper (Indian Chiefs of Alberta 1970) and sought the affirmation, not the abolition of their special status and rights. Under pressure of an unprecedented public outcry, Prime Minister Trudeau publicly suspended the policy in June 1970.[4] In a predicament over the White Paper and the lack of policy direction that followed its suspension, the government established a policy to fund Indian political organizations at the provincial and national levels. Mainly a response to native demands, this policy launched the second stage in developing native policy-advising mechanisms.

Australia

The first attempt to develop a national Aboriginal advisory committee in Australia was made in a highly charged political climate during the height of the controversy over Aboriginal land rights during the last months of the Liberal/Country party government in 1972. Following Prime Minister McMahon's Australia Day speech on Aboriginal policy,[5] Aboriginal activists from eastern cities founded the internationally publicized Aboriginal Embassy by erecting tents on the Parliament House lawns in Canberra to protest the government's denial of Aboriginal land rights. Six months later the government forcefully removed the tents, hospitalizing some Aborigines in the process and provoking renewed controversy (Harris 1972:28-30). The federal initiative to establish an Aboriginal advisory body to the minister came within days of the government's removal of the tent embassy, and was prompted by Peter Howson, minister for the Environment, Aborigines and the Arts, at a conference he called in Canberra in August 1972. Against the advice of officials in the Council for Aboriginal Affairs (CAA), the advisory body to cabinet, he restricted Aboriginal representation to delegates from the state-appointed advisory bodies—bodies which many Aborigines and the CAA considered suspect in all three senses of representivity. During the meeting Howson informed the delegates that in previous sessions with Aboriginal groups, ''I have never been completely sure whose views they were expressing,'' but after recent discussions with state ministers for Aboriginal affairs, he was assured by them that ''this conference, structured as it is, is the best means available of obtaining a truly representative expression of Aboriginal views throughout the nation at this time.''[6] Howson was promoting a national body composed of delegates from state-appointed advisory bodies, but his proposal was rejected by the delegates and activists from the embassy who wanted, instead, to set up ''a fully representative national conference.'' They decided that in the future, ''there be no Government appointees on Aboriginal Councils or at Aboriginal conferences and that all adult Aborigines and Islanders be eligible to vote for representatives without Government interference.''[7]

Howson's efforts were seen by some Aboriginal activists and the CAA as a transparent device to manage Aboriginal conflict and divert public attention from the explosive land rights issue (Cooper 1976:37-38). Indeed, the members of the CAA, who were by that point in open conflict with the government over Aboriginal land rights, were highly skeptical of Howson's motives. After hearing him refer to the proposed body as a ''durbar'' they became convinced the government did not intend to grant it any real authority, but only the semblance of power held by durbars in colonial India.

During the subsequent campaign leading to the December 1972 national election, the Liberal/Country party promised to establish, in consultation with the states, an elected national Aboriginal advisory body,[8] but the government was defeated. The incoming Labor party, despite its massive reform program in Aboriginal affairs, made no reference in its platform to a national aboriginal body of any form.[9]

By 1972 Aboriginal activism was well developed, most forcefully in the southeast by urban Aborigines who created service-oriented organizations having a political (pressure group) capacity, such as the Aboriginal Medical Services and the Aboriginal Legal Services. In contrast, Canadian Indian activism produced territorially oriented political organizations. Both Indian and Aboriginal activists viewed advisory committees as ineffectual in influencing government and as devices in which native representation was manipulated by governments for their own purposes.

The latter view was particularly strong in Australia, where government appointees to advisory committees were preferred.

For governments, advisory committees have a certain appeal because they are government-managed committees whose members are expected to address matters of government concern. They are even more attractive if the members are government-appointed, for this allows governments to select 'representatives' from a range of public organizations or interests, and to be reasonably assured that the members will behave in circumspect fashion: that they will deal privately with government, avoid public criticism and resign quietly if they disagree with government positions.[10] In short, advisory committees allow governments to secure advice on their own conditions and terms, from persons with whom they can work comfortably. For these very reasons they are unacceptable to native activists.

The second stage in developing native advisory mechanisms began when both governments provided funds for native groups to create their own national organizations.

Although both the Trudeau government in Canada and the Whitlam Labor government in Australia (1972-75) fostered pressure groups in various areas (e.g., conservation, urban affairs, poverty groups), such policies are difficult to rationalize because it is known by ministers that these groups, if they become effectively organized, will bring exacting pressure to bear on the governments.

The problems in fostering native pressure groups stem from (1) the conventional belief that pressure groups should be publicly, not government-funded; (2) the provision of funds which may not be properly accounted for by the native groups; and (3) bureaucratic resistance in the line departments (DIAND and DAA) to competing native advice and to ministerial access (Weaver 1985:203-04). These problems were encountered in Ottawa and Canberra in the early 1970s as native activists sought government funding to establish their own national organizations. But government approaches to the organizing initiatives differed significantly, as did the form of organizations that emerged.

Canada

The National Indian Brotherhood (NIB) was founded by Indians in 1968-70 as a loose federation of the provincial and territorial

(Yukon, Northwest Territories) organizations, known as PTOs. Government funding was precipitated by (1) the convergence of the demands by Prairie Indian leaders for funds with the desire of certain government officials to expand their programs by establishing a new clientele;[11] (2) the support for Indian political development *per se* among key officials in non-DIAND departments and the PCO; (3) the commitment in the early Trudeau years to participatory democracy; and (4) the government's need, generated by the White Paper and its rejection, to have Indian organizations to consult.

Consequently, in 1970, the Secretary of State's[12] "core funding" policy, under its "citizenship" mandate, enabled Indian leaders to organize provincially and nationally, to choose their own structures, to set the pace and style of operations, and to define and promote their own issues.[13] The NIB emerged as the national spokesman for Indian interests.[14]

Although fiscal restraint in Ottawa and factors internal to the NIB have limited its activities, there is no evidence to suggest that government funding has compromised NIB positions on issues. Indeed, NIB presidents have been persistently outspoken critics of government policies and practices to the increasing displeasure of certain prominent cabinet ministers. Over the years, the NIB has become more skilled in lobbying governments at home and abroad and in expanding its contacts in Ottawa's bureaucracy.

Throughout the NIB's history, the question of its representivity, particularly its capacity to obtain and transmit grassroots views to the government, has been an issue. The NIB is aware of government attempts to discredit its representivity in order to refute its demands and undercut its legitimacy, but it has experienced its own dilemmas in this regard. The task of unifying Indian demands at the national level, by necessity, involves NIB leaders in *creating* symbolic and ideological issues (e.g., Indian government, Canadian constitutional amendments) as a way of seeking government and societal affirmation of the unique status of Indians in Canada: the *raison d'etre* of the NIB. On ideological submissions, the government finds NIB demands too vague and open-ended for serious attention, and the NIB can be readily criticized for being too radical and therefore not reflecting the more conservative positions often held at the grassroots. In addition, like any federally structured pressure group (Dawson 1975), the NIB is faced with the unenviable task of reconciling regional differences in aspirations and needs, and when it is unable to resolve these differences, it is considered ineffective in defining the interests of its constituency. Yet regionalism pervades the entire Canadian political system, and is unresolved by national political parties in many instances; in this sense, the government is guilty of a double standard with regard to representivity, and NIB leaders have pointed that out in recent federal elections where the Trudeau government has failed to secure elected representatives from the Prairies.

In order to broaden its basis of representivity the NIB developed a policy secretariat in 1977, whose task was to research and substantiate the needs and aspirations of its constituency. But it was hampered by the PTO's disregard of its advice, lack of coordination of its activities and initially by the inability to attract the type of educated Indian personnel sought (Weaver 1982). The NIB's ability to produce position papers that reflect Indian views *and* have the endorsement of the PTOs has been uneven. But again the NIB is placed in a no-win situation, since government officials feel that the NIB should hire consultants to prepare more coherent and pragmatic submissions, but when (white) consultants prepare submissions, officials discredit the papers, claiming they are not the work of, or the views of, the NIB.

Over the years the NIB has consistently demanded that the government consult it on policies and programs. However, when government departments comply, the NIB is overburdened with requests, and risks becoming reactive to government priorities and timetables rather than initiating its own priorities. And when the NIB does not respond to consultation requests, officials, including sympathetic ones who believe Indians should be involved in policy or program development, charge the NIB with "not doing its job," meaning that it is not promoting the interests of its constituents to the government.

Central to the question of NIB's representivity is its structure and procedures. Each PTO brings its own structure and style of operation to the NIB federation, and some PTOs may not consult their reserves on issues, or even have systematic relations with Indian communities. In addition, some PTOs have collapsed (e.g., Union of B.C. Indian Chiefs in 1975 and Manitoba Indian

Brotherhood in 1979), weakening regional participation until such time as new leaders emerge. Another related problem is that some PTOs have stronger organizations with more immediate grassroots support than the NIB, as a federation, can ever demonstrate.

All aspects of the representivity question were evident in the Joint Cabinet/National Indian Brotherhood Committee, a unique experiment begun in 1975 to develop mutually acceptable policies for Indians in Canada (Weaver 1982). But two became particularly prominent: the NIB's formal authorization to act on behalf of its constituency, and the NIB's responsiveness to the "needs" of its constituency. The first aspect was reflected in the judgment of government officials that the NIB lacked "a mandate" to negotiate policy issues in the Joint Cabinet/NIB forum. The second was shown in their belief that if the NIB were genuinely concerned about the conditions of Indians in Canada, it would have accepted the cabinet's offer, for example, to grant Indians "maximum access" to educational services, rather than pursue its demands for the "Indian right" to education. Each side defined Indian interests differently, and when the NIB definitions did not concur with those of government, the NIB was judged to be unresponsive to the needs of its constituents—the third meaning of representivity.

Government officials, particularly in DIAND, have been increasingly skeptical of the NIB's representivity. Briefly, DIAND knows that certain Indian organizations are not members of the NIB and, further, that the Prairie PTOs play a powerful role in influencing NIB positions; hence the NIB cannot be relied on to obtain a wide spectrum of Indian opinion in Canada. Second, through its administrative networks with PTO presidents and band chiefs, DIAND can and does compare NIB positions with those it receives directly from bands and PTOs, which provides DIAND with enough input to question the NIB's stands on both substantive and ideological grounds. Third, when DIAND learns that the NIB is not consulting the grassroots on issues it is promoting, the NIB's claim to represent Indian views is discredited on procedural grounds. Fourth, in discussions with PTO presidents, DIAND officials often experience the PTO's undermining of NIB positions. The PTOs are highly competitive and often distrustful of each other; such behaviour erodes any credibility the government might place in the claim of the NIB office to speak for its component organizations, let alone its grassroots constituents.[15]

Despite the government's awareness of the NIB's limited representivity, it continued to grant funds to the NIB to provide advice on the Indian Act revisions and to prepare its position on reforming Canada's constitution (see Sanders, this volume). And it continues to seek the NIB's advice and endorsement of its policies and programs. On issues of priority to Indians and on matters which relate to the ideological base of the Indian movement—special rights and status—the NIB has convincingly articulated Indian demands. This has occurred often enough, with important results (e.g., court intervention against changes affecting the status of Indian women, Indian control of Indian education, and aboriginal land rights) that the NIB cannot be disregarded. In such cases the demands from reserve and regional levels were seen as consistent with the NIB position. But when officials and ministers want a broad spectrum of Indian views on issues of priority to the government, or when they need to rely on the NIB for a nation-wide Indian position, they are understandably frustrated in their dealings with the NIB. More significantly, when government simply wants to use the NIB's public endorsement to promote a policy, or when it decides to pursue an issue it values, the representivity question is overlooked. Furthermore, the government's more general need to consult with some Indian body at the national level has meant that it cannot discredit the NIB *per se*; as one official explained, "it's all we've got." In this sense, the government *assigns* representivity to the NIB on the basis of its own self-interest.

Australia

In Australia, concerns about representivity have been far more controversial. The government's attempt in 1972 to create a national advisory body left a legacy of manipulation of Aboriginal representivity which made Aboriginal activists particularly conscious of the need to protect future organizations from such practices.

More significantly, representivity, as it relates to a definable Aboriginal population (potential constituency), is far more problematic than it is in Canada. The legal distinctions between "full-bloods" and "half-castes" used historically by the states (Rowley 1972a:341-64) were unacceptable to the federal government in 1967 when it assumed responsibility for Aboriginal Affairs. These distinctions were dropped and Aborigines (and Torres Strait Islanders) were defined as persons of Aboriginal descent who identify as Aborigines, and are considered such by the community in which they live. But the historic categories had become so institutionalized among Aborigines, and in society generally, that they could not be expected to disappear quickly (Rowley 1972a:341). Consequently, any national Aboriginal organization, in addition to its other challenges, would have to accommodate the deeply rooted division between northern traditional Aborigines (who are more commonly of full Aboriginal descent) and southern urban Aborigines to claim representivity in all three senses.

Equally relevant to representivity was the fact that Aborigines, whose one percent of the population (like Indians) is scattered throughout the country, had no nation-wide system of identifiable Aboriginal communities or local councils that could function as building blocks for regional or national organizations—as did Indian reserves and band councils in Canada[16] (see Beckett's paper, this volume). For these and other reasons, the first national Aboriginal organization, the National Aboriginal Consultative Committee (NACC) (1973-76), emerged under much more difficult circumstances than the NIB.

The NACC developed within the orbit of the new Labor government in 1973, in that it was promoted by Gordon Bryant, the first minister of the newly created Department of Aboriginal Affairs (DAA), and organized by Charles Perkins, an Aboriginal activist then employed in the DAA (Cooper 1976). Bryant, a long-time advocate of reform in Aboriginal Affairs, intended the NACC "to advise on and develop policies for my Ministry," and in February 1973, at the founding conference he held in Canberra, he gave Aborigines the mandate to organize the NACC "to decide on the role of the Committee, its structure and method of representation."[17]

Representivity was a central concern for the NACC organizers. They felt that if the new body represented Aborigines in all regions and if its membership were recruited by a method which ensured representativeness, it would have a greater capacity to influence government decisions and be seen by Aborigines to be free of government manipulation. Hence it was resolved that the NACC would be nationally elected by Aborigines,[18] a "truly representative body'' to act as ''the Aboriginal voice'' in Australia.[19] Regional meetings were held throughout the country (June-August 1973) to promote the idea of the NACC to Aborigines and to map the electoral areas. After visiting New Guinea, the organizing team adopted the roving ballot-box method to enable Aborigines in isolated areas to participate in the election. Strong Aboriginal support for the NACC was shown in the November 1973 election, when almost 78 percent of the enrolled Aborigines voted for the new 41-member NACC.[20]

Aboriginal organizers had a heterogenous native constituency to mobilize and represent, akin to one that combined status Indians, Metis, non-status Indians, and the Inuit. Nor did the NACC organizers have the same impetus to organize nationally that the White Paper provided in Canada.[21] More notable was the lack of support within government for NACC organizing activities, both in terms of sympathetic and cooperative key officials inside or outside the DAA, and of government funding for their organization's operations. And ministerial support vanished when the prime minister dismissed Bryant as minister of Aboriginal Affairs, thereby removing the sole source of commitment to the NACC within cabinet.[22]

The circumstances of its origin, as much as its operations, made the NACC's representivity, in all three senses of the concept, suspect from the government's perspective. DAA officials had not supported the idea of the NACC from the outset, preferring instead a government advisory committee.[23] They felt that the NACC was premature in the absence of effective local political organizations, and that Bryant's founding conference ''did not represent Aborigines'' but was rather a collection of the minister's Aboriginal friends and contacts through FCAATSI. Bryant's dismissal renewed Aboriginal demonstrations against the department and the new NACC became involved in open conflict with the DAA and its new minister. The NACC's short three-year history was devoted to securing recognition as an independent body and obtaining government acceptance of its constitution, which, in the end, the Labor•government withheld (Hiatt 1976:22-27). The DAA had rarely sought advice from the NACC, and the NACC had not perceived itself as an advisory body.

In terms of its operations, the NACC experienced many dif-

ficulties, which affected its claim to be a truly representative body.
Its 41 members (salaried on a full-time basis by government) were
uncertain of their roles and unable to maintain contact with their
constituents and thus were vulnerable to charges of not securing
grassroots opinions. To remedy the situation, the NACC sought
government funds for establishing state-level branches and a
newsletter to communicate its activities to its constituency. But
the funds were denied.

But more significant was the fact that a small core of urban
Aboriginal activists held the NAAC leadership roles. Generally,
urban Aborigines are regarded as unable to represent the views
of tribal Aborigines, given their limited knowledge of traditional
Aboriginal customs. In addition, their militancy alienated some
of the tribal Aborigines in the NACC. Despite attempts by its president, Jim Stanley, the NACC did not advance tribal interests,
although the need to do so and to improve tribal participation in
the body was developing at the end of NACC's existence.[24]

Government negation of the NACC's representivity focused
on the urban activists. DAA officials viewed the NACC as the "personal political platform" of urban radicals who "represented no
one." And the attempt by Senator Cavanagh, Bryant's successor,
to make the NACC constitution more "democratic" was primarily a strategy "to dilute the domination of [the NACC's] public image and its meetings by the activists" (Cooper 1976:60). In other
words, the NACC was judged incapable of representing a wide
range of Aboriginal views and disinterested in responding to the
needs of its constituency. As Cooper noted, "representation
became an issue focused on the organization of the NACC as a
body and its internal conflict rather than on the representativeness
of members in relation to characteristics of the Aboriginal population" (p. 58).

The third stage in the development of native advisory
mechanisms began when the national native organizations were
restructured. Native leaders in both the NIB and the NACC were
dissatisfied with the ineffectualness of their organizations to influence government and to demonstrate contact with their constituents. And both governments, concerned more with fiscal
restraint and the economy than social policy issues by the
mid-1970s, were increasingly intolerant of native activism. Changes

in governing parties in both countries became important turning points for national-level organizations when the federal preference for dealing with native peoples at the local level, rather than through national organizations, emerged clearly. Representivity was a key issue in reordering both national organizations.

Canada

The restructuring of the NIB into a new body, the Assembly of First Nations (AFN), began in 1978-79—a deliberate attempt by Indian leaders to strengthen its representivity. The intent was to develop a national organization "which is more representative and accountable to the Indian people" by creating a direct relationship with its constituency at the *local* level through band chiefs.[25] The "re-strengthening process," as it is called, has involved three forces: those internal to the NIB, those involved with government and those internal to government. These forces have intersected in complicated ways, and although the process is still unfolding at the time of writing (June 1982), some of the representivity factors can be briefly identified.[26]

Internal forces that prompted reorganization of the NIB originated in 1975 when its constitution (1970) was amended to bring it in line with its operations, and again in 1977 and 1978 when resolutions of the annual general assemblies called for the need to improve "the equality of representation" among the PTOs.[27] The conviction that reorganization was necessary, however, evolved not from a grassroots demand, but from within the NIB office in Ottawa during the last years of Noel Starblanket's presidency (1976-80). He and his predecessor, George Manuel, had become keenly aware of the need for the NIB to develop the ability to formulate and sustain positions on issues and to demonstrate more effective grassroots knowledge and support of its positions. This need became particularly evident when the Joint Cabinet/NIB Committee (1975-78) failed to foster "political discipline" and "unity" in the NIB.

Consequently, within days of the NIB's withdrawal from the Joint Cabinet/NIB Committee, Starblanket announced the first nation-wide All Chiefs Conference to be held that summer (1978). The conference was an "attempt to obtain grassroots opinion on future relations between the federal government and the Indian people.''[28] Seeing this as a "pioneering effort," Starblanket hoped that "when federal politicians finally hear the views from the community level, they'll begin to understand the frustrations and anger building up in Indian communities." Although the planned meeting did not take place, Starblanket's idea of an All Chiefs forum set in motion a series of such conferences in 1980 and 1982,[29] which served to secure a broad mandate on specific issues such as the Canadian constitution, and to establish the new Assembly of First Nations.

Factors in Indian/government relations that prompted NIB reorganization are complex, but two major issues served as catalysts: the Canadian constitution renewal process (1978-82) and Indian Act revisions.

Amending and patriating the Canadian constitution raised the serious possibility that the unique status and relationship Indians have had with the federal government under the BNA Act might be eroded. (See Sanders' paper in this volume for an analysis of this issue.) The link between the constitution and the NIB's reorganization and representivity was pointed out by the NIB executive: "If changes [in the Constitution] are underway and Indians are caught unprepared to provide *credible and broadly supported input* to those changes, we could lose our unique status and be dealt out of official existence . . .''[30] Thus the constitution renewal process reinforced the NIB's original mandate to promote and protect Indian rights at the same time as it constituted *a strategy* for the NIB to secure a mandate for reorganization.

The second issue was the planned revision of the Indian Act. In its various discussion papers, DIAND proposed revisions to enhance band council powers, whereas the NIB advocated a broader notion of "Indian Government" (NIB 1979). Although the notion of Indian government has yet to be clearly conceptualized, it represents an effort by Indian leaders to define a new relationship between Indians and the nation-state. Substantively, the notion stems from (1) the principle of self-determination, which is linked to the idea of "sovereignty" or Indian "jurisdictions" for managing their own affairs and their own resources; and (2) on the principle that legitimacy for Indian government derives from the Indian people, not from the federal government through the delegation of authority to band councils, as was being suggested

(Long *et al.* 1982). The legitimacy would derive from individual Indian governments: ". . . on each reserve, the People should develop a way to govern their own affairs so that there is a solidness and a strength when their nation gathers in the Assembly of First Nations."[31] Whatever form the Assembly of First Nations eventually takes, it has been stressed that its power "rests with the people we are elected by to serve and represent."[32]

Finally, factors internal to government that have influenced the NIB's reorganization are equally important, even though they have not been publicly visible. By the late 1970s there were a growing number of critics of Indian organizations among both sympathetic and unsympathetic ministers and officials. Some of these critics cast Indian organizations as "creatures of government" which "don't represent Indians." Others privately expressed concern that representation has become problematic because Indian organizations are funded directly by government, and not indirectly through the bands, which would then either keep the funds or assign them to those organizations they chose to represent their interests.[33] Thus, funding assumed many problematic dimensions for the government and the NIB: as an instrument of government retaliation against Indian organizations for their unpopular actions, as a pressure tactic for Indian organizations to be more accountable to Ottawa than to their constituents, and as a factor in the future existence of Indian organizations, given the impending review of the core funding program. To these were added the view that Indians have had a decade in which to develop organizations that could operate in a representative, responsible and consistent fashion, and that it was now reasonable to expect such behaviour from them.

Although Indian political organizations have always been criticized by government and by Indians (e.g., Wuttunee 1971; Burke 1976), open public criticism of the NIB had not been pronounced until 1979, when the Beaver report was released.[34] Critical of both DIAND and the NIB with regard to their structures and operations, the report condemned Indian political organizations, especially the NIB. Despite acknowledging that some Indian organizations were "structured to be responsive and responsible to bands," Beaver implied that most were not (Beaver 1979:iv). He felt Indian bands had "abdicated" their responsibilities of questioning ''the structure, the mode of operation, or the effectivenss of their Indian organizations in representing their interests'' nationally and provincially (p. 77). Beaver defined Indian interests in terms of local-level economic development, and recommended Indian self-government at the reserve level and community-based planning and development. He argued that Indian bands should ''decide the nature and form of the representation they require, and fund their political organizations accordingly'' (ibid.).

Although the Beaver report was not implemented, being no more popular in DIAND's bureaucracy than among Indians, it broke the public silence on Indian representivity and struck a receptive chord in the new minister of Indian Affairs in the new Progressive Conservative government[35] (June 1979 - February 1980) and in the new 'super-ministry'—the Ministry of State for Social Development—created in 1979 to improve the coordination of policy advice to the cabinet. Both the minister and the agency believed the government should deal with Indians at the local band-level, not through provincial and national organizations, in which they had no confidence. More generally, the report was consistent with the change in overall government priorities from social to economic issues, with minimal priority assigned to consultation with Indian organizations.

The negative attitudes toward the NIB increased markedly after the return of the Trudeau government in 1980, when the NIB continued its political lobby against patriation of the constitution. Officials describe ministers as ''tired of being kicked in the back-side by Indian leaders.'' One angry minister commented to the press: ''It's the maximum of democracy when you finance your own critics.''[36] The government's dilemma in funding Indian organizations has consequently become acute at times, for there are forces within government that dislike the confrontationist behaviour of Indian organizations and argue that their funding should be stopped or significantly diminished. Funding in some form will undoubtedly continue, if for no other reason than, as one official explained, ''we need these organizations as interlocutors for the next two years at least for the purposes of constitutional discussions.''[37]

The NIB's awareness of the governments' doubts about its

representivity, together with the concern over the future of core funding, the government's new focus on local-level relations and the unworkable federal structure of the NIB precipitated the restructuring process. At present, the NIB will remain the administrative wing and secretariat of the new Assembly of First Nations. The NIB's constitution has been altered to ensure that the NIB is responsible to the executive of the assembly, a body composed of seven chiefs elected from specified regions, and the national chief. The 573 band chiefs meet annually and establish, or sanction, policies to be carried out by the executive and the national chief, who is elected by the chiefs for a three-year term. As the reorganization continues, various options will be proposed and political support sought for them in the remaining difficult issues, such as the structure of the executive and the role of the PTOs in the new body. If the process is carried to completion as planned, the Assembly will be able to demonstrate far greater contact with, and support of, its constituency, thereby enhancing its representivity in all three senses of the term.

Most important is that although the restructuring was in part induced by government reaction to NIB behaviour, the reorganization has been Indian-instigated and Indian-implemented, an adaptive learning process by Indian leaders at all levels, intended to strengthen the efficacy of Indian political organizations in influencing government.

In Australia this political learning and adaptive process was *denied* Aborigines in the context of the NACC's reorganization. Government intervention came with the December 1975 election of the conservative Liberal/National Country coalition government, whose firm business-as-usual approach to governing signalled tighter government control of Aborigines and Aboriginal Affairs.

Australia

Following its election promise, the new Fraser government (1975-1983) appointed a committee of inquiry in 1976 to assess "the effectiveness with which the NACC has represented Aboriginal opinions to Government," and either to recommend changes in the NACC, or to propose new bodies for providing the government with Aboriginal advice on policies and programs (Hiatt 1976:iv). The inquiry team, headed by Dr. Les Hiatt, an an-

thropologist at the University of Sydney, and composed of three
Aborigines, including the NACC president, held public hearings
throughout Australia to obtain Aboriginal opinions on the NACC.
Its report, which was highly sympathetic to the NACC, stated that
"the great majority of Aborigines know practically nothing of the
formal activities of the NACC, and thus are in no position to judge
whether it has represented their opinions adequately to the
Government or not" (Hiatt 1976:viii). The inquiry was a means
for government to secure external policy advice, but it was also
a strategy for justifying the replacement of the NACC by a new
body, since it was publicly established that the NACC had not provided the government with widely based Aboriginal views, nor
sought to be an advisory body.

The central recommendation of the Hiatt report was that
government continue supporting the NACC as a government-
funded pressure group, and that it be enlarged from 41 to 46
members to increase tribal membership and participation. As the
NACC had sought previously, Hiatt recommended the creation
of state branches within the NACC and the continuation of election as the method of recruitment, stressing that tribal Aborigines
could in time adapt to this procedure. Although sympathetic to
the NACC activists, he wanted to ensure that their participation
did not overshadow that of traditional Aborigines in the executive
or general meetings. Hence he recommended that the national executive be composed of state branch delegates (not elected at large
from the full membership as the NACC had done), and that the
national executive not be bound by the decisions of the annual
meeting (full membership). In short, Hiatt proposed non-
accountability within the new structure, a weak organizational
form of a pressure group which would be vulnerable to charges
that its executive's decisions and policies were not representative
of the views of its own membership.

Although the government accepted many of the organizational
features proposed by Hiatt, it did not accept the spirit or the constructive intent of the report. Hiatt sought to renew and strengthen
the NACC by giving it more stature and prominence, and to increase the role of Aborigines in policy-making by creating a Commission for Aboriginal Development, a ten-member statutory body
with executive powers at the departmental level in government.

Instead, the government developed a policy which created two new bodies: a Council for Aboriginal Development (CAD) with purely advisory powers, and a National Aboriginal Conference (NAC), a government-structured consultancy body, not a pressure group, to replace the NACC (Viner 1977). Although still nationally elected, the NAC was to be "a forum for expression" of Aboriginal views on policies and programs, and its size was reduced to 35 members, in disregard of Hiatt's attempt to make the electoral areas smaller to facilitate tribal members in both the electoral procedures and in the scale of the meetings. In contrast to Hiatt's vision of NAC members' role as "politicians" and "referral agents," the policy cast members as "local representatives" responsible for conveying Aboriginal views to the NAC itself and to local DAA planning conferences.

In developing the NAC policy, the minister and senior DAA officials sought to prevent urban Aboriginal activists from overpowering tribal members and "dominating" the new body, particularly its executive, through resolutions at the annual meeting. They argued that the new body's credibility with government and the public rested on the containment of activists, which was necessary if the NAC were to convey a full range of Aboriginal views. However, many of Hiatt's recommendations for enhancing tribal participation were not adopted, including his recommendation that electoral area boundaries, which he drew up along cultural and tribal lines, be reconsidered in consultation with the NACC. Instead, electoral boundaries were determined along the lines of DAA's administrative boundaries and by the department.

The policy-makers held very negative views toward urban activists, and the NAC policy reflected this distrust. The stated desire to protect tribal Aboriginal representation in the NAC was used by government to justify the curtailing of activists' influence in the new body. As a consequence, the NAC was structured to provide government with unaggregated Aboriginal advice in that each of its three components—the six state branches, the national executive and the annual assembly— could not bind the others by their decisions. As the policy stated, the intent was to create "a group of bodies" to provide views and advice "which represents the genuine feeling of the Aboriginal community at *each level*" (Viner 1977:211; author's emphasis). Consequently, under the govern-

ment charter (constitution) for the NAC, its national executive is
not bound to convey the views of its elected membership to the
government or the public.

Both the government and the NAC have encountered difficulties over the NAC's representivity in all three senses, and many
of these problems are directly attributable to the government's
NAC policy (Weaver 1983). The very act of government intervention preempted Aborigines from restructuring the NACC
themselves, either through an internal reorganization or through
an election process. By creating the NAC, the government made
it, as some policy-makers intended, unattractive to urban
Aboriginal activists, few of whom ran in the 1977 election, and
some of whom boycotted the election. Electoral support for the
NAC dropped noticeably in urban centres, compared to the NACC
1973 election, and of the two activists elected, one resigned within
a year. The government extended the nomination period in the
Northern Territories to encourage the participation of more tribal
Aboriginal candidates in the election, but like the NACC, the NAC
experienced difficulties in bringing tribal interests effectively into
the NAC. These problems have been compounded, moreover, by
the emergence of the Northern and Central Land Councils, created
in 1976 by the Aboriginal (Northern Territory) Lands Act (1976),
which have more resources and authority than the NAC has.

The NAC is essentially a rural Aboriginal body, and despite
the dedication of its members to making it work, it has yet to
develop a role for itself at the national level. Its political passivity
has led to private criticism from urban Aborigines and from some
sympathetic government officials, both Aboriginal and non-
Aboriginal, who feel that it should speak out forcefully on issues
and advocate Aboriginal interests, such as those raised in the controversial Aurukun and Mornington Island 'affair,' when the
Queensland State government took control of these communities
in the face of Aboriginal protest and initial federal opposition (Tatz
1979:66-81).

Internally, the NAC's capacity to cull Aboriginal opinions and
define a national, or even regional, position on issues has been
limited by many factors, among them the individual members' inability to develop contacts with their constituents, the lack of a
policy-research capacity in its national secretariat and leadership

skills. The executive members have been deeply concerned about these weaknesses and disappointed with their efforts to correct them. Finally, the NAC's image as an Aboriginal body independent of the government was initially damaged when the executive, allegedly under the influence of a government official in the Public Service Commission, hired a non-Aboriginal as its secretary-general. The ensuing public controversy occurred before the NAC had a chance to get its own bearings, and it was unsettling for the executive members who were trying to establish a separate administration and terminate the interim DAA secretariat, an arrangement which neither the executive nor the DAA officials found comfortable.

The government did not see the NAC (1977-80) as a useful or reliable source of advice on Aboriginal opinion, or as an effective lobbying group. Initially, DAA officials thought the NAC "was going the same route the NACC did" in being concerned over their salaries and benefits rather than issues relating to their constituents. Then, officials became aware of the internal conflicts that have at times preoccupied the NAC's national executive. New officials, not involved in developing NAC policy in 1976/77, as well as Aboriginal officials in the DAA, point to the secretariat as a prime source of the NAC's organizational difficulties, even though they are aware of the limited resources the government initially provided the NAC for its secretariat. For some officials the NAC charter itself militates against the NAC's being perceived as "a nationally representative forum" for Aboriginal views. These officials also receive evaluations of the NAC's state branch activities from DAA regional directors, who generally have found that NAC members are not knowledgeable about government or effective in advocating their constituents' interests at the bureaucratic level. Finally, DAA officials realize that some of the NAC's submissions to government have been based on the views of individual NAC executive members, not the views of the membership. Generally, the new DAA officials have been supportive of the NAC, and initially some hoped it would become politically more assertive (e.g., in Queensland) in promoting Aboriginal interests—and backing federal actions. Although they do not want militancy, some officials acknowledge that a well-organized NAC that is seen by government to convey a broad spectrum of Aboriginal opinions

would benefit the department as well as Aborigines. Referring to
the utility of pressure groups to government, one DAA official commented, "You can't operate without them."

Thus the NAC is privately censured for political inactivity, and
yet it was designed by government to discourage activism, and it
was not provided with resources that would enable it to be an effective lobbying organization.

As in Canada, however, the government overlooks the NAC's
representivity problems when it is politically expedient to do so.
Thus, for example, Prime Minister Fraser, who, like his
predecessors, is sensitive to Australia's international image in dealing with questions of race and minority groups, has said that the
NAC will be the body he deals with regarding the Treaty of Commitment, a concept promoted by non-Aborigines, which proposes
that the government acknowledge the past injustices of dispossess-
ing Aborigines from their lands and provide fair and just compensation to them (Harris 1979). As a result, the NAC has been funded to travel and collect Aboriginal views on the idea of a treaty.
The NAC has also been consulted by ministers on issues (but by
no means to the extent the NIB has been in Canada). And the
current minister, Senator Baume, has agreed to consider the NAC's
long-standing desire to change certain aspects of the charter to increase its representivity (e.g., Queensland's membership in the executive).[38] However, the first real test of the NAC's legitimacy in
terms of a formal mandate from, and accountability to, its constituents is likely to come if the government should ever decide to
negotiate a Treaty of Commitment.

The Australian experience with the NAC policy illustrates the
problems encountered by governments when they structure native
organizations to serve their own purposes. The very act of structuring new bodies creates in the public/Aboriginal perception "a
government" rather than "an Aboriginal" organization, regardless
of whether the membership is elected and regardless of how committed its members are to making it succeed. Aborigines are unlikely to identify with the NAC as an Aboriginal organization until
they perceive that it can advocate their defined interests effectively to government and the public. And until the NAC secures
legitimacy from its own Aboriginal constituency, it will be of
limited utility to the government in terms of providing it with ad-

vice and information, and in carrying out tasks the government may legitimately wish it to undertake.

In Australia, as in Canada, the social-microcosm notion of representivity was not identified as a major problem. Rather, governments focused on the native organizations as vehicles for political communication, vehicles that could ensure continual grassroots input as the basis for formulating a national position on issues. However, the two countries differed markedly in the extent to which the governments provided resources to the native organizations to enable them to be representative, and in the extent to which they used the notion of representivity as a strategic weapon in their relations with the organizations. Canada needed Indian organizations to consult; therefore resources were forthcoming and the government avoided public criticism of Indian organizations *per se*. Australia, by contrast, was much more interventionist and manipulative; it had no need for consultation at the *national* level; it provided minimum resources to the NACC, which it openly criticized, and subsequently structured the NAC as a nonrepresentative body in its internal operations in order to manage government conflict with urban Aboriginal activists.

CONCLUSIONS

This paper has identified some of the difficulties experienced by both governments and native groups over the matter of native political representivity at the national level in Canada and Australia from the 1960s to early 1980s. The concept of representivity is seen to embody three related functions: to represent the views and interests of constituents to government and society, to be representative of the constituency in its social composition, and to be responsive to the needs and aspirations of the constituency. As an ideal concept in the political culture of Canada and Australia, representivity, in all three senses, is sought but rarely achieved by either governments or the national native organizations. Instead, the concept exists in the field of native/government affairs in two forms: as a belief that representivity is an attainable and demonstrable condition of native organizations, through which communication between native organizations and government can be improved, and as a political resource used by both governments and native groups in their efforts to influence the behaviour of the other.

Accordingly, the paper has argued four points. First, that political representivity of native organizations at the national level is as much a problem for governments as it is for native groups because governments find it difficult to communicate with unorganized sectors of the public that are unable to define and articulate their interests to government. Difficulties ensue for governments when they genuinely seek native advice. In these instances governments have little choice but to work with the advice they are provided, and by comparing it with internal advice they obtain from their own administrative systems at all levels, they judge its representivity accordingly, often concluding that advice obtained through bureaucratic channels is more representative of the broad range of native opinion than that provided by native organizations. These judgments are significantly influenced by bureaucratic self-interest, by government definitions of native ''interests,'' by the political climate and general policy priorities prevalent in government at that time, and by a knowledge, however limited, of the structure and internal operations of native organizations.

The second point argued in the paper is that representivity of native organizations is a political resource which governments can assign and withdraw from native organizations to serve their own interests, and that in this sense representivity is an *assigned* political status rather than an empirically demonstrable condition. When governments are pressured by native demands (backed by the public) which they dislike or disagree with, government personnel will use representivity as a weapon to discredit the demands, and under particularly persistent criticism, they will use representivity to discredit the native organizations *per se* if they do not need them for their own consultative purposes. But when governments decide to pursue a policy regardless of native opinion, they will overlook representivity in their desire to seek native organizational endorsement and support for their actions. In this sense representivity becomes a strategic weapon in the power relations between governments and native organizations.

The third point argued is that from the Indian and Aboriginal perspective, political representivity may, in certain situations, be neither possible nor desirable. Two situations in which these circumstances prevail are the following: when native movements are initially being shaped by emerging spokesmen, neither the demands nor the leadership can be considered representative because spokesmen are engaged in the very processes of defining the issues and creating the constituency. And when native organizations emerge at the national level, they not only operate at a distance removed from the grassroots, they must also shape issues and interests of national applicability, and given their desire to secure a unique relationship with the nation-state, their ideological demands may not always reflect more conservative grassroots opinion. Compounding these problems are those created by the need to accommodate to other often competing and more specialized national or regional bodies, and to resolve regional differences in an attempt to achieve a national position. If national native organizations are to continue to promote the unique interests of their constituents, particularly in their relationship with the nation-state, these organizations and their leaders face the persistent denial of their representivity, unless governments share their definition of native interests.

The fourth point is that Indian and Aboriginal leaders use representivity as a political resource in their attempts to protect themselves against government manipulation of their organizations and their advice, and to enhance their capacity to influence governments. Thus, when governments are seen to structure native advisory bodies or organizations to serve their own purposes, astute native activists use representivity to discredit government actions either by actively boycotting the bodies or by withholding participation. It was also shown that when native leaders, like other pressure-group spokesmen, seek to increase their influence in government, they will use representivity, if given the opportunity, to strengthen their organizations.

In conclusion, representivity is an illusive and complex ideal in the political culture surrounding native/government relations; it is constantly in motion in the process of being assessed, assigned, withdrawn, and disputed.

Notes

1. This paper is based on research in Canada (1979-82) and Australia (1979-80) on the emergence of native pressure groups in the 1970s.

Financial support from the Social Sciences and Humanities Research Council of Canada is gratefully acknowledged. I am grateful to Noel Dyck for his valuable critique of the draft paper and to members of the NIB for their constructive comments.

2. Although I do not examine the degree to which the federal governments are representative of their indigenous minorities, it can be noted in passing that native and public pressures were brought to bear on both governments to employ natives in their bureaucracies, especially in DIAND and DAA, in an effort to develop a more ''representative bureaucracy'' (e.g., Matthews 1976:346; Kernaghan 1978). Also, Indians and Aborigines have on occasion demanded separate political representation in Parliament, a demand often derived from or supported by the New Zealand example of four Maori seats in Parliament (e.g., Jackson 1973; McRobie 1978; Stokes 1981).

3. Because there was a core of ministers and other officials who placed little value on the need for native advice, the commitment within both governments to the advisory committee mechanism was uneven at the outset. Furthermore, it is worth noting that in both countries the first impetus for seeking native advice came primarily not from administrators and ministers, but from senior officials who advised the federal cabinets and who were highly dissatisfied with the current direction of native policy in general; these were officials from the Privy Council Office (PCO) in Ottawa and from the Council for Aboriginal Affairs (CAA) in Canberra, the three-man advisory body to the cabinet established in 1967 (Coombs 1978). Both groups of officials were activists in their own right, and they opposed sham efforts by government to consult with native peoples. In neither case did they support their governments' first initiatives at the national level.

4. ''Statement by the Prime Minister at a Meeting with the Indian Association of Alberta and the National Indian Brotherhood, Ottawa, June 4, 1970.'' Toronto: Indian - Eskimo Association.

5. ''Australian Aborigines: Commonwealth Policy and Achievements: Statement by the Prime Minister, 26 January 1972.'' Canberra: Government Printer.

6. Proceedings of the National Conference of Aboriginal Advisory Councillors, Canberra, 10-11 August 1972, p. 1.

7. *Ibid.*:8-9.

8. William McMahon, Federal Election 1972 Policy Speech, p. 21.

9. ''Australian Labor Party Policy on Aboriginals,'' ALP Conference, June 1971.

10. ''Submission to Committee of Inquiry into the Role of the National Aboriginal Consultative Committee, August 9, 1976.'' Department of Aboriginal Affairs, Canberra.

11. This was particularly the case with the first federal department to provide funding to Indian organizations—the Department of Forestry and Rural Development—which in 1969 became the Department of Regional Economic Expansion.

12. According to officials, the core funding policy was devised with little serious forethought about the future political consequences for government, the aim being to develop Indian leadership to enable Indian participation in the political system. Participatory democracy was a key concept in Ottawa at that time, and cabinet approved the policy readily despite some reservations that it might create unrealistic expectations of government compliance with native demands. This policy process contrasted with Australia, where the Whitlam cabinet approved the NACC just before the NACC election, and where neither the Labor nor the Liberal coalition governments purposely supported government-funded Aboriginal pressure groups at the national level. The Whitlam cabinet, for example, did not endorse DAA submissions for additional funding of the NACC, and in 1974 the minister of Aboriginal Affairs publicly threatened to cut off NACC funds if it did not behave as an advisory body.

13. At the same time the PCO, at the NIB's request, funded land claims research (1970-72), and DIAND, which took over this program in 1972, funded specific programs undertaken by Indian organizations (e.g., education, community development, Indian Act consultation).

14. Compared to Aboriginal organizations, Indian organizations were well funded and allowed to operate independently of government. Despite this relative independence, the NIB inevitably became enmeshed in the government's financial management procedures, in problems of accountability of funds, in delays of approved funding, and in the covert (and as yet not publicly researched) influence government exerted through funding (e.g., Ponting and Gibbins 1980:226; Loney 1977).

15. For example, NIB research on Indian Act revisions in 1974 was allocated to the Indian Association of Alberta, which confined its work to that province and informed the government of this fact in submitting its proposals. Minister of Indian Affairs Jean Chrétien found this unacceptable and wrote NIB president George Manuel that NIB "recommendations must be based on the views of the Indian people generally, and not on the opinions of a selected few who would produce the papers you propose" (28 March 1974). He stressed that studies on the Indian Act under way in many of the provincial Indian associations "should be brought together and welded into one comprehensive, national proposal for legislative change."

16. The Metis in Canada have experienced similar problems with regard to an identifiable population, and this has led to recent efforts by the Native Council of Canada to secure changes in the 1981 national census to enable it to determine the number of native people who identify as Metis and non-status Indians.

17. Statement by the Minister of Aboriginal Affairs, DAA Media Release, 20 February 1973.

18. "Proceedings of the National Aboriginal Consultative Committee Conference, 21-23 February 1973," Department of Aboriginal Affairs, Canberra.

19. Minutes of the NACC Steering Committee meeting, 19-23 March 1973, p. 1.

20. "Chief Returning Officer's Report of the 1973 National Aboriginal Consultative Committee Elections," Australian Electoral Office, Canberra 1974.

21. The central issue in Aboriginal politics at this time was land rights, but it was being addressed by the government-appointed Woodward Commission (Woodward 1973) whose mandate confined its inquiry to the Northern Territory. It should be also noted that the closest approximation of mobilizing native peoples in Canada on the scale the NACC was attempting was the creation of the National Indian Council in 1961. Strains between the Indian and Metis members were evident in the council from the outset, and native leaders disbanded it in 1968 when they began organizing the NIB to represent status Indians and the Native Council of Canada to represent Metis and non-status Indians (Wuttunee 1971).

22. Department of Aboriginal Affairs, "Submission No. 1 to the Joint Committee of Public Accounts: Inquiry into the Financial Administration of the Department of Aboriginal Affairs," 26 March 1974.

23. Department of Aboriginal Affairs, "Submission to Committee of Inquiry into the Role of the National Aboriginal Consultative Committee, 9 August 1976."

24. Although the NACC remained organizationally undeveloped, it was a beginning. Its members were aware and often explicit about its shortcomings. Had the NACC and its constituency, through elections, been given the freedom to re-organize and the necessary resources, in time it might well have developed into an organization with which Aborigines could have identified.

25. "The Re-Strengthening of the National Indian Brotherhood." NIB brochure, 1982, p. 1.

26. At the time this article went to press (October 1983) the Assembly of First Nations was continuing to modify its new structure. The evolutionary nature of the reorganization is to be expected, for the changes

do not involve simply drawing new structural charts on paper, but of re-ordering power relationships between the local, provincial and national levels.

27. "Re-Strengthening of the National Indian Brotherhood: Organizational Structure of the Assembly of First Nations," presented at the 12th Annual Assembly of the NIB, August 1981, section D, p. 1.
28. "First National All Chiefs Meeting Called." NIB Press Release, 17 April 1978.
29. First Nations Constitutional Conference, 28 April 1980, Ottawa, Resolution 4, Appendix B, p. 3. Transcript: Constitutional Strategies for Entrenchment of Treaty and Aboriginal Rights, NIB Assembly of First Nations Constitutional Conference, 30 November 1980, Ottawa, Resolution 28, Appendix A, p. 19. Resolutions Report, prepared for April 1982 Assembly of First Nations meeting in Penticton, Resolutions 13 and 17, pp. 16 and 31. "Resolutions Passed at the 3rd Assembly of First Nations, April 20 -22, 1982. Penticton, British Columbia," Ottawa, NIB.
30. "Executive Organizational Report to the General Assembly of the National Indian Brotherhood, August 1979 - August 1980," p. 10 (author's emphasis).
31. "The Re-Strengthening of the National Indian Brotherhood," p. 5.
32. "Organizational Structure of the Assembly of First Nations," Assembly of First Nations, Penticton, April 20 -22, 1982, Beige Section, p. 2.
33. This idea was initially proposed in the White Paper (DIAND 1969:13) and periodically brought up in DIAND since then, although it was not adopted by the Secretary of State in its core funding policy in 1971 or in its renewal of this program in 1976. In 1981 an attempt by regional officials to implement this approach among some bands in British Columbia created a furor among Indians, who saw it as a blatant strategy to erode the economic base of the Union of British Columbia Indian Chiefs. The federal body handling the constitutional process intervened in an attempt to stop the activity, fearful that it would endanger the existence of Indian organizations which were necessary for the post-patriation talks on the constitution.
34. Jack Beaver, a highly successful professional engineer and businessman, was appointed jointly by DIAND and the NIB in April 1978 as special adviser to review and recommend policy directions in socioeconomic development. His actions in legally incorporating his Board angered the NIB, which then withdrew its support from his inquiry in April 1979. He terminated the Board's research activity at this point, and six months later produced the report which reflected his bitterness over NIB actions.

35. Speech notes for the Honourable Jake Epp, minister of Indian Affairs and Northern development, at the Annual Assembly of the National Indian Brotherhood, Montreal, 20 September 1979; and Notes for a Speech by the Honourable Jake Epp, to the Executive Planning Committee, Quebec City, 20 November 1979, DIAND Press Release.
36. *Toronto Star*, 19 February 1982.
37. Government funding has continued to allow the Assembly of First Nations to participate in the ''ongoing'' constitutional meetings with the federal and provincial governments, scheduled until 1986.
38. At the time this article went to press, the NAC was considering how it might re-organize to become ''an umbrella organization'' for the various specialized national Aboriginal organizations (e.g., sports, education, hostels). It was responding to a request from the new Labor government's minister of Aboriginal Affairs, Clyde Holding, a request consistent with party policy to strengthen the NAC and make it ''an effective advisory body to the Government'' (*Aboriginal Treaty News*, No. 7:3, 1983).

The Indian Lobby and the Canadian Constitution, 1978-82 *

6

DOUGLAS E. SANDERS

OVERVIEW: INDIAN STATUS, 1945 - PRESENT

As the political struggle over patriation recedes into the past, it becomes clear that the least expected and most exotic part of the story was the Indian lobby. The Canadian constitution became the dominant political issue for Indians, Metis and Inuit in the years 1978 to 1982. They pursued a complex and expensive strategy, which many politicians dismissed as naive and quixotic. They sought recognition as political actors within the Canadian state and piggybacked the campaign on a legal issue not of their making. In the effort to block or transform patriation, they sought to change their role within the Canadian federation.

---

*Editor's Note: The patriation of the Canadian constitution from the British Parliament to Canada in 1982 marked the end of more than a decade of negotiations between federal, provincial and British authorities. Sanders examines how Indian, Metis and Inuit organizations succeeded in becoming participants in these negotiations.

Following patriatiation another constitutional conference between provincial premiers, the prime minister and leaders of native organizations was held in Ottawa in March, 1983. The main accomplishment of this meeting was an agreement to hold future conferences to consider enshrinement of aboriginal rights in the Canadian constitution.

This chapter appeared originally in Keith Banting and Richard Simeon (eds.) *And No One Cheered: Federalism, Democracy and the Constitution Act,* published by Methuen Publications. This edited version appears with permission of Methuen Publications.

The Key Organizations Comprising the Indian Lobby, 1978-81
National Organizations

NIB - National Indian Brotherhood (the representative body of provincial and territorial associations of registered Indians, 1968-82)
AFN - Assembly of First Nations (the national body that grew out of and eventually succeeded the NIB in 1982)
NCC - Native Council of Canada (the national organization of Metis and non-status Indians—persons not recognized as Indian under the terms of the federal Indian Act)
ICNI - Inuit Committee on National Issues
NWAC - Native Women's Association of Canada

Provincial and Territorial Organizations

Union of British Columbia Indian Chiefs (UBCIC)
Indian Association of Alberta (IAA)
Metis Association of Alberta
Federation of Saskatchewan Indians (FSI)
Four Nations Confederacy (Manitoba)
Grand Council of Treaty Nine (Ontario)
Dene Nation (Northwest Territories)
Council of Yukon Indians
Aboriginal Rights Coalition (ARC) (body formed by the Dene Nation and the the Council of Yukon Indians)

The Indian lobby occurred at a particular stage in the evolution of Canadian aboriginal policy which has had a history of tremendous intolerance, symbolized most graphically by the campaigns against Indian languages in Indian schools. In the years since the Second World War government policy progressed, particularly in the areas of legal equality and cultural rights; more recently the focus has shifted to special economic and political rights.[1] In the first decades after the war, Canada ended its formal discrimination against the Indian populations and began extending them normal social services. They gained the vote, access to liquor and Family Allowance. The church/state alliance in Indian education was ended and students were increasingly integrated into provincial school systems. The end of discrimination and beginning of 'normalization' of Indians within the Canadian state were accompanied by a partial dismantling of the special status of Indian reserve communities. Although racism in Canadian society placed limits on this process, by the 1960s, the right of Indians to equal treatment had been accepted, at least in theory. In the 1970s, the federal government officially approved Indian language instruction, Indian control of Indian education and the funding of Indian cultural-educational centres.

Progress in economic issues has been slower. Indian reserves were originally envisaged as a transitional arrangement designed to transform Indians into farmers; but in practice they perpetuated and increased Indian marginality. After World War II, economic-development programs for Indians were individualistic or assimilationist in character. Gradually, as conditions on reserves became a public embarrassment, the government was forced to shift its concern to the plight of the reserve communities. Indian demands focused on special economic and social rights using arguments based on treaty and aboriginal title. The government resisted these. The White Paper of 1969, which proposed the end of special status for Indians, dismissed aboriginal title claims and trivialized treaty rights. But after a period of litigation and controversy, the government eventually developed a more accommodative policy toward Indian land claims. Aboriginal and treaty claims would be dealt with by a process of negotiation and settlement.[2] A major settlement was negotiated in 1975 by the Cree and Inuit of northern Quebec, facilitating the James Bay hydro-electric project (see Feit, this volume). But progress in settling other claims has been stifled by legal issues, intergovernmental differences, bureaucratic delay, and an insufficient politicization of the aboriginal population. The government response, political in its origins, became legalistic in practice.

The aboriginal organizations came to see that they had to adopt an explicitly political strategy. The first major aboriginal political statement was the Dene Declaration of 1975, which asserted Dene nationhood within Canadian federalism.[3] The 1976 Nunuvut proposal envisaged an Inuit-controlled territory north of the treeline, and in 1977 the Federation of Saskatchewan Indians pioneered the term "Indian government." The concept quickly became national in scope. Between 1980 and 1982 the National Indian Brotherhood (NIB) was reorganized as the Assembly of First Nations (AFN).

The federal government became apprehensive about this development in ideology. In 1975, Minister of Indian Affairs Judd Buchanan rejected the Dene Declaration as "gobbledegook"; and two years later the federal cabinet rejected "political divisions and political structures based solely on distinctions of race."[4] In April 1980, Prime Minister Trudeau acknowledged an Indian demand for "internal native self-government," but refused to accept terms such as "self-determination" or "autonomy."

This progression in Canadian aboriginal policy since World War II forms the background to the constitutional issues of 1978-82. Recognition of Indian governments as a distinct order of government within Canadian federalism was the central thrust of Indian demands and it underpinned native strategy in the constitutional wars.

GETTING IN THE DOOR

In 1978, it seemed unlikely that Indians, Inuit and Metis would play any substantial role in the Canadian constitutional reform process. After all, constitutional reform was basically a response to Quebec's demands for sovereignty; the actors in the reform process were the First Ministers, and no interest-group participation was envisaged. Most politicians assumed that aboriginal issues could be handled by legislation and were not of a constitutional order. (They also saw the aboriginal group as factionalized and politically unsophisticated.)

However, there was an awareness that some constitutional issues did involve Indians. The most persistent constitutional problem was the provision of social services. How could Indians, a federal responsibility, be included in the modern range of social services being provided to Canadians by the provincial governments?[5] As well, there were constitutional issues concerning hunting and fishing rights.[6] The federal White Paper of 1969 proposed the repeal of section 91 (24) of the British North America Act, which gives the federal government jurisdiction over "Indians, and Lands reserved for the Indians." But after strong Indian opposition the White Paper was officially withdrawn a year later. The Clark government in 1979 recognized that Indian and Inuit land claims were a factor to be dealt with in any transfer of ownership of offshore resources to the coastal provinces; and the constitutional evolution of the two northern territories involved aboriginal questions as well. But there was little else. Indians, Inuit and Metis were not on any government's list of major constitutional issues.

Indians, meanwhile, had become interested in the constitution. They argued, as always, that federal jurisdiction must continue, reflecting both the Indian focus on special status and a history of provincial indifference or hostility. In addition, on the Prairies, there was a well-established Indian belief that the treaties were, in effect, constitutional documents and thus, should be protected by, or incorporated in, the constitution. In 1978 the National Indian Brotherhood identified constitutional reform as an issue affecting all Indians—transcending the traditional treaty and non-treaty divisions within the organization. In one sense, the Indian approach was rooted in history. Indians knew they had a special constitutional status and believed it was inadequately recognized by both federal and provincial governments. In addition, Indians asserted a special relationship with the Queen, which was to become a distinctive feature in their later arguments and strategies. But, in another sense, Indians were free from history. As Noel Starblanket, president of the NIB, testified in 1978, "We are now prepared to consider the negotiation of the terms and conditions upon which we will develop our relationship with Canada."[7] He also wrote to Trudeau saying, "our relationship with the rest of Canada remains to be defined."[8]

These initiatives were given at least vague symbolic recognition in constitutional discussions. The Trudeau government's constitutional amendment bill, introduced in June 1978, included a provision to ensure that its Charter of Rights did not erase Indian rights based on the Royal Proclamation of 1763. The accompanying White Paper, *A Time for Action*, stated that "the renewal of the Federation must fully respect the legitimate rights of the native peoples."[9] Other studies and initiatives, such as the 1978 Canadian Bar Association study and the 1979 report of the federal government's Task Force on Canadian Unity, also identified Indian questions as part of the constitutional reform agenda. The Quebec Liberal party's 1980 Beige Paper, for example, said that native people "must become the authors of their own destiny and not mere subjects of jurisdiction."[10]

The NIB formulated two basic and specific demands. First, a new constitution must entrench aboriginal and treaty rights; and second, the Indians must themselves be involved in the process of constitutional reform. At its General Assembly held in Fredricton, New Brunswick, in August 1978, the Brotherhood threatened that, if these demands were not met, it would travel to England to ask the Queen to block patriation of the constitution.

There was a limited, but accommodative response on the part of government. Representatives of the three national aboriginal organizations were invited to the October First Ministers' meeting as observers in October 1978. The NIB represented status Indians, the Native Council of Canada (NCC) represented Metis and non-status Indians, and the Inuit Committee on National Issues (ICNI) represented the Inuit. Federal thinking insisted that status Indians could not be invited without the non-status Metis and Inuit being present as well. The federal government did not accept the distinction between status and non-status Indians, even though it was the product of earlier federal Indian policies, and it could not understand the NIB's refusal to cooperate with the NCC. Although the Inuit were as far from the understanding of federal politicians as Baffin Island, their right to be equally involved with the Indians was assumed. Nevertheless, the NIB was the major actor as far as government was concerned.

Since the October meeting was public, the invitation to be observers simply meant that the aboriginal representatives had seats in the conference centre. As Noel Starblanket often said later, he could have seen the proceedings just as well on television. Indian distrust of the reform process was clear. In March, 1978, Starblanket spoke at the Task Force on Canadian Unity:

> The federal government has continually hammered the Indian people with as much vigour as it has the Parti Québécois. In Ottawa's minds, a move to undermine the special status of Indians is a move to undercut the special status of Quebec. The Indian people greatly resent this government's willingness to fight the Parti Québécois on the backs of the Indian people.[11]

Similarly, Joe Dion, president of the Indian Association of Alberta came away from the First Ministers' meeting "concerned that treaty rights may not be safeguarded by a new constitution and that the ending of Canada's colonial status could also mean the ending of the Indian people's special relationship with the crown."[12]

For the next First Ministers' meeting in February, 1979, the three national aboriginal organizations were again invited to send observers. The invitation was particularly meaningless, since most of the sessions were closed. At the meeting Prime Minister Trudeau proposed a new agenda item, "Canada's native peoples and the constitution," to which all premiers agreed. The Prime Minister's Office insisted that "the federal government does not wish to abdicate its special trust relationship with native peoples," and emphasized the need for "frank discussions between all the parties concerned."[13]

Despite this declaration, the NIB took the position that it was excluded from the constitutional reform process, and proceeded with its plan to visit the United Kingdom and petition the Queen. The federal government, meanwhile, tried several strategies to avoid potential embarrassment. The minister of Justice wrote to the NIB on May 8, offering participation in the fall meeting of the Continuing Committee of Ministers on the Constitution. Indians would be allowed to participate at the ministerial level, but not at the level of First Ministers. Soon after, however, the Liberals were defeated in a general election. At its first cabinet meeting, the new Conservative government, headed by Joe Clark, decided to instruct the Queen not to meet with any Indian delegation.[14] The Clark cabinet apparently had not wanted to convey the impression to Quebec that they regarded the Queen as having any real power. In a last minute letter to the NIB, Federal-Provincial Relations Minister William Jarvis seemed to offer substantial Indian involvement in constitutional reforms. The letter was hand-delivered to the NIB offices on July 3, but the Indians had already left for England.

The trip was a success.[15] As many as 200 Indians made the journey. Though they were unable to meet with the Queen, the prime minister or members of the cabinet, they did meet the leader of the Opposition, members of the House of Commons and the House of Lords, various High Commissioners and a senior official in the Foreign Office. Moreover, the event was well covered in the Canadian media. The Indians had a hidden card in the London strategy. The romantic notion of the noble red man has a deep hold in Europe. The Indians were the first, and remain the classic victims of European colonialism. Labour backbencher Bruce George, in particular, had a lifelong interest in North American Indians. He was active in a London-based group, Survival International, which was intensely involved with issues affecting South American Indians. His support was essential to the London trip, and it continued to the final debate on the Canada Bill in 1982.[16]

The Clark government's promise of aboriginal involvement in the constitutional reform process was confirmed at a meeting between the executive council of the NIB and the prime minister in September, 1979. Clark rejected the idea of having the NIB as ''an 11th province at all discussion tables,'' but did contemplate having ''the NIB or Indian representatives speak at the First Ministers' table on matters that have clear legal impact on Native people.''[17] Starblanket was positive. ''Our request for ongoing and full participation has been accepted.''[18] Having achieved this breakthrough, Starblanket and the NIB pressed the point: almost everything on the First Ministers' agenda affected aboriginal people, they argued, and therefore should come within the native agenda item. Starblanket argued: ''We are not willing to accept exclusion from debate on a matter simply because it affects everybody in the country and not exclusively Indians. Nor can we accept the idea that there can be an arbitrary separation of 'Indian issues' on the one hand and non-Indian issues on the other hand.''[19]

These federal initiatives took place without consulting the provinces, however. At a meeting of provincial officials on July 31,

> General concern was expressed that the Jarvis letter had pre-cast the nature of Indian/Native involvement and may preclude any recommendations from the Annual Premier's Conference. Some officials stated their belief that the Jarvis letter was not so much a policy statement but rather more so the product of a nervous, quick Federal reaction to the NIB prior to the England trip by Indian chiefs.[20]

Some provinces were hesitant about the openendedness of the aboriginal involvement in the constitutional reform process.[21] Howard Leeson, Saskatchewan's deputy minister of Intergovernmental Affairs, complained of unilateral federal initiatives in vigorous terms:

> These meetings were ill-considered and unfortunate. The subsequent telexes from Arnold Goodleaf and Noel Starblanket give ample evidence of how quickly misunderstandings can develop. I wish to register my formal objection to the way in which federal officials have acted in this matter. The expectation level on the part of the native organization and their subsequent disappointment, can be directly traced to these previous federal initiatives.[22]

Linking the federal/provincial process to a government/Indian process clearly would not be easy.

Nor, in general, were the provinces well informed on aboriginal questions. The minutes of a meeting of provincial officials in July, 1979 concluded that ''other than Saskatchewan, no provinces have a clear policy position regarding 'rights' of Indians by virtue of Treaties of 'special status,' ''[23] As late as June or July, 1980, a federal-government background paper commented: ''at this stage very little can be said about the positions of each of the Provinces on the various issues relating to Natives and the Constitution.[24] In all the detailed constitutional position papers put forward by the provinces, there was only one reference to the subject of native people and the constitutions. Despite these problems, the provinces did agree to go along with the federal initiatives.

The national aboriginal organizations and Continuing Committee of Ministers on the Constitution met on 3 December 1979. The ministers spoke of the meeting as a significant advance. In

contrast, Noel Starblanket spoke bluntly. He had agreed with the
prime minister on full, equal and ongoing participation in the constitutional talks, limited only to the native agenda item. To meet
with the committee at all was itself a concession on the part of
the NIB. He rejected any process of negotiation or compromise:

> I am not here to negotiate. I cannot compromise the position
> my colleague, Chief Dion, has espoused or anything mandated
> by our annual meeting resolutions. It is pure and simple. You
> must now go forward to your continuing committee and report
> that that is our position. There has been no compromise as far
> as we are concerned and you will report that accordingly.[25]

Starblanket asserted that the Indians should be involved in the
constitutional negotiations as governments. In the place of negotiation and compromise, Starblanket talked of a Canadian Indian
Constitutional Commission which would hold hearings and con-
solidate an Indian position. The First Ministers would eventually
be faced with a package developed by the commission and a demand for acceptance. Starblanket also made it clear that governments would have to deal separately with the three national
organizations. Whereas the Native Council of Canada clearly
sought a unified front of all the aboriginal peoples' organizations
vis-à-vis government, the NIB followed its traditional rejection of
common-front strategy. Finally, Starblanket predicted failure:

> Not a Liberal government and not a Conservative government,
> has not and will not in the near future anyway accede to treaty
> rights and aboriginal rights in this country . . . we know very
> well what your government's position will be, what it is, has been
> and what it is going to be.[26]

Starblanket's position with respect to NCC and ICNI would
have come as no surprise to the ministers; but his insistence on
meetings with First Ministers, the rejection of negotiation or compromise and the prediction of failure must have seemed extreme.
Places at the federal/provincial bargaining table had never before
been opened to any but government executives.

Shortly after the December meeting, the Clark government fell,
and the constitutional renewal process stopped. After Trudeau
regained office in February, the Quebec referendum on sovereignty
association became the overriding federal preoccupation. Mean-

while, the Task Force on Canadian Unity recommended that "Both central and provincial should pursue direct dicussions with representatives of Canadian Indians, Inuit and Metis, with a view to arriving at mutually acceptable constitutional provisions that would secure the rightful place of native peoples in Canadian society."[27]

In April, the NIB held a national all-chiefs conference in Ottawa, which was attended by an estimated 376 chiefs and another 2,000 Indian people.[28] The assembly was called the First Nations' Constitutional Conference and was held in the largest conference room in Ottawa. The federal government hosted a banquet on the second night where Prime Minister Trudeau spoke of the "remarkable progress in mutual understanding which has taken place between native peoples and the federal government during the 1970s," including the "valuable and historic precedent" of involving aboriginal representatives directly in the constitutional reform process.[29] Trudeau was claiming credit for this innovation. But, in fact, his White Paper on Indian policy had made no reference to the "involvement of Indian, Inuit and Metis representatives." Nor did the documents issued after the First Ministers Conference of February 1979. In effect, Trudeau was distorting history to take credit for a policy initiated by Prime Minister Clark. But at least all three federal parties now had the same stated positions, and no federal or provincial politicians publicly opposed aboriginal participation in the reform process nor provisions for aboriginal rights in a new constitution.

THE SHORT LIST: PARTICIPATION DELAYED

The defeat of the Quebec referendum on sovereignty association in May 1980 was followed by new initiatives in the reform process. The First Ministers met in June and agreed on a two-stage strategy. The Continuing Committee would work on a list of 12 items over the summer and present their conclusions to a September First Ministers' meeting. Other constitutional issues would be put off for a "second stage." Aboriginal issues did not make the short list.

The accelerated schedule, with its attendant deadlines, worked against the aboriginal organizations. Extensive work had been done on constitutional questions such as a charter of rights, the

Senate and family law, but no comparable work had been done on aboriginal questions. The NIB and NCC proposals for commissions of inquiry needed a year or two to carry out. The strategy had made sense when Clark was in power, but it could not accommodate the new Trudeau agenda.[30] The government was aware of the dilemma in which it placed native peoples. An internal federal memorandum, written probably in early July, commented:

> The short list, together with the agreed upon time schedule, leaves open the distinct possibility that Native interests and positions may be compromised or ignored in the rush to achieve general consensus under most of the items. It is this possibility amongst other factors that has led to increasing demands by the Native leadership (especially the NIB) for "full ongoing and equal" participation in all discussion relating to the short list items in addition to the "Natives and the Constitution" item. The fact that governments have issued no formal statements on the status of the item "Natives and the Constitution" has compounded this problem for the Native leadership.[31]

Nothing was done, however, to ease the problems. In only one token meeting did a subcommittee of the Continuing Committee of Ministers on the Constitution meet with the representatives of NIB, NCC and ICNI. The organizations were all concerned with the process being followed. Harry Daniels, NCC President, stated that he was:

> . . . puzzled at how this form of our participation in the constitutional review process has come to pass and why we are being asked to comment on a list of priority items distilled from over two years of federal and provincial meetings and negotiations from which we have been excluded.

Del Riley, the new president of the NIB added:

> At no point have there been discussions about the process involved. In our view we should be invited to participate in the September meeting of the First Ministers and in all future First Ministers' meetings. In addition, in our view, we should be given a seat on the Continuing Committee of Ministers on the Constitution, which would mean ending the need for a special subcommittee of the CCMC on native questions.

Jean Chrétien, representing the federal government, repeated the pledge that aboriginal representatives would be at the table with the First Ministers *when the time came to discuss the native agenda item*. The fact that financial support to assist the aboriginal organizations in the constitutional process had just been paid was used to justify the delay in dealing with the aboriginal issues. But Chrétien clearly rejected the idea of Indian groups constituting a third order of government in Canada as a "non-starter" in constitutional discussions.[32]

While the First Ministers were meeting from September 8 to 13, the NIB held a parallel conference, rather than simply accept observer status. The NIB announced that it would "begin a systematic and timely dialogue with the provinces on our mutual Constitutional interests." An advance team was mandated by the NIB executive council to go to England to prepare for a systematic lobby of the Queen, parliamentarians, Commonwealth embassies, and the European Economic Community. The NIB also planned to join other indigenous nations in an international forum in Canberra, Australia, in March and to lobby at the United Nations. "And we will attempt a much needed public education program in Canada."[33]

A MILITANT REACTION: FALL 1980

When the Trudeau government decided to move unilaterally, its resolution contained only two sections affecting aboriginal groups. A general clause allowed affirmative action programs; and another provision protected "the rights and freedoms that pertain to the native peoples of Canada" from the Charter of Rights and Freedoms. The document was consistent with the federal position that aboriginal questions were to be kept for the second stage of constitutional reform.

Aboriginal organizations knew they had been left out of the action and out of the constitution, and there was an aggressive response. The Union of British Columbia Indian Chiefs took on the cause with a vengeance. In September, they initiated a lawsuit in Canada, asking for a judicial declaration that Indian consent was necessary before the constitution could be patriated. They also planned further actions:

> The Union of British Columbia Indian Chiefs is presently investigating the possibility of taking legal action in Great Britain

and also within the terms of the United Nations. In Great Britain we are seeking to bring an action asking that the British courts declare that Britain is still in a trust relationship to the Indian people and cannot patriate the Constitution without Indian people's consent.

On a world level, we are seeking to have world courts declare that the Treaties entered into between Great Britain and the Canadian Indians cannot be extinguished on the request of the Federal Government of Canada.[34]

George Emanuel, head of the Union of British Columbia Indian Chiefs, accused the federal government of trying to terminate Indian rights. He saw the egalitarian provisions of the Charter of Rights as designed to make Indian rights illegal.[35]

The measures which are now underway to patriate and amend the Canadian Constitution appear to be designed to remove all constitutional impediments to an accelerated termination of the special status and rights of Indian Nations by eliminating Canada's administrative responsibilities now carried out on behalf of Britain. Canada seems intent on nothing less than the total assimilation of Indian peoples and the complete destruction of Indian Governments.

Current Canadian intentions with respect to Constitutional amendment should not come as a surprise. The fact that a new Constitution appears geared to a termination policy, rather than to any recognition or enhancement of Indian rights is entirely consistent with long-standing Canadian objective and practices.[36]

In October, the union announced plans for a "Constitution Express," a protest train to travel from Vancouver to Ottawa. The federal government had established a Special Joint Committee to hold hearings on their constitutional proposal, and the NIB had called an emergency First Nations Assembly. The Constitution Express would arrive in Ottawa for both events. Then a delegation would go on from Ottawa to New York to petition the United Nations. In addition, the NIB announced that it would establish an "embassy" in London.[37] At the urging of Bruce George and other British supporters, the term "embassy" was dropped in favour of the "Office of the First Nations of Canada." The NIB talked of establishing an office in New York.

Additional forums became available. The Foreign Affairs Committee (the Kershaw Committee) of the British House of Commons began hearings on November 12 on British responsibilities concerning the Canadian constitution. Indian groups sent briefs and asked to appear as witnesses, but the committee heard no witnesses from Canada. The Fourth Russell Tribunal was held in Rotterdam from November 20 to 24 on the situation of the Indians in the Americas. Briefs were submitted on the constitutional issue, and Indians from British Columbia, Alberta, Saskatchewan, and Ontario attended.

Again the federal government tried to counter the Indian international lobby. The prime minister wrote to the aboriginal organizations on October 30, assuring them that patriation was not a threat to their rights and repeating the government's promise to involve them in the second stage of constitutional talks.[38] He also proposed a meeting in the spring of 1981 to discuss how to involve the aboriginal groups in the First Ministers' meetings.[39]

Clearly, aboriginal lobbying placed the government in a difficult political and moral position, as an internal federal document written at this time reveals:

> There is likely to be a major effort by Canada's Native Peoples to win national and international support (especially at Westminster) for their stand against patriation. If the Native Peoples press forward with their plans and if they succeed in gaining support and sympathy abroad, Canada's image will suffer considerably. Because Canada's native Peoples live, as a rule, in conditions which are very different from those of most other Canadians—as sample statistics set out below attest—there would well be serious questions asked about whether the Native Peoples enjoy basic rights in Canada.

Moreover, the document acknowledged the unreality of the government's second-stage strategy: "Native leaders realize that entrenching their rights will be enormously difficult after patriation, especially since a majority of the provinces would have to agree to changes which might benefit Native Peoples at the expense of provincial power."

Nevertheless, in public, the government maintained its stated reason for a delay on aboriginal questions: the difficulty of formulating precise constitutional provisions. As the prime minister observed, "the simple claim of aboriginal rights without anyone knowing exactly what it means, is not a matter which one can convincingly argue should be put in the Constitution at this time."[40]

Indian British strategy also hit a reef. On November 12, the Foreign Affairs Committee of the British House of Commons heard its first witness, Mr. J. R. Freeland, a legal adviser in the Foreign and Commonwealth Office. When Sir Anthony Kershaw asked if Britain retained treaty or other responsibility for Canadian Indians, Freeland replied, "In our view, all relevant treaty obligations insofar as they still subsisted became the responsibility of the Government of Canada with the obtainment of independence, which at the latest was with the Statute of Westminster of 1931."[41] The report of the Foreign Affairs Committee the following January adopted Mr. Freeland's views on the treaty issue, and its judgment had great impact both in England and in Canada.[42]

In the meantime, 500 Indians arrived in Ottawa on the Constitution Express in late November. Two days later, the Assembly of First Nations met with perhaps 2,000 Indians, again in the largest convention room in Ottawa. The Indians had established a remarkable presence in Ottawa at a crucial time in the constitutional reform process. But their presence confused observers and politicians. The Assembly of First Nations, rather than charting a war plan, drafted a general manifesto, called the Declaration of the First Nations, which was presented to the governor-general:

> We the Original Peoples of this land know the Creator put us here.
> The Creator gave us laws that govern all our relationships to live in harmony with nature and mankind.
> The laws of the Creator defined our rights and responsibilities.
> The Creator gave us our spiritual beliefs, our languages, our culture, and a place on Mother Earth which provides us with all our needs.
> We have maintained our freedom, our languages, and our traditions from time immemorial.
> We continue to exercise the rights and fulfill the responsibilities and obligations given to us by the Creator for the land upon which we were placed.
> The Creator has given us the right to govern ourselves and the right to self-determination.
> The rights and responsibilities given to us by the Creator cannot be altered or taken away by any other Nation.

The parliamentary committee had altered its schedule to hear both the NIB and the Constitution Express leaders. But at the last minute both groups boycotted the committee hearings, and a delegation from the Constitution Express went to New York to the United Nations. The NCC and ICNI, however, did testify before the committee, as did regional groups such as the Council for Yukon Indians and the Nishga Tribe.

The lobbying in Ottawa and England produced some cooperation between the three national organizations. British supporters stressed that the aboriginal case would get greater support if the Canadian groups had a unified strategy there. In November, a single submission went to the British Foreign Affairs Committee on behalf of the NIB, NCC and ICNI. In addition, staff in the three national organizations developed a common position on constitutional provisions which would entrench treaty and aboriginal rights, recognize aboriginal self-government and require aboriginal consent to constitutional amendments affecting their rights. But this cooperation quickly foundered. A formal NIB executive-council resolution of September, 1980 had opposed cooperation with the Metis, and prairie leaders, particularly from Alberta, were furious that the NIB would defy their views in this way. Their organizations had long seen the Metis as rivals, and the following August the General Assembly of the NIB resolved that the organization would ''work alone on the constitution.''

The thinking of one key group, the Union of British Columbia Indian Chiefs, had changed in an important direction during the Constitution Express. The idea of the entrenchment of Indian rights in a Canadian constitution was rejected as inconsistent with the national status of the tribes. As the union later reported to the NIB:

> If Indian people choose entrenchment, Indians are Canadian citizens, forever, and the emphasis will be to get the best possible arrangements for citizenship, remembering that we will always be in a minority.

> If Indian people choose nationhood, and if we are unsuccessful in achieving a negotiation structure prior to patriation, the fallback position must be to lobby to keep section 91(24) and Section 109 of the BNA Act in Britain, while the rest of the Canadian Constitution is patriated. We will then negotiate directly

with Great Britain, on our own behalf, for our land, resources and for the settlement of the trust owing to us.[43]

As a result, the union, with a mandate from the NIB, began to explore the legal strategies open to Canadian Indians to achieve these goals. The union sought an opinion from an international law expert at Oxford University on whether or not a case could be made in England. They also explored the possibility in the European Court of Human Rights, the International Court of Justice in the Hague and the Human Rights Commission of the United Nations.

"THE SHORTEST TREATY IN HISTORY"

The federal government's own strategy was encountering heavy weather. The Kershaw Committee reported in January, 1981, that the federal government was not constitutionally authorized to go ahead with patriation against the opposition of eight provinces. Although Trudeau and Chrétien had consistently maintained that they had the power to petition the British Parliament without provincial consent, they had been, in fact, far less confident of their constitutional position. They faced more opposition from the provinces and the other federal political parties than they had expected. The Indian opposition was only one of many problems facing the government, but it was particularly troubling because of its combination of moral and legal arguments. The government knew that the Indian cause had significant appeal in Canada and in Britain.

The embattled federal government tried to broaden support for its position at the federal level.[44] The joint committee became a central vehicle for building that broader federal consensus, and aboriginal rights became a bargaining issue within that forum. The NIB were told that the government would agree to positive entrenchment of aboriginal and treaty rights, and between January 28 and 30 the deal was struck by the three federal parties and the leaders of the national Indian organizations. The key new section in the resolution read:

> 34.(1) the aboriginal and treaty rights of the aboriginal peoples of Canada are hereby recognized and affirmed.
>
> (2) in this Act, "aboriginal peoples of Canada" includes the Indian, Inuit and Metis peoples of Canada.

Section 25, protecting the rights of aboriginal peoples from the egalitarian provision of the Charter of Rights, was strengthened. A new Section 35(2) required that a future First Ministers' meeting involve the participation of aboriginal representatives and discuss aboriginal issues.

The amendments were in line with what the organizations had requested. The alteration to section 25 and the provision in 35(2) came directly from the NIB's submission to the joint committee in December.[45] Although the agreement was still a compromise, since there was no response to the aboriginal positions on self-government and a clause requiring their consent to future amendments, it was generally seen as a dramatic reversal of policy. Indian, Inuit and Metis leaders declared they were beginning a new era in which they would at last take control of their own destiny. It was, said Del Riley, "an historic moment, a recognition of the right of native peoples to self-determination," and "a new beginning for Indian people in Canada." Native leaders announced they would join Prime Minister Trudeau in demanding that the British Parliament approve patriation. "I'll carry it back for him now," said Harry Daniels of the Native Council.[46] The emotional moment was shared by members of all parties, and the committee vote was unanimous.

The euphoria was short-lived, however. The breakthrough took place on Friday, and by the following Monday Jean Chrétien was circulating additional provisions that would have allowed section 34 to be amended in the northern territories by Parliament alone. In the provinces the general amending formula would apply. Chrétien explained that these provisions were part of the Friday agreement. There were heated denials from the organizations and the opposition parties. Although Chrétien withdrew the provision, there was a sense of betrayal. One NIB employee referred to the January 30 bargain as the shortest treaty in history. To the aboriginal organizations the dispute emphasized the need for a consent clause on amendments. But a consent clause was unacceptable to the federal government.[47]

Ed Broadbent, national leader of the New Democratic party, advised the aboriginal leaders that the government would not move on a consent clause and that the general amending formula gave the aboriginal groups sufficient protection. He feared that the demand of the Progressive Conservative party and the majority of provinces for simple patriation without a charter of rights might succeed, and therefore asked aboriginal groups to accept their gains and support the government's package.

Nevertheless, within days, the government was using the January 30 concession to build support. On February 6, Chrétien testified before the joint committee: having agreed to entrench rights for the handicapped, natives and Quebec anglophones, we cannot "play politics on their backs."[48] In Britain, the Canadian High Commission quickly disseminated the news of the January 30 agreement, circulating a document rebutting "myths" about the Canadian constitution.

> MYTH: That the rights of native people in Canada would be adversely affected by "patriation" of the Constitution.
>
> FACT: The Constitutional proposal actually marks a dramatic step forward in the relationship between aboriginal peoples and other citizens of Canada. For the first time, there would be a positive affirmation of aboriginal and treaty rights. In addition, the commitment of the Government of Canada to invite representatives of the aboriginal peoples to a Conference of First Ministers to discuss constitutional matters that affect them would be confirmed in the Constitution Act.[49]

But the January breakthrough quickly fell apart. There were hostile reactions from some of the member organizations of the NIB. Alberta chiefs unanimously rejected the agreement, calling for Del Riley's resignation.[50] The NIB executive council forced the organization to reverse its stand. A moderate grouping, including the Dene of the Northwest Territories and the Council for Yukon Indians, lost in their bid for continued NIB support. In March, the Indian Association of Alberta withdrew from the NIB, alleging collusion with the federal government and with Metis and Inuit groups.[51] The Four Nations Confederacy in Manitoba also severed their ties with the Brotherhood, on constitutional matters.[52] Actual leadership had shifted to organizations in the western provinces as early as October, 1980. The NIB was discredited in the eyes of its member organizations, and any appearance of NIB coordination of the Indian strategy was destroyed.[53]

THE LONDON LOBBY

The drive for international political support intensified. The Union of British Columbia Indian Chiefs announced a second Constitutional Express, this time to Europe. Indians would visit Germany, France, the Netherlands, and Denmark, gathering support on their way to London. The Union also called an emergency general assembly for May 14 and 15. President George Manuel warned: "We are in a state of emergency . . . We expect you to be at this meeting because the end of your Indian reserves, Indian governments and all your Indian rights is very close . . . This is the final showdown."[54] A delegation of Alberta Indians left for England in May. A Saskatchewan group left in June.

Indian legal and political initiatives increasingly focused on the London lobby, which had begun as a continuous strategy that spring. The organizations did not participate in the litigation before the Supreme Court of Canada in the spring of 1981,[55] and the Canadian suit brought by the Union of British Columbia Indian Chiefs was not actively pursued. Canadian courts were the proper forum for Canadian governments and Canadian law, but Indians were better off litigating in England. Earlier, the union had provided leadership on the strategy of litigation in England and over the summer there was cooperation between the union and Alberta and Saskatchewan groups.

In the fall, however, cooperation fell apart. The Indian Association of Alberta initiated its own litigation. The Nova Scotia and New Brunswick organizations joined the Alberta suit, allowing both pre-Confederation and post-Confederation treaties to be involved in the arguments. The Union of B.C. Chiefs was joined by the Four Nations Confederacy in Manitoba and the Grand Council of Treaty Nine, a regional group in Ontario. British Columbia and Saskatchewan continued to cooperate, though Saskatchewan launched its own suit.

Legal action was reinforced by political action. Lobbyists were in London continuously from June until the following March. The NIB's London office was taken over by the western Indian organizations, and from September, 1981 to March, 1982, the lobby met about 250 members of the House of Commons and the House of Lords. There was, however, little media coverage of this activity in Canada.

An attempt to re-establish national coordination of Indian strategy was made in July. The Joint Council of the NIB and the Assembly of First Nations[56] hired Joe Dion, former president of the Indian Association of Alberta, and Wilton Littlechild, an Indian lawyer, to coordinate the lobby nationally and report to the annual General Assembly of the NIB. Dion and Littlechild spent a week in London, meeting with significant actors in the constitutional drama. Their report gave an interesting picture of the thinking of various individuals at that time. Gilles Loiselle, agent general in the Quebec delegation in London, apparently expressed interest in a joint Quebec/Indian court case in Britain, if they had similar positions. Member of Parliament Sir Bernard Braine was planning "a short, sharp, rampant speech" in Parliament against the Canadian proposals. Bruce George advised them they could "lobby on the emotional side but (they) must also come up with a definite legal argument that the British Parliament has a legal responsibility."

Dion also wrote a paper on "Indian Statehood" that proposed consolidating the Indian reserve communities in Canada into a national government, with powers equivalent to a province. An executive or cabinet would be comprised of chiefs or ministers of various departments and agencies established to serve Indian people. It would report to an elected legislature, with possibly an additional chamber to accommodate a council of elders. There would be a judiciary and a public service staffed with people recruited by the Indian state to carry out the work of the various departments and agencies. Fiscal arrangements with the federal government would be similar to those of the provinces with equalization payments and "would be purely intergovernmental in nature." Under Dion's plan the Department of Indian Affairs and the Indian Act would cease to exist. Indians would no longer be identified by the province in which they lived, but rather as citizens of an Indian state.[57]

Although the idea of provincial status had been explored before, the paper was a bold proposal that went well beyond any existing political consensus among Indians. At the General Assembly of the NIB, the paper was supported by Indians from the northern territories. However, opponents from Ontario and British Columbia argued that the paper dealt with postpatriation plans and was therefore tacitly admitting an Indian defeat in the fight against patriation. After a heated debate, the document was tabled for future discussions. They never took place. This new effort by the NIB to coordinate Indian strategy on the constitution failed, leaving the initiative with the three western organizations.

BETRAYAL IN OTTAWA

The Supreme Court of Canada gave its decision on federal unilateral strategy on 28 September 1981, setting the stage for the climactic First Ministers' meeting in November. As the governments jockeyed for position, native leaders also began to organize.

The Union of British Columbia Chiefs held a general assembly on October 28 - 30 to launch the second Constitution Express. Union President George Manuel circulated a letter he had written to the prime minister:

> Our indictment of your administration of our affairs can no longer be restrained. At this critical juncture in our relationship, your legacy of mismanagement and neglect coincides most remarkably with the hidden agenda of your government which is to try to achieve the termination of our aboriginal title and our sovereign rights.
>
> In all the corruption and attempted destruction of our ideals by your government, we must point our accusing finger at you, Mr. Trudeau, as the Head of this government. It is impossible for us to disregard the hard evidence which is our daily companion. Daily, these assurances, promises and guarantees of your government are shown as lies.

British Columbia Indians flew to Europe on November 1. The next day, a 21-member delegation of Saskatchewan Indians flew to London—the sixth trip to England by Saskatchewan Indians in two years. Indians from both Quebec and Saskatchewan met French officials in Paris. Later in the struggle, an Alberta delegation met the Pope.[58]

As the First Ministers gathered in Ottawa for their fateful November meeting, the native groups supporting the government package, such as the ICNI, were fearful lest section 34 be traded off in some bargaining session. Chrétien assured them the section was safe. But he was wrong. On November 5, a political compromise was announced at the end of the First Ministers' meeting.

The accord was worded to avoid any direct reference to the fact that section 34 was gone; and when Trudeau tabled the accord in the House of Commons, his speech did not mention the fate of the section.

There was immediate confusion. Who was responsible for the killing of section 34? Chrétien stated that the section was dropped because the Indians had objected to it. Trudeau said that seven premiers had opposed it.[59] Mr. Broadbent understood that the prime minister had supported the removal of the section.[60] *Macleans* magazine wrote that Trudeau "tried briefly to reinstate native rights"[61] Another journalist reported that Trudeau asked if aboriginal rights had been omitted by mistake. When told it was not a mistake, he "shrugged and moved on to the next agenda."[62]

The federal government had solved its main problem, but at some cost. Because of section 34, it lost at least one Liberal M.P.[63] and some opposition support. Both the Progressive Conservative and New Democratic parties committed themselves to clauses on sexual equality and aboriginal rights. But only the NDP said it would vote against the package if these sections were not added. The government had been using the aboriginal and treaty rights section to assure Indian supporters in the United Kingdom that Indian rights were being respected. Indians had continually relied on conspiratorial arguments and to challenge the good faith of the government. Now the conspiratorial arguments looked good. Canadian governments were prepared to gang up on Indian rights.

John Munro, Minister of Indian Affairs, met with the NIB on November 5. The strident Indian opposition was deeply resented by the major federal politicians. Munro told NIB leaders that they had "pissed and shitted" on him over the constitutional issue. Ever the politician, however, Munro offered to meet with the cabinet the next morning to try to get section 34 restored, at least to apply at the federal level. But the NIB were uncertain whether they could support the reinstatement of section 34, given the aggressive campaign of the provincial organizations.

The political initiative was taken by others first. The NCC, IC-NI, the Native Women's Association of Canada, the Dene Nation organization in the Northwest Territories and the Council for Yukon Indians joined together as the Aboriginal Rights Coalition

(ARC). On November 9, the prime minister met with Inuit leaders, to whom he expressed his regret that the aboriginal rights section had been dropped and suggested the possibility of restoring it for the northern territories where Ottawa had full jurisdiction. Charlie Watt of ICNI rejected this proposal as unfair to other native groups and suggested a three-year delay for a restored section 34, giving time for the governments to negotiate specific provisions on aboriginal rights. Trudeau replied that if the aboriginal groups could agree on some proposals, the cabinet could consider them later in the week. Proposals were submitted. They were considered and rejected at a cabinet meeting on November 12:

> The Prime Minister and Cabinet would not restore section 34 even with a delay in coming into force; they would ask government lawyers to "study" the idea (which they themselves had earlier proposed to the Coalition) of applying section 34 to federal jurisdiction; they would make no attempt to persuade the provincial premiers to change their positions; they urged the natives to press the provincial premiers to change their positions; and they lamented the divisions in the native movement between the NIB and the coalition . . . [64]

Chrétien offered to entrench section 34 at the federal level if the NIB, NCC and ICNI indicated their support for such an action by November 24. He repeated that section 34 could not be fully restored without the consent of the nine provinces that had signed the accord.

Lobbying in Ottawa was going nowhere. The ARC and NIB began to plan public protests. On November 16, the anniversary of the execution of Louis Riel, ARC supporters demonstrated in Ottawa, laying a wreath at the conference centre where the accord had been signed. The NIB declared November 19 as National Indian Solidarity Day and spent two days preparing a statement of constitutional principles, which they presented to the governor-general.[65] November 19 saw Indian demonstrations in nine cities across Canada. In Vancouver, Indians occupied the Museum of Anthropology. Five thousand Indians demonstrated in front of the Alberta legislature in Edmonton. Premier Lougheed addressed the crowd, saying the province supported existing Indian rights, which in his view were adequately protected without section 34. If the aboriginal groups were seeking more rights, then the government

wanted to know which additional rights were being sought.[66] On
November 19, Premier Lévesque, referring to the deletion of section 34, called English Canada "hypocritically fundamentally racist
. . ."[67]

The premiers gradually swung around. On November 17, Sterl-
ing Lyon was defeated in the Manitoba election, and the new
premier, Howard Pawley, announced his support for the restoration of section 34. On November 19, Premier Blakney of Saskatchewan, in political trouble for his alleged opposition to a sexual-
equality section, offered to support that clause if other premiers
agreed to restore section 34. Premier Davis stated his support for
section 34. The next day, Premier Bennett announced British Columbia's support at the same time that Indians were addressing the
provincial Social Credit convention. And the same day Premier
Lougheed, after negotiations with the province's Metis organizations, announced support for a modified section 34, limited to "existing" rights.[68]

The nine provinces agreed to the new wording. Chrétien stated
in the House of Commons that his legal advisers assured him that
the addition of the word "existing" did not alter the meaning of
the section. What had been implicit was now explicit.[69] Ten
governments had agreed and the matter was settled.

In one sense, the massive pressure had worked. But,
remarkably, the new wording had the agreement of only one
aboriginal organization, the Metis Association of Alberta. The Inuit, who had supported the government from January 30 to
November 5, opposing the new wording. The three national
aboriginal organizations were now fully united against the whole
constitutional package.

THE FINAL DRAMA IN LONDON

The very day Chrétien announced the new wording for section 34
(renumbered as section 35), the Indian Association of Alberta filed its action in the English courts. Alberta argued that the treaties
had been signed with the Crown, and the responsibility for them
remained in the United Kingdom. The suit directly challenged
Freeland's testimony to the Foreign Affairs Committee the previous
November, which had been adopted as the position of the government of the United Kingdom. Freeland had taken an orthodox

British constitutional position on the evolution of legal arrangements, which held that Canadian independence had evolved through custom and practice. At some point the authority over Indian affairs had shifted to Canada. It was unnecessary to find a date or a document, as long as one could argue that the process of transfer was over.

Nevertheless, the Alberta argument had two strengths. It did not require arguments about Indian sovereignty or international law, both of which would have been difficult. Rather, it accepted the treaties as being "domestic," not international in character. The argument therefore only required asserting that the treaties were significant legal documents within Canadian federalism, an argument easily accepted in Britain. Second, it was argued that there had been imperial responsibility for Indian affairs, but never any explicit transfer of that responsibility to Canada.

Both Saskatchewan and British Columbia were preparing legal arguments, asserting that Indian consent was necessary for patriation. Saskatchewan Indians were highly critical of Alberta for discarding the idea that the treaties were treaties in the international sense.[70] They based their arguments firmly on the status of the treaties. British Columbia, however, argued that the tribes were part of the constitutional order within Canada, and their consent, along with that of the provinces and the federal government, was necessary by the terms of the Statute of Westminster of 1931.

Underlying these legal arguments was a fundamental distrust of the Canadian government. Indians involved in the London lobby argued that while Canada was talking of entrenching aboriginal and treaty rights, it had a government bill in the wings to undercut Indian self-government, and had introduced legislation hostile to Indian land claims in the northern territories. The larger threat was the terminationist policy espoused by the federal government in 1969, which was often alleged to be its hidden agenda. Canada, the Indians argued, did not have a free hand to terminate Indian rights as long as the treaty link to the United Kingdom existed and as long as the constitution contained its one provision on Indians—section 91(24). Patriation would both sever the treaty link and enable Canada to repeal that section.

The Alberta case was thrown out by a judge of the British Court of Queen's Bench on December 9. But on December 21, Lord Denning, the maverick chief justice of the Court of Appeal, granted leave to appeal. An elite populist Tory, a defender of the 'little man,' Denning had taken jurisdiction on the plea of the Red Indians of Canada. But he was such an unusual figure that normal predictions of success meant little. The first reading of the Canada Bill took place in the House of Commons on December 22, when the Thatcher government announced that a second reading would be delayed until the Alberta appeal was completed. The appeal was argued on January 14 and 15, and judgment was given on January 28.

The decision was a disappointment to the Indians. Lord Denning upheld the treaties, but as Canada's responsibility. The Freeland argument accepted the premise that the treaties were with the Crown in the right of the United Kingdom but asserted that the latter had transferred its responsibilities to Canada. This was problematic in terms of the law of treaties. How could one party to a treaty shift its obligations to another state without the consent of the other party to the treaty? To avoid this problem, Lord Denning, in the Court of Appeal, ruled that what had been a unified Crown had divided into the Crown in the right of the United Kingdom and the Crown in the right of Canada. There had been no transfer. That part of the Crown with which the Indians had dealt, split off and continued to be the treaty partner of the Indians. Clearly, this was a mythical concept, cloaking a non-explicit transfer of power.

Lord Denning went on to note Indian distrust of the Canadian government, but argued that it was unjustified.

> There is nothing, so far as I can see, to warrant any distrust by the Indians of the Government of Canada. But, in case there should be, the discussion in this case will strengthen their hand so as to enable them to withstand any onslaught. They will be able to say that their rights and freedoms have been guaranteed to them by the Crown—originally by the Crown in respect of the United Kingdom—now by the Crown in respect of Canada—but, in any case by the Crown. No Parliament should do anything to lessen the worth of these guarantees. They should be honoured by the Crown in respect of Canada ''so long as the sun rises and the river flows.'' That promise must never be broken.[71]

Judicial defeat left the British Parliament as the last forum. Sol

Sanderson, President of the Federation of Saskatchewan Indians, proposed a legislative strategy to the other Indian organizations. His organization had drafted an "Indian Rights Amendment Bill," based on the Treaty and Aboriginal Rights Principles that had been agreed to by the NIB/AFN the previous November.

> The Amendment Bill (if) passed by the British Parliament would make patriation of the Canada Act conditional upon recognition by Canada of Indian rights set out in the schedule. In other words, the British Parliament could pass the Amendment Bill in Britain and say to Canada, You can have your Canada Act if you recognize Indian rights and your Secretary of State is satisfied that you meet the conditions set out in the Indian Amendment Bill.[72]

The joint council of the NIB/AFN supported Saskatchewan's strategy in mid-February and approved lobbying both in Ottawa and London.[73] But time was running out. On February 17, debate began in the British House of Commons on the Canada Bill. The parliamentary debate was a kind of victory for the Indian lobby:

> In the House of Commons, a total of thirty hours were devoted to debate on the Canada Bill over several days, and of these twenty-seven hours were on Indian matters. Approximately 90% of the time was exclusively spent on Indians. In the House of Lords, over 80% of the debate was concerned with our rights.[74]

But in the end the bill was passed. The Queen went to Canada and gave royal assent to the legislation on April 17, and later in the same month the British courts struck out the remaining Indian court cases.

The NIB declared April 17 a day of mourning. Robert Manuel said that any Indian participating in the celebration would be committing a "treasonous act against the Indian nations and their citizens."[75] The Queen, in her speech, referred to the Indian issue. She was pleased that "the rights of the aboriginal people are recognized with full opportunity for further definition."[76] Trudeau stated that the constitution "offers a way to meet the legitimate demands of our Native peoples . . . The two orders of government have made a solemn pledge to define more precisely the rights of Native peoples."[77]

Patriation was over. In June, Trudeau met separately with the leadership of the three national organizations as part of the preparations for the First Ministers' Conference that would consider aboriginal questions.

CONCLUSIONS

From 1978 to 1982 the political initiatives on aboriginal questions had come from aboriginal organizations. There was important support from the federal constitutional studies and from maverick M.P.s at Westminster. In Canada, all governments, at least nominally, accepted the legitimacy of aboriginal provisions and aboriginal participation. But it was not obvious that this acceptance would produce anything more than pleasant words in a new preamble. In the real world of federal/provincial bargaining, surely the aboriginal organizations could not be real players.

The NIB took an aggressive line, interrupted only by the short-lived agreement of 30 January 1981. The aggressiveness of the stance seemed a cover for internal divisions and a lack of Indian politicization. If so, a process of political negotiation was never a real possibility, since a truly accommodative response of governments would have exposed the political weaknesses of the organizations. But, almost predictably, the governments broke their promises of aboriginal involvement. The process, in the end, was not reasoned negotiation but public bargaining over symbolic provisions. In that process the aboriginal organizations *could* be real players. In the end, they achieved increased recognition in the new constitution without delivering any political agreement. It was surprisingly like the granting of the federal vote in 1960. Indians could later assert that any political implications of having the franchise had not been agreed to by the tribes. In the same way, no political questions on the Indian issue were settled in the new constitution.

Indian strategy, in retrospect, had serious problems. It was expensive: one estimate put the total cost of the London lobby at $4.5 million.[78] More important, the lobbying and litigation, in the end, could not win. The continuation of the strategy beyond January, 1981 endangered the gain achieved with the original section 34 and resulted in the restoration of a weakened section. The strategy severely antagonized the federal government, the only Canadian government likely to support Indian issues against other Canadian governments. It did not win allies among the provincial governments, which, while sometimes supportive, officially kept their distance. It also risked losing nongovernmental support in Canada by its opposition to patriation.

Some blamed the Indian strategy on their lawyers. Reeves Hagan, the federal government's representative in London on the constitution, was reported to have made this argument: "While acknowledging that the Indian rights problem 'can only be a source of regret and shame,' he suggested that Indians lobbying in London 'have been advised by very sharp lawyers and PR people who should probably be strung up by the heels.' "[79] As well, two prominent Canadian constitutional authorities blamed the lawyers.[80] These opinions had the advantage of avoiding criticism of the Indians, but they were misguided: the Indian groups had obtained advice from leading British academics and had hired leading counsel. According to the information available to me, the lawyers consistently advised their Indian clients that it was unlikely or highly unlikely that they could win in the British courts. The Federation of Saskatchewan Indians estimated they had a 10 percent chance of victory.[81] Other estimates were somewhat higher, others lower.[82] Although lawyers may have given conflicting signals and Indians may have had undue faith in British justice, the basic reality is that litigation in Britain was pursued as a political, not a legal strategy.

What was the political strategy? In the controversy that has surrounded this issue, it is possible to discern an aboriginal thesis and a government thesis.

The aboriginal view asserts that the aboriginal groups had a coherent and explicit set of demands. They were formulated in the briefs presented to the special joint committee in December, 1980, repeated in the Treaty and Aboriginal Rights Principles in November, 1981, and reworked again in the Indian Rights Amendment Bill in January, 1982. The reality was not that the government was confused about what the aboriginal groups wanted, but that it was never really prepared to consider provisions on aboriginal self-government or a consent clause. This left the aboriginal groups with a simple choice between continued struggle or capitulation. Del Riley made an error by agreeing to the January 30 compromise, but it was soon reversed.

On the one hand, the aboriginal view argues that it was the federal and provincial politicians who were disorganized and inconsistent over time. The politicians wanted to have it both ways. They wanted the political credit for involving aboriginal representatives, but they could never organize the reform process in a way that allowed them to live up to their promises. They promised participation, then denied it. They pledged that section 34 was non-negotiable, then negotiated it away. They responded not to principle but to the federal political crisis of January, 1981 and to massive Indian demonstrations in November, 1981. In contrast, the aboriginal groups were much more consistent and principled in their approach to the reform process.

The government view, on the other hand, asserts that the aboriginal leaders could not negotiate because their constituencies were not sufficiently politicized for a unified position to be developed or political agreement to be delivered. The unwillingness or inability of the groups to negotiate and accept compromise was a sign of political immaturity, not of principle. Why was consent delivered on January 30 and then withdrawn? Such a turnabout proved—in the government view—that Del Riley was an ineffectual leader. He could not deliver his constituency and did not realize that he could not deliver it. No coherent grouping would elect such a weak leader. How was the federal government to understand the ensuing campaign that focused on a demand for a consent clause? Would a consent clause satisfy the groups, or would their demands simply escalate to recognition of aboriginal self-government? Some Indians were on record as saying that the Canadian constitution should not even mention them. Indians had parallel governments under the Crown and were no more a part of Canada than was Australia.

According to government analysis, Indian activity was not simply disunited, it was chaotic. Del Riley was a startlingly weak leader. The London lobby was uncoordinated. The provincial Indian leaders adopted widely differing approaches to the negotiations: Sol Anderson of Saskatchewan was smooth and deliberate; Eugene Steinhauer of Alberta played the radical and always avoided negotiations; Wayne Christian, the main organizer of the Constitution Express, called Trudeau a liar in a confrontation with the prime minister before television cameras, an act that did not encourage reasoned negotiations. On top of these divisions, the NIB would not cooperate with the NCC, and the Inuit were playing what seemed a different political game.

In my opinion, both the aboriginal and the government views miss the mark. The aboriginal groups were seeking recognition as political actors within Canadian federalism. Their nationalist political positions had been developing since 1975, or earlier. Although governments had moved, to some extent, on questions of aboriginal and treaty rights, there had been little acceptance of the aboriginal redefinition of the issues in Canadian aboriginal policy. Both the demands for a recognition of aboriginal self-government and for a consent clause were political demands, which, if fulfilled, would have made aboriginal peoples equal to governments. The federal government's response to the politics of the situation was to offer a concession on the less controversial questions of aboriginal and treaty rights. Such a concession was not perceived as painless, or it would not have been delayed so long and offered only when the federal government felt it was in serious political trouble. But the government had already defined aboriginal and treaty claims in nonpolitical terms. The Canadian legal system had delivered only limited recognition of these claims, and it was doubtful that section 34 would seriously alter the character of that recognition. Aboriginal title claims were uncertain with or without section 34.

The political goal of Indians was not to get and protect section 34. The goal was to achieve power by becoming political actors in the constitutional game. By this analysis, Del Riley was wrong in agreeing to section 34, not because it was a compromise and not because he did not have the authority to bind the member organizations of the NIB; he was wrong because agreement ended the political role of Indians in the constitutional game. By playing the game through to the end, Indians were unmistakably political actors in the drama. They were the final domestic issue, along with women, in the November controversies. They were the final issue in England. Indian litigation there delayed patriation by two months, and the Indian issue occupied most of the British parliamentary debates.

The Canadian government could dismiss the Indian lobby as incoherent. Prime Minister Trudeau said in exasperation, "I honestly don't know what the Indians want. I just don't know."[83] But Bruce George, the romantic, knew: "I believe that their campaign . . . will be seen by future generations as an important stage in their political development, and in the inevitability of the Indian nations of Canada playing an infinitely greater role in the governing of their affairs."[84]

Notes

1. The Hawthorn Report gives some background on Canadian Indian policy: Hawthorn (1966; 1967); and Weaver (1981) is a valuable account of the development of the White Paper.
2. The policy was announced on 8 August 1973, and has been recently restated in two booklets published by Supply and Services Canada (1981; 1982).
3. The Dene Declaration is reprinted in M. Watkins (1977:3).
4. Terms of Reference, Special Government Representative for Constitutional Development in the Northwest Territories, 19 July 1977, P.C. 1977-2227.
5. The issue was discussed at a conference of federal and provincial officials in 1963 and at a conference of ministers in 1964: see Sanders (1975:99-102). The Hawthorn Report considered these problems and contained two chapters on constitutional and legal issues. The 1969 federal White Paper aborted any continuing discussion of the provision of services by proposing a termination of federal responsibility.
6. These issues entered the constitutional discussions of 1978-82 in two ways. The federal government was conscious that the judicial decisions and the Indian Act meant that provincial hunting laws were limited by treaty rights, whereas federal hunting and fishing laws were not. The federal government was conscious that the provinces could argue fairly that the burden of these rights should be equally respected or equally ignored. Second, there was the real possibility of a transfer of jurisdiction over fisheries from the federal to the provincial level.
7. Starblanket, Testimony to the Special Joint Committee of the Senate and House of Commons on Bill C-60, 23 August 1978, p. 4.
8. Starblanket to Trudeau, 27 September 1978.
9. Supply and Services Canada (1978:8).
10. Constitutional Committee of the Quebec Liberal Party, *A New Canadian Federation* (1980), p. 84.
11. Starblanket, NIB presentation to the Task Force on Canadian Unity, 2 March 1978, p. 3.
12. *Kainai News*, Standoff, Alberta, November No. 1, 1978, p. 3.
13. Office of the Prime Minister, Release, 12 February 1979, p. 6.
14. The decision to block the meeting with the Queen was curious. If the Queen had no power, as bureaucrats often reminded the NIB,

a meeting was simply a piece of symbolic politics. Indians, in full regalia, had always been part of royal visits to Canada. Prince Charles was made an honorary Kainai chief in a special ceremony in southern Alberta. Alberta Indian leader Harold Cardinal gave a political speech to the Queen on a royal visit in 1973 (the speech and the Queen's reply had been fully negotiated before the event). In 1976, Indians visited the Queen on the occasion of the 100th anniversary of Treaties Six and Seven.

15. The only account of the trip is Sanders (1980:6).
16. Bruce George became a controversial figure among Indians. He recommended to the Indians that they argue in terms of human rights and avoid talk of sovereignty. Duke Redbird of the Ontario Metis and Non-Status Indian Association accused George of paternalism, saying he wanted to be known as ''Bruce of the Breeds.'' Other British M.P.s were involved. Sir Bernard Braine, known as a supporter of non-mainstream causes, was active in the Alberta lobby. M.P. Mark Wolfson spent two years teaching at a Nishga school in British Columbia. M.P. David Ennals, a former Labour cabinet minister, supported the Indian cause since 1979.
17. Meeting with Prime Minister Clark/Cabinet Ministers and the NIB executive council, 28 September 1979 (minutes probably prepared by the NIB), p. 5.
18. Starblanket to Clark, 2 October 1979.
19. Meeting of the Steering Committee of the Continuing Committee of Ministers on the Constitution with the representatives of the national aboriginal organizations, 3 December 1978 (Canadian Intergovernmental Conference Secretariat, Document 830-77/014, p. 15.)
20. Provincial officials meeting, Winnipeg, 31 July 1979, minutes, p. 2.
21. Preliminary meeting of officials at the NCC offices, 15 November 1979, minutes (taken by the NIB).
22. Leeson to Dick Gwyn, 13 December 1979.
23. See note 20 above, p. 6.
24. Background and Discussion paper, ''Natives and the Constitution,'' written sometime after 19 June 1980, informally released.
25. Steering Committee of the CCMC, see note 19 above, pp. 54, 89.
26. The text of Starblanket's prepared speech was more positive than his comments at the meeting. The speech indicated hope for mutual trust and accepted involvement at all levels. It contained the positive statement: ''Indians now have an opportunity to become partners within Confederation.''
27. This theme of aboriginal participation in the reform process was repeated in a resolution passed by the National Liberal Convention in Winnipeg, 4 July 1980. It also appeared in a background paper

prepared by the Constitutional and International Law Section of the
Canadian Bar Association for the bar convention in August, 1980.

28. The idea of a national gathering of chiefs mooted within the NIB for
a number of years. The meetings in London in 1979 were described
as an all-chiefs meeting, and a resolution passed there for the con-
vening of another such meeting in Canada, was approved by the
General Assembly of the NIB in September, 1979.

29. Office of the Prime Minister, Release, Ottawa, 29 April 1980.

30. The NIB never established their commission of inquiry. In July, 1980,
the NCC established the Metis and Non-Status Indian Constitutional
Review Commission. The NCC President Harry Daniels acted as the
commissioner, with other leaders acting as deputy commissioners for
particular hearings. A report was published (NCC 1981).

31. See note 24, above.

32. The CCMC subcommittee's report of the August 26 meeting was conveyed to the First Ministers' meeting in September. The report recommended that the item "Canada's Native Peoples and the Constitution" be on the agenda in future First Ministers' meetings on the constitution, that native leaders meet directly with First Ministers at that
time, and that all parties accept the possibility that constitutional
amendments in favour of native peoples could result from those
discussions.

33. *Kainai News*, Standoff, Alberta, September, 1980, p. 2.

34. Statement of the Union of British Columbia Indian Chiefs, approximately 25 September 1980.

35. *Vancouver Sun*, 15 October 1980.

36. Union of British Columbia Indian Chiefs (1980:7-8).

37. *Vancouver Sun*, 22 and 30 October 1980.

38. Trudeau to Riley, 30 October 1980.

39. This is stated in "Briefing Materials on Canada's Native Peoples and
the Constitution."

40. Government of Canada (1980:3a).

41. Minutes of evidence taken before the Foreign Affairs Committee, 12
November 1980, p. 39.

42. Canadian constitutional expert Edward McWhinney later rebutted
Freeland's testimony before the House of Commons committee in
London. This seems to have been important in sustaining the Indian
legal arguments in London. The Foreign Affairs Committee issued
a second report in January, 1982, saying that with the agreement of
nine provinces, it was proper for the British Parliament to pass the
Canada Bill. The report referred to the First Ministers' conference
on aboriginal issues, promised in the Canada Bill, as the "proper

forum'' for the discussion of the concerns of the aboriginal people of Canada (*Vancouver Sun*, 18 January 1982).

43. Union of British Columbia Indian Chiefs (1981:4).

44. One account says that Broadbent informed Trudeau in December, 1980, that he could not deliver one section of his caucus without a provision on aboriginal rights. (*Vancouver Sun*, 1 December 1980 and 26 January 1981.

45. The NIB brief to the Special Joint Committee on 16 December 1980, said: ''Section 32 formally institutionalizes the First Ministers' conferences and requires certain meetings to be held. A requirement of Indian participation, at least on matters affecting Indian people, should be included in any such provision.''

46. *Ottawa Citizen*, 31 January 1981.

47. *Ontario Indian* (1981:16).

48. *Vancouver Sun*, 6 February 1981.

49. ''Canada - the facts,'' Canadian High Commission, London, n.d.

50. *Kainai News*, February No. 1, 1981, p. 1; *Native People* (Edmonton), 13 February 1981, p. 1.

51. *Native People*, 20 March 1981, p. 1.

52. *First Citizen* (Winnipeg), May, 1981, p. 1.

53. Del Riley came to deny that he had ever supported the January 30 package. Harry Daniels of the NCC came to describe the January support as conditional on a satisfactory resolution of the consent clause issue. On April 20 he announced NCC's opposition to the package as it then stood (*The Forgotten People*, Spring, 1981, p. 10; *The Native People*, 24 April 1981, p. 7).

54. *Coyote Prints* (Williams Lake, B.C.) April/May 1981, p. 3.

55. The Four Nations Confederacy of Manitoba was represented in the Manitoba Court of Appeal and in the Supreme Court of Canada. No distinctively Indian legal arguments were presented.

56. From April, 1980, to the spring of 1982 the NIB went through a reorganization to become the Assembly of First Nations. From December, 1980, an interim committee of the AFN met jointly with the executive council of the NIB to form the joint council, referred to in the text. This unusual transitional structure does not seem to have been a significant factor in the performance of NIB leadership.

57. *Native People*, 28 August 1981, p. 1.

58. *Native People*, 12 February 1981, p. 1 and also 13 November 1981, p. 6.

59. *Vancouver Sun*, 6 November 1981.

60. Stated on the CBC radio program ''As it happens,'' 6 November 1981.

61. *Macleans Magazine*, 16 November 1981, p. 32.

62. *Vancouver Sun*, 13 November 1981. Gwyn named the four western provinces, Newfoundland and New Brunswick. Gwyn's analysis is

partly confirmed by Chrétien in the House of Commons *Debates*, 9 November 1981, p. 12636.

63. Warren Allmand, former minister of Indian Affairs, was a constant ally of the Indians.

64. Jull (1982:89).

65. This document, "Treaty and Aboriginal Rights Principles," is reprinted in *The Saskatchewan Indian*, 4 December 1981, p. 5.

66. Exerpts from Premier's Address, *Native People*, 27 November 1981, p. 2.

67. *Vancouver Sun*, 20 November 1981.

68. Meetings took place on November 16 and 19, 1981, and involved the premier, other provincial officials, leaders from the Metis Association of Alberta, Clem Chartier (legal adviser to the NCC), and Rod Hope (legal adviser to the Metis Association of Alberta).

69. There was major controversy over whether the change in wording mattered. *Financial Post*, 5 December 1981.

70. *Saskatchewan Indian*, January, 1982, p. 2.

71. Court of Appeal, 28 January 1982.

72. *Saskatchewan Indian*, January, 1982, p. 28.

73. *Saskatchewan Indian*, February-March, 1982, p. 2.

74. *The First Nations*, Federation of Saskatchewan Indians, 1982, p. 28.

75. *Vancouver Sun*, 15 April 1982.

76. *Native People*, 16 April 1982, p. 1.

77. *Native People*, 16 April 1982, p. 3.

78. *Vancouver Sun*, 27 May 1982. The Canadian government has funded Indian, Metis and Inuit political organizations since the early 1970s. It was often assumed that this funding went into the London lobby, though this was denied by some Indian leaders (*Vancouver Sun* 3 February 1982). Substantial funding came from the natural-resource revenues of the Blood and Samson bands in Alberta. The Federation of Saskatchewan Indians negotiated a provincial tax rebate on gasoline and asked bands to donate the interest on the amounts to the constitutional struggle. The two Constitution Expresses organized by the Union of British Columbia Chiefs were largely paid for by the individual participants. The union also organized an auction sale of artifacts to raise funds. At the end of the campaign, both the NCC and the NIB were seriously in debt.

79. *Vancouver Sun*, 25 February 1982. In Vancouver, Bob Manuel, president of the Union of British Columbia Chiefs, countered with the observation that the Canadian government is getting some bad advice from shoddy bureaucrats.

80. McWhinney, (1982:129); Professor Dale Gibson, one of the counsel for the federal government, was quoted as saying that the Indians

were badly advised if they proceeded with litigation in England (*Edmonton Journal*, 9 February 1982).

81. *Saskatchewan Indian*, January, 1982, p. 3.
82. Representatives of the Union of British Columbia Indian Chiefs and the Federation of Saskatchewan Indians were told that the chances were ''certainly less than even,'' perhaps 30 to 40 percent. The solicitor speculated that a judge might say that the Indians had rights, while ruling that no English court had jurisdiction to deal with them. Such a ruling could have ''some political effect.'' Interview with J. Rosenheim, 24 July 1981, in Dion, ''Report on Constitutional Lobby in London,'' England, 5 August 1981.
83. Quoted by Premier Lougheed in his speech on 18 November 1981 to the Indian demonstration at the provincial legislature (*Native People*, 27 November 1981, p. 2).
84. Quoted in *Toronto Star*, reprinted in *Saskatchewan Indian*, February-March, p. 4.

Ethnodrama and the 'Fourth World': The Saami Action Group in Norway, 1979-81[1]

7

ROBERT PAINE

PRINCIPAL CONCERNS

The first concern of this essay is with moral opposition as an instrument of Fourth World politics. I view moral opposition as a mode of political opposition.[2] Whereas opposition in politics is ordinarily conducted in accordance with accepted procedures of the nation-state, through the ballot box, for example, moral opposition uses alternative (often innovative) channels in the knowledge of powerlessness to register one's will *directly* through the ballot box. The alternative means chosen are moral in the sense that there is an appeal to values which are widely recognized as intrinsic and thus supra-transactional; a common occasion for the use of moral opposition is when a group (or individual) believes that it is being mistreated with respect to a supra-transactional value;[3] but in such a case, the actual action taken must not itself do violence to the normative moral code.

Accordingly, when the Saami Action Group (SAG) in Norway wished to impress upon the government that the Saami of the country were not being given a "fair deal" (Henriksen 1983), they resorted to a hunger strike and thereby successfully placed a claim on the public conscience. In effect, two messages reached the public simultaneously: the one promulgated powerlessness and the other a new source of power. In like manner, much of Fourth World politics is about turning physical powerlessness into moral power and then putting that to good political account.

The other principal concern of this essay is with ethnodrama, for much of the cutting edge of moral opposition is in its dramatic presentation. The hunger strike was not simply a newsworthy event; it also had an important dramatic structure, and I hope to demonstrate the crucial role of drama—more precisely, ethnodrama—in the *making of* a Fourth World point of view and lobby. In general, there is good reason to see the public side of Fourth World politics as dramas.[4] For with but meagre corporate power, or none at all, a Fourth World may exist only in its own stagings of the 'fact'; only by such means can certain political truths be experienced. In short, the Fourth World is linked to what I am calling drama by its efforts to express its version of reality and thereby possibly cause the rearrangement of the experience of others.

The phrase Fourth World carries strong connotations concerning the circumstances of certain aboriginal or autochthonous *peoples* (see Introduction, this volume), but the focus in this essay is upon individuals. Thus some Saami among Saami are 'Fourth Worlders,' and they like to believe that eventually their work will be recognized as being on behalf of all who consider themselves Saami. But difficult questions about representativeness arise. Because Fourth World leaders or activists shape new demands and work at creating (probably with innovation) a new constituency, they are unlikely to be "representative of" the constituency they wish to represent (see Weaver, this volume). It seems, then, that for a Fourth World ideology to possess a political life it is necessary for it to attract the broadest public by an event of particular force. The hunger strikers created just such an extraordinary event—and in doing so they were helping to maintain, or even *make*, a Fourth World situation.

Their strike took place in Oslo, in protest against the Norwegian government's intention to dam a river (for hydro-electric development) in the Saami homeland in the far north of the country—the Alta/Kautokeino River (Paine 1982). Their defiant presence in the capital demonstrated for all to see that "We are . . . ." Using the river as an ethnic symbol, they transformed government action into an ethnic insult. At the same time as they impugned the morality of the state, they confronted Norwegians with the question of whether the Saami in their country were being treated properly.

There were other events of civil disobedience on this account too, but these took place primarily in the north and, paradoxically, were Norwegian (rather than Saami) in inspiration. So I will compare the handling of some of the events in the north with the hunger strike in Oslo in order to identify factors of success and failure in moral opposition, in general, and in the staging of political ethnodrama in particular.

OSLO, 1979

Background

The Alta/Kautokeino River is one of two major watercourses running through Saami areas of settlement in the province of Finnmark, Norway. At some 140 kilometres from the sea, it passes through the village and county seat of Kautokeino (here it is known as the Kautokeino River). Over 80 percent of the 2,000 villagers in the area use Saami as their mother tongue; they are reindeer breeders, farmers (combined with hunting and fishing), and employees in diverse administration and service jobs; included among the monolingual Norwegian-speakers in Kautokeino are NATO personnel. Downstream and about halfway to Alta—but still inside the county of Kautokeino—the river runs through Masi, a small village (pop. 400) that is virtually totally Saami-speaking.

Downstream from Masi the watercourse becomes the Alta River, signalling marked topographic, ecologic and cultural changes. The open tundra—with its vast bed of lichen providing winter pasture for the 60,000 reindeer in Kautokeino county—is replaced first by wooded escarpments through which the river winds, and then by meadow and pine forest along both banks. Here the Saami presently form a small minority, compared to the immigrants from North Finland and South Norway who began arriving in numbers two centuries ago. The primary occupations are farming—on a conspicuously more profitable basis than upstream—slate-quarrying and salmon-fishing in various combinations (but there is a markedly differential access to the salmon-fishing). The river reaches the sea at the town of Alta (pop. 3,000), a modern, urban and regional growth centre. In earlier times, even the area around the lower reaches of the river was exclusively Saami, with transhumant reindeer pastoralists, and hunters before them, camping and moving in the terrain. Still today, the area is important to Saami reindeer pastoralism (Paine 1982).

In 1970, the Norwegian Water Resources and Electricity Board[5] (hereafter, the Board) announces a project that includes the flooding of Masi. The project is approved by the province and the "importance" of the village of Masi, when weighed against the development of the province, is disparaged by the provincial governor (*Altaposten, 10* September 1970). But in Masi itself, an action committee is formed, and a parliamentary delegation visiting the village that summer are met with banners that read: "We Were Here First." "We Will Not Leave." This has its effect and in 1973 Parliament declares Masi a heritage area. But otherwise the plans of the Board are forwarded to the next procedural stage.

In 1974, an official report commissioned by the Board warns of "catastrophic" consequences for reindeer pastoralism. In 1975, both of the two national Saami associations that exist in Norway at this time[6] declare themselves against the project. In 1976, the two counties directly affected vote against the project.[7] During 1977-78 several government departments work together to produce revised legislation, and in November 1978 Parliament legislates into existence a considerably reduced project.[8] (But the river will still be dammed.) Even at this late hour, the whole matter is still seen by some as simply "another hydro" project.

Early in June 1979, Parliament, responding to protests from various Norwegian and Saami sources, debates a proposal to re-open the debate over the Alta River project; the Labour-Conservative parliamentary alliance on this matter defeats the proposal. It is then widely supposed that this would be the last that Parliament would hear of the matter—any further developments could be left to the police to handle—and a month later the bulldozers are ordered to begin work on the 36 kilometres of access road to the dam site.[9]

The Saami Action Group emerged in 1979 in a mood of disgust and frustration over the failure to have the rights of Saami, as a people, taken seriously. Several of the group were from Masi itself. Another decisive factor in the formation of SAG was the realization that action against the hydro project was being presented to the general public as, first and foremost, a Norwegian movement to save a *river*. In 1978 a nationwide Peoples' Action Group (PAG) had been formed to oppose all plans to dam the river. Throughout the summer of 1979, the PAG used civil disobedience methods to prevent the bulldozers from carrying out their work; a PAG camp in the area, it is claimed, was visited by up to 5,000 people, foreigners among them.

Among the few Saami PAG members that summer were two who decided that "something *big* had to be done—*by us Saami.*" They settled on the idea of getting a small group of friends together to go to Oslo (3,000 kilometres away) to demonstrate. It took a little longer to decide what form the demonstration would take. A small number of people, including some members of the *Norske Samers Riksforbund* (NSR) executive, a Saami organization, were told something of their plans, but the SAG would not be dissuaded from carrying through their action: "We are representing ourselves only" (and therefore were answerable only to themselves). They decided to stage a hunger strike in Oslo—a secret so surprisingly well kept that their appearance on 8 October on the lawn outside the parliament building was a surprise even to many Saami in the Kautokeino area. There they erected a Saami tent (*lavvo*).

Narrative[10]

Norwegians, even those who have never visited their capital, are likely to be aware of the national symbolism associated with Karl Johansgate—the principal street that runs from the central railway station to the spacious grounds of the royal palace. Across from the shops on the east side of "Karl Johan" there is an open space of lawns, flowerbeds and paths; the national theatre is situated in the middle of this area, and outside stand the busts of Björnsen, Holberg and Ibsen. Facing the theatre, on the east side of the street, is the Faculty of Law of the University of Oslo. The theatre and university are overlooked by the palace to the north, and a few hundred yards to the south is the parliament building, a more recent structure. The lawn in front of this building is known as Eidsvolls *plass*, for it was at Eidsvoll, a Norwegian village, that the Norwegian constitution (according independence from Denmark) was adopted in 1814 and the first Norwegian parliament of modern times was convened. The steps of the parliament building lead down to the lawn and within a few paces there is the traffic of Karl Johan. It was on this lawn that Saami hunger strikers pitched their tent.[11]

Monday, 8 October. Seven young Saami, in traditional dress and speaking Saami as they work, erect the tent. One of them goes up the parliament steps to deliver a written ultimatum to the government: it must rescind its authorization to the Board concerning the Alta/Kautokeino River project until Saami status and rights (including land rights) are settled by the courts. If no positive response is received from the government by noon the next day, the SAG will start a hunger strike (which will continue until such time as the government accedes to its request).

The group's ages range from the early twenties to early thirties. All of them are from Finnmark, the northernmost province where the Saami population is concentrated. None of them has any notable background in politics. There are two women in the group, one of whom, a recent graduate of the Royal Academy of Art, has her studio in Masi; and her parents are Saami from the coast. The other woman is a schoolteacher in East Finnmark, where her parents were one-time reindeer owners. One of the five men is from a reindeer-owning family but he himself is no longer engaged full-time in reindeer herding; the other men are from sedentary families in the interior of Finnmark.

In the north, the PAG still defies the bulldozers, so that work on the access road has not been able to begin.

Tuesday, 9 October. The government rejects the demands of SAG and the hunger strike begins. Within a few hours the celebrated Norwegian arctic explorer and writer, Helge Ingstad, already an octogenarian, is at the tent where he is photographed with the SAG; two members of Parliament (left-wing) also sit around the tent for a while, giving public expression of their support for "the Saami cause." Indeed, it seems that the Oslo public and the media accept the strikers as *bona fide* representatives of the Saami cause against the injustices of the Norwegian state. Several thousand people in Oslo have already signed a statement of support for the strikers. The World Council of Indigenous Peoples (WCIP) and International Work

Group for Indigenous Affairs (IWGIA) send a joint appeal to the prime minister, asking him to recognize the legitimacy of Saami interests in the Alta/Kautokeino River controversy. The mayor of Kautokeino, however, tells the media that the demonstration in Oslo does not represent "Saami interests." Meanwhile, NRL (see note 6) ask the government not to begin work on the access road until its consequences for reindeer management have been properly assessed; further, they ask for an extension of the deadline for the statement of their case in this matter. NRL have not issued any statement of support for hunger strikers.

Wednesday, 10 October. Already informed by the police that their 'occupation' of Eidsvolls *plass* is illegal, the strikers are told that they will be allowed to hold their demonstration on the other side of Karl Johan (the side of the shops) around the statue of a celebrated artist (Christian Krogh) for one day only, from 9 a.m. to 9 p.m. in accordance with the city by-laws. The strikers' lawyer accepts the change of venue but rejects the one-day restriction, and the Saami themselves insist that they must be allowed to stay in their tent at night. The situation with the police remains deadlocked. There is no statement from the government. Meanwhile, there is friendly interaction between the strikers and the crowd around their tent at Eidsvolls *plass.* The media watch and report. Particular note is taken of the "valuable and varied 'instruction' *(oppvisning)* in Saami culture" which the strikers—with megaphone in hand— offer: communal singing, Saami poetry, *joik* (ballad) and historical legends. Sometimes a person steps out of the crowd, grasps one or another of the Saami group and tells him (in Saami) that he himself is a Saami—adding that this is something he had kept secret since coming to live in Oslo.

The Saami group already shows concern lest the crowd turn in anger on the police should they come to take them (the strikers) away. They remind everybody that "our action is one of passive resistance. The Saami people are a nation with strong traditions of passive resistance."

Thursday, 11 October. Around noon the police take the seven strikers into custody; their tent is dismantled and confiscated. Also arrested with them is one of the members of Parliament who had demonstrated his solidarity with the Saami on Tuesday. Released later in the day, they make their way back to Eidsvolls *plass* and, among much jubilation from the crowd, raise another tent.

In their reporting from the scene, journalists mention ''black'' and ''silent'' figures standing inside the large window of the parliament building overlooking the tent and the milling crowd on Eidsvolls *plass.* The dark silhouettes are those of members of Parliament. The imagery and the contrast is unmistakable: inside the building all is dark and, for once, the politicians are not talking; outside all is light and life. A clenched fist is waved at the window—and the dark silhouettes withdraw from view.[12]

In the evening, the strikers bind themselves loosely together with a thin chain. Outside the tent, their supporters, arms interlocked, form a protective circle. The group has made it 'officially' known that one of their number, Mikkel, is their spokesman in any business conducted with the authorities: he will not continue his fast.

Friday, 12 October. Early in the morning the strikers are taken into custody again. This time as many as 200 supporters are driven away in police vans, as well. The arrested are not held for long and they return to Eidsvolls *plass.* But the police maintain a security cordon around the parliament building, preventing another tent from being raised on the lawn. For a while the traffic is halted on the thoroughfare running parallel to Karl Johan (Rosenkrantzgate) by about 200 demonstrators sitting on the road. The crowd chants the PAG slogan ''Let the river Live!'' Among the demonstrators is a well-known (as radical) law professor, who is interviewed by the media. The strikers appeal to these people to remove themselves: ''It is no longer our action. We do not wish to obstruct the traffic,'' says one of them.

Mikkel makes a public statement about the difficult situation in which the police are placed, but he also states that "the two actions which the police have undertaken against us show, quite clearly, that we are an oppressed people." He comments bitterly that "our action was one of passive resistance but it was met with force." He assures journalists that they are not going to give up but intend to continue their hunger strike "quietly—in the Saami way." He wants to make this quite clear to the prime minister. The prime minister says that he respects the right to demonstrate, but that this group—like any other—must respect and obey the instructions of the police in the matter.

There are, to date, 20,000 signatures on the statement of support. Members of the SAG who are not taking part in the actual hunger strike sell the first issue of the action group's own newspaper, *Charta 79*, on Oslo streets. It is said that a printing of 8,000 copies was sold out within hours.

The group considers erecting a tent elsewhere in the centre of Oslo. "We have to have some place to sleep while we fast."

Saturday, 13 October. The strikers slept in a private apartment the previous night, and today erected a tent, with the permission of the police, by Christian Krogh's statue. The group also accepts the police regulation that they leave the street each evening at nine o'clock. There are still large crowds of sympathizers, and Mikkel continues to urge restraint upon them. The strikers remain the centre of attention of all media.[13]

SAG is now winning recognition from Saami organizations (note 6). NSR has issued a statement of unqualified support, and NRL, clearly impressed by the joint statement from WCIP and IWGIA, recognizes the hunger strike as a "peaceful" action that poses no threat to the democratic system; a sympathetic statement is also expected from tomorrow's meeting of the Nordic Council.[14] But SLF, of course, condemns the action in Oslo.

In Parliament, five questions are tabled concerning Saami and the Alta/Kautokeino controversy. All come from the smaller parties (of the centre and left); all are critical of the government.

Julie Felix, the American singer, arrived in Oslo today for an engagement; she immediately made her way to the parliament building where she declared her solidarity with ''the Saami people'' and led the crowd in the singing of ''We Shall Overcome.''

Sunday, 14 October. A week of popular support for the SAG climaxed this evening with a charity concert at the Chateau Neuf Theatre. Among the many performers were Julie Felix and Saami musicians; one of the women strikers made a moving appearance on stage. The text of a telegram from WCIP president George Manuel (of Canada) to the prime minister was read out.

In sombre contrast are reports that full-scale police action is imminent in the north against the PAG. Already there are several hundred police in Alta, and it is believed that more will arrive tomorrow. The government has already said that it will not wait upon the pending court case against the Board[15] before taking action to remove the PAG demonstrators; nor will it grant the NRL an extension of the deadline for submission of its statement (to the Board) regarding the threat that the Alta/Kautokeino project may represent to reindeer pastoralism.

Almost lost between these events comes the expected appeal by the Saami section of the Nordic Council to the Government of Norway: the council makes much the same substantive requests—but in more polite language—as did the strikers in their original communication to government.

Veteran Helge Ingstad flew north to Alta and sat with the PAG demonstrators, in front of the bulldozers for a few hours.

Monday, 15 October. The government retreats: authorization of the Alta/Kautokeino project is withdrawn (for the time being). The prime minister says that this is not because of the hunger strikers—he would not allow them to determine government policy—but out of concern for Saami interests (thereby acknowledging, it seems, the principle of special Saami interests). He warns that his government has had no change of heart with regard to the project; however, in many circles (on both sides of the controversy) the prime minister's statement is regarded as a capitulation.

Respected legal opinion is reported as saying that the government, by its action, has accepted "the principal demand of the Saami, namely, land and water rights." Indeed, the prime minister himself reputedly refers to "the legitimate rights" of the Saami in the area, adding how important it is that the Saami feel sufficient time is being taken to afford protection of these rights. The government proposes to resume talks with representatives of Saami reindeer interests; moreover, the whole matter will be brought before Parliament again before the government re-authorizes construction work. Even the more 'serious' Oslo newspapers write of this reversal of government will as being for "an indefinite period."

The days immediately following. The mayor of Kautokeino, still holding to the opinion that the strikers are not representative of Saami in Finnmark, now adds: "but I have noticed how they seem to have the whole country behind them . . . I only hope that the people who support the hunger-striking Saami . . . will also give [other] Saami their support when this whole business is concluded." And the president of NSR says, "We now look forward to discussions with the authorities concerning the rights of Saami as an aboriginal people and as a minority [in Norway], and not just as reindeer owners." A striker reflects: "my best moment was when we sang our ballads (*joik*)—it was quiet in the streets of Oslo then, and people began to understand that the Saami culture is quite different from the Norwegian." Collectively, the SAG note that their demands, to which the government acceded, are the same as those which the Saami organizations have been making over the years. Asked what they would do if the government continued with the project as before, their answer is "then we come back again." The PAG halt their civil disobedience in the north, but they, too, will be watching carefully to see that the government keeps its word.[16]

Interpretation

The significance of the hunger strike is that instead of shaping themselves to the politically dominant reality—to the world outside them—the strikers shaped it to themselves, and they attained *their* reality in the very act of portraying it.[17] What the drama 'said' to the Norwegian public in the south was that they could either kill the ethnic minority in their midst or let it live, but it could only live on its own terms. The effect was electric. And in one week this handful of Saami ("we represent ourselves") achieved the victory that had evaded Saami organizations for some time. The government stopped construction work and took up discussions about Saami interests in the area, and Norwegians were confronted with the prospect of having to accommodate a Fourth World in their own country.[18] In other words, by expressing reality as they saw it, the strikers led many Norwegians to rearrange their own experience concerning their nation so that the prime minister was eventually forced to back down by the tidal wave of Norwegian support that the Saami hunger strikers had generated.

This particular ethnodrama was played out against a history (Paine 1985, *passim*) of Norwegian codification of Saami culture and Norwegian tutelage of individual Saami: not only have successive governments ignored the questions of Saami rights to land and water, but generations of bureaucrats—controlling education, social welfare, housing and even reindeer management—have defined the limits and even the content of Saami culture. The hunger strike reversed the process, momentarily at least; Saami ethnicity was demonstrated on a basis of *self*-ascription and *self*-advocacy. "The will behind the vision of the hunger strikers prevailed over that of the prime minister" is how a well-known Saami preacher in Finnmark summed up the event for me.

The achievement of the SAG, then, is best explained as a public performance which radically rearranged the conventional relation between centre and periphery, that is, between Norwegian and Saami society. Ordinarily, Oslo civil servants issue directives to Saami communities in the north—but the drama forced the prime minister to accede to a group of Saami in Oslo. The point can be put more strongly: the hunger strike confused the perception of centre/periphery relations so that even people who are ordinarily not concerned about what is happening in Saami/Norwegian relations were challenged to question the issue, or at the very least were thrown into doubt over it. Norwegians even began to scrutinize their own institutions (aside from how they looked at the Saami, alias the SAG): a prolonged public debate began in all the media, particularly the newspapers, on such issues as the difference between law and justice, civil disobedience in a democracy, the roles of different levels of government, and—of course—the notion of aboriginality.[19]

So the hunger strike became a *Norwegian event*—one of general, or national, concern even though staged by Saami. This is an important development from the Fourth World perspective, for it serves to advance the process whereby the premise of Saami/Norwegian relations is changed: before the hunger strike, issues affecting Saami interests and principles were dealt with according to 'set' Norwegian principles, but after the strike we find Norwegian principles being re-examined in the light of the SAG's action.

The drama focused on the perceived unfairness of the 'deal' offered to the Saami by the Norwegian state, as well as upon differences between Norwegian and Saami value systems. It is important to note that the SAG selected the state—and sometimes the government—as its target rather than the Norwegian people, for this allows the public to side with them more easily. The status and potency of the state is reduced by symbolic means.

Thus the ministry of Justice, ordinarily a taken-for-granted office, and the law enforcement of the police, ordinarily a taken-for-granted activity, came under critical scrutiny by the general public, and comparisons were made between the ministry and the SAG. Personalities and 'moralities' were compared rather than anything else, and the public showed a strong bias in favour of the SAG. Whereas Mikkel and his fellow hunger strikers were depicted as prepared to accept the greatest sacrifice for their ideals, the minister of Justice (lampooned by cartoonists) was seen as an insensitive, 'hardline' bureaucrat, and the Oslo police as nothing but his minions. The only act that would have legitimated (popularly) police action in these circumstances was aggressive, physical resistance; it seems Mikkel knew this well. Even the conduct of the crowds of SAG supporters was revealed as morally inferior to the SAG themselves, for the crowd would probably have resorted to physical aggression against the police (there were attempts to pull the police off their horses) had they not been restrained by Mikkel. Indeed, the nonviolent ideal of the hunger strikers—demonstrated in deed and word—so impressed the general (and TV-viewing) public in the south that although the SAG were technically engaged in civil disobedience, their action was not reported primarily in those terms—but as nonviolent. This means that their public image, at that time, was unaffected by the opprobrium ordinarily attached to civil disobedience in this country which has "a strong obedience streak" (Anderson 1981:7). By contrast, Parliament—the ostensible symbol of democracy—suffered some public opprobrium for its alleged overbearing exercise of power.[20]

The key to the impact by which these processes were set in motion is the power of metaphor about the SAG at Eidsvolls *plass*. In placing their tent in front of the parliament building, the SAG not only took for themselves the kind of leap of the imagination associated with metaphor,[21] they also enabled a broad section of the Norwegian public to make the leap after them. Separately, "parliament" and "tent" are metonyms of Norwegian and Saami societies, respectively, and by physically juxtaposing them at Eidsvolls *plass*, the SAG successfully provoked a number of questions about the ways in which the two societies are alike, or unlike, each other.[22]

I suggest that there is a discernible sequence in the way this key metaphoric relationship between parliament and tent worked its will—under SAG orchestration—upon the public. When the SAG came to Eidsvolls *plass* it was in defiance of Parliament—indeed of Norwegian society. Placed alongside the parliament building, the tent 'stated' how *unlike* are Saami and Norwegians. Parliament and tent, then, were enveloped in what we may well call a *polemic metaphor.*[23] In this case its purpose was to enable the SAG to dramatize a we-versus-they situation and to recruit support. As the SAG won this support, the possibility arose for the character of the metaphoric tie between the parliament building and the tent to change. People then began to see the tent as the structural equivalent of Parliament, and the metaphor evoked complementarity, as much as opposition and mutual exclusion.[24]

Of course it is on the basis of complementarity, rather than dichotomized opposition, that a people such as the Saami of Norway stand the best chance of obtaining recognition of legitimate rights. Probably for this very reason, the government was brought unwillingly into this relationship; indeed, it wished to disregard the tent from the time it was erected. The police were instructed to behave as if it were bereft of any symbolic value. But public reaction in Oslo was, as we saw, quite different: SAG-at-Eidsvoll sensitized many people to what they took to be a disparity between political ideals and social practice on the part of the state, and helped to reinterpret their responsibilities toward the Saami people (cf. Eidheim 1971:73; Thuen 1983:22).

The question remains, *how* did this change—in the space of the seven days—take place? Through Mikkel, the spokesman, SAG-at-Eidsvoll challenged Norwegians about the morality of their politics, more than anything else. Mikkel talked to Norwegians in terms of (putative) Saami ideology. He quickly became the 'idol' of the media, but, more subtly and more importantly, he was also a combination of moral 'tutor' and political 'text' for the Norwegian crowd that circulated around the tent. What was achieved in this way at the informal and interpersonal plane is comparable to the scrambling effect that we have already suggested the SAG had, at a higher level, on the perception of centre/periphery relations.[25]

But there is also an indispensable second stage in the making of complementarity and the success of the SAG's mission. The Norwegian public watched on their television screens the empathetic interaction between Norwegians and Saami; they observed the response of the crowd to Mikkel; they saw how casual passers-by—"ordinary" people (not "radicals")—were moved to identify with the SAG. The next morning they could read about what they had seen, and the newspapers assured them that the SAG had won the hearts (at least) of all. The government took note.

The drama closed in a fittingly symbolic way with the prime minister *coming out* of the parliament building and walking over to the animated circle of Mikkel, the hunger strikers and their supporters (*Nordlys* 16 October 1979).

Backlash

The cornerstone of SAG strategy was to put themselves above the issue of representativeness; and we have seen how they achieved this. In the north, however, there was as much an outrage, even in Saami circles, over the SAG as there was support. The symbolic use of the Saami tent (of reindeer nomadism) was particularly upsetting; the mass support that the SAG won in the south, on behalf of "the Saami," was editorialized as "beyond belief" and "on the edge of hysteria;" and the government's "surrender" was regretted in SLF circles as "the capitulation of democracy" (*Finnmark Dagblad* 18 October; *Nordlys* 16 October; and *Sagat* 24 October 1979).

In short,[26] the element of make-believe about SAG-at-Eidsvoll was self-evident for most northerners. Some applauded it but probably more were scandalized. But for the SAG, it was the public in the south that mattered in this confrontation with the government on its own doorstep.

ALTA, 1981

A good deal more can be learned about SAG-at-Eidsvoll—and the politics of morality generally—by comparing their civil disobedience with that staged by the PAG (Peoples' Action Group), with SAG participation, outside Alta in January 1981. In general, my principal concern is how public credibility is achieved (or lost) and I will continue to examine—comparatively, this time—the two crucial dimensions of this process: construction of symbolic oppositions and mediation of experience. An Oslo/Alta comparison also raises two other issues of considerable importance in Fourth World terms: (1) involvement of non-Saami (e.g., Professor "M") in Saami causes and (2) the cost to the SAG of its working partnership with the PAG.

The essential narrative from Alta is presented below, followed by the comparison.

Background

Nullpunktet or "Zero Point"[27] was what the PAG called the place where they had stopped the bulldozers. It was on a hillside in the sub-arctic terrain a few miles outside Alta, a little north of the Alta/Kautokeino River but in the path of the planned access road to the dam. In the summer of 1979, the PAG erected a stone barrier there, and in January 1981 an ice barrier with the slogan ELVA SKAL LEVE (THE RIVER SHALL LIVE),[28] fashioned in large letters out of frozen birch branches set in the ice. Zero Point was always manned, and by the end of the summer of 1979 it was the police who had to retire, defeated. Zero Point stood. A larger force of police was about to be dispatched to the area in October when the government backed down in its confrontation with the SAG in Oslo, as a result of which the PAG withdrew voluntarily from Zero Point. However, the belief that the government really had capitulated in October 1979 (beyond symbolically re-stating the democratic process of listening to the electorate) proved illusory. Early in January 1981 it was known that the government intended to resume construction work that month on the access road. PAG supporters began to collect (from all areas of Norway) in Alta; Zero Point was re-established.

The story of how this impasse built up can be told quickly. Early in 1980, the government had appointed a Commission of Inquiry to examine Saami rights. The commission had a wide mandate and particular attention was to be paid to rights to land and water; it was headed by a distinguished legal scholar, and its members included representatives of the principal Saami organizations (NRL, NSR and SLF).[29] The government believed (it is said) that in this way it had discharged its promise to take account of Saami interests before continuing with the hydro project, and a short while later Parliament supported the government in its intention to re-authorize construction on the access road to the dam. The question then was when would the work begin? This time (compared to 14 October 1979) the decision was taken to wait for the judgment in the court case concerning the legality of action taken by the Board. A decision, favourable to the government, was given on 5 December 1980, but an appeal was immediately lodged at the Supreme Court (see note 15). It was then clear that work on the access road would resume early in the new year; that is to say, orders would be given to the police to remove the PAG from Zero Point at about that time. The government stood firm in this decision, against pleas by each of the NRL, NSR, SAG, and PAG to wait until the Supreme Court heard the appeal and, especially, until the Commission of Inquiry delivered its report.[30] Only then, could it be said that the government had properly discharged its promise to take Saami interests into account.

Narrative[31]

> *Monday, 5 January.* It is minus 33°C. Several hundred PAG and some 40 journalists have reached Alta. PAG headquarters is in the town, but the camp is at Zero Point. The media find Professor "M"—one of three senior Norwegian academics who are expected[32]—already there, together with a couple of veteran opponents of other hydro schemes in Norway. These men are household names in a considerable sector of the national population.
>
> *Aftenposten* announces that D-day for the police, under Superintendent E, is Wednesday, 14 January. Parliament has voted the government two million kroner (about $375,000 U.S.) daily, until further notice, for this operation. The Kiel-Norway ferry, MS Janina (9,400 tons and 600 berths), has been requisitioned and is sailing north to Alta, where it will serve as police headquarters.
>
> The leader of the PAG, a local person, holds a small news conference this evening at a farm (not all the press found their way there; no Saami were present). He says his sources confirm the D-day date; he is not alarmed: PAG have "resources" and the government "underestimates us."
>
> A journalist on his first assignment to the north assured me that had the SAG been alone in protesting this issue again there would have been a "colossal backlash" in the south; as it was, the PAG "engages," divisively, many different groups and classes of people throughout the country. He was astounded at the "racist" undercurrents here: between "Norwegians," "Finns" (immigrants from the previous century) and, especially, "the Saami."

Tuesday, 6 January. When I visited the PAG camp at Zero Point this morning, there were no Saami in evidence. I was asked, "When are they coming?" I watch a rehearsal of a "chain gang drill" in one of the tents behind the ice barrier: they sit in line, side by side, and each person puts on a tight-fitting metal belt, locking it to the heavy chain that is bolted to the rock at each end. M says that the "chain gangs" (one for each of the several tents behind the ice barrier) are prepared to remain sitting there, chained and exposed to the elements, even if the police remove their tents. He wants this to be known in Alta so that public opinion will exert pressure on the government and the police. He also thinks that on the 14th, the Saami at Zero Point should place themselves *in front* of the ice barrier and not chain themselves. Then the police would remove them first and without any difficulty—which would be "symbolically and historically correct."

"It's a kind of language," says M, referring to the different actions being taken by the PAG and the police during this pre-D-day week. He is troubled, though, by the poor connection of the field telephone with the PAG in Alta.

This evening I watch the television news at the home of Nils, one of the hunger strikers from 1979: the PAG leader, "L," tells the interviewer that the news about MS Janina coming to Alta, as a police ship, awakens bitter memories of the war, when German warships and prison ships were anchored in Alta harbour. Nils comments: "*We've* had a ship here before that," referring to the naval vessel that brought soldiers to Alta in 1853 following the killing of the sheriff and a merchant in Kautokeino by some Saami religious zealots. Several of the Saami were executed in Alta and others given life sentences in the south.

The radio interviewer this morning asks Police Superintendent "E" whether a state of emergency now exists. E replies that he does not like that phrase and would not use it himself.

Wednesday, 7 January. Another PAG news conference, this time in the main hotel in Alta, is well attended. An Oslo journalist complains that after visiting Zero Point certain things are not at all clear to him. He asks L: ''How long will you people stay sitting up there, should the police remove your tents?. . . Until you freeze to death?'' L replies: ''It is up to the police whether any of us freeze to death!'' Those present are momentarily stunned at the possible implication; then questions are asked: Is this the decision of the PAG *leadership?* Will some of the leadership be in the ''chain gangs''? Will any Saami be in them? They are told that individual PAG members, and L himself, will be in a chain gang; at all events, one Saami will be included (it is immediately assumed that this is the Saami who is in the top echelon of the PAG). A PAG spokesman diverts attention to the chains that will be used: ''the strongest chain from last time [Zero Point, 1979] was but child's play to what we have now.'' L himself concludes: ''We are not prepared to bargain [with the police]. *Our tents must stay.*''

Thursday, 8 January. FIFTEEN MEN IN DEATH GANG screams an important national daily across its front page. Beneath this headline is a large photograph of Professor M and others, sitting in their tent, wrapped in arctic clothing. The chain gangs have become ''the death gang,'' and all editorials express horror. COME TO YOUR SENSES demands one (this from a newspaper that consistently opposed the Alta/Kautokeino project).

Superintendent E holds a press conference.[33] In a brief opening statement he assures us that Zero Point will be cleared on the 14th, and that it is also part of his duty to see that no one will be injured. He invites questions. To reporters' attempts to draw him out concerning the PAG, his reply (more than once) is: ''You should ask the Justice minister.'' He is telling us that these are not proper questions to put to a police officer, they are political. He is relaxed and well prepared. The one line of questioning that does upset him a bit concerns reporters' suggestions that police from the Special Branch are in Alta, that PAG phones are being tapped and that the police have infiltrated Zero Point. These things are not true, he says, but of course, some threats to individuals have been made and the police have always to be concerned about that. He concedes that police are stationed around Zero Point on snow scooters, but he is not sure "how they are dressed"—he hasn't asked. He promises that he will not spring unfair surprises, and will keep the press (and television reporters) informed. He seems to wish to impress upon us the *routineness* about what a policeman is asked to do.

Nearly lost in the fuss is the announcement in an Oslo paper that "the same group of Saami who went on a hunger strike outside parliament in the fall of 1979 intend to begin new 'actions' in Oslo on the 14th of January." The Saami would not divulge details but the newspaper supposed it unlikely that there would be a hunger strike again.

Friday, 9 January. The 'news' from Zero Point centres on a press interview (conducted yesterday) with Professor M: "There is no 'death gang'; at any rate I am not a member of any. The PAG is concerned with the preservation of life." But even if the police removed the protective covering of their tents (each has a wooden stove inside) he and others will stay there, chained, for "as long as possible."

At Masi, teachers plan to go out on strike the first day that work is renewed on the access road. The villagers seem uneasy about the PAG: it is "strange," they say, that some Norwegians would die for the river; others tell me it is "not easy" for Saami to join Norwegians in their demonstrations. Will the mood change as soon as there is a Saami tent at Zero Point?

In Oslo, Mikkel and another hunger striker from 1979 have asked for an audience with King Olav—"he's our king, too."

Saturday, 10 January. As the 14th approaches there is a kind of 'big fight' excitement building up. In 1979, at Zero Point, 200 PAG defied 40 policemen, but this time—we are constantly being reminded—there will be 800 or more PAG and 500 or more police. On most days the progress of MS Janina is plotted on the television news.

The mayors of Alta and Kautokeino appeal to the government to suspend the planned police action; the local supporters of the PAG, says the mayor of Alta, are not "extremists" but "solid, law-abiding citizens;" and the mayor of Kautokeino,[34] is apprehensive—the earlier assurances of the government not withstanding—about the fate of Masi. Superintendent E and PAG leader L are interviewed together on television—over coffee and cakes! The studio presentation seems self-consciously concerned not to be seen favouring one side, or one man, over the other. And as one would expect, the two protagonists are polite to each other without either suggesting that there is the possibility of giving an inch.

Another journalist (this time a veteran reporter with the Saami section of Swedish Broadcasting in north Sweden, and a Saami himself) remarks on the "racism" in north Norway, particularly concerning the reindeer-owning Saami. In his view, radio and television (state-owned) in north Norway are agents of this state of affairs.

Sunday, 11 January. Saami are beginning—in small numbers—to collect at Zero Point, and there are now three tents outside the ice barrier. Among those present are Saami from Finland and Sweden. Meanwhile, in Alta, supporters of the hydro development present Superintendent E with a bouquet of flowers. It is estimated that 600 persons were in the procession to police headquarters, including Saami (traditionally clad) from Kautokeino.

I ask a member of the PAG executive (he has a farm in the river valley outside Alta) what is at stake for him in this struggle. He replies: "one, farming; two, the salmon fishery; three, nature; four, reindeer pastoralism." Professor M's answer to the same question is "first, Saami rights; and second, [exposure of] the judicial swindle [by which the Board were given the go-ahead]."

Monday, 12 January. Probably over a thousand PAG supporters have reached Alta, but only a quarter of this number at Zero Point. The police have closed the road to it and have skidoo patrols out. (But under cover of darkness it will still be possible to get through by skidoo or on skis.) The media are surprised to see the blue, gold and red Saami flag at Zero Point.

Police preparations are proceeding apace with convoys carrying personnel and motorized equipment by land and air. Despite efforts to be discreet, there begins to be an aura of a military operation about it all.

Tuesday, 13 January. MS Janina arrives. The Supreme Court delivers two judgments: the appeal of the 1979 hunger strikers is rejected (the judgment of Oslo Magistrate's Court is upheld), and the earlier decision of the County Court in Alta, acquitting three PAG leaders for their part in the demonstrations during the summer of 1979, is *reversed.*[35] Mikkel and his associate are granted their audience with King Olav.

There are processions through the streets of Alta this evening: one organized by NSR and NRL, expressing their sharp dissatisfaction with the government, and a larger one —an hour later—organized by a group of Alta citizens calling themselves ''the Committee for Order and Work'' to express support of the government. All day long people have been converging on Zero Point, especially Saami: at least 800 people in all, with seven tents in front of the ice barrier.

A past president of NSR, who is now active in the SAG, tells the media that ''We Saami are positioning ourselves in front of those [Norwegians] who sit, chained, in their tents behind the ice barrier; for this is a way of impressing upon people that we were here first [in the land], and that there is more at stake than saving a river—there is also an important issue regarding [the future of] Saami.'' He adds that even if the government breaches Zero Point tomorrow, the struggle will continue elsewhere. A member of the Saami Rights Commission, himself a Saami, declares: "All that we Saami are asking is for the Norwegian state to confirm our rights to the land and water of the tundra *(Finnmarksvidda)*." And SAG spokesmen at Zero Point—in a message to the prime minister in the eleventh hour—demand the suspension of all construction on the Alta/Kautokeino hydro project until the Saami Rights Commission presents its findings to the government.

Wednesday, 14 January. The police action begins a little before 9 a.m. (it was too dark earlier). From in front of the ice barrier come the words and melodies of Saami ballads, and from behind the barrier, the police are greeted with *their* national anthem: "Yes, we love this country." On each side of the barrier there are flags: Saami and Norwegian. But also in Alta today there are more flags than usual—the Committee for Order and Work has urged citizens to fly the flag of Norway out of respect for the government and the police.

The police first encircle the immediate area and then attempt to penetrate Zero Point by bypassing the ice barrier and, in particular, the Saami 'camp' in front of it. But they run into difficulties. First of all, they have to contend with the extreme slipperiness of the slope (the PAG had made certain it was properly 'iced'), and then, as they begin to make some progress, scores of Saami leave their camp and throw themselves in front of the police. Superintendent E admits to being frustrated: "We didn't wish to remove the Saami first, and they were obviously disappointed over that: some of them even shouted that we were discriminating against them. But when they began to throw themselves down at the feet of our people, we had no choice but to carry them away. In this way they had their wish fulfilled" (Hansen and Pihlström 1981:113)—and the media were there to witness this little ethnodrama.[36]

After these Saami, hundreds of other demonstrators (some Saami among them) are bodily removed; it all takes a great deal of time as the police 'work' with great care and self-restraint. As daylight falls, the work continued under floodlighting, and there is one real challenge left: the release and removal of the approximately 70 persons in the four chain gangs. But this is accomplished with unexpected ease.[37] The entire operation is completed after 15½ hours. At a quarter past midnight, a bulldozer drives through Zero Point. Of a probable total of 800 demonstrators, about 150 are Saami, including 17 from Sweden and 6 from Finland.[38]

Thursday, 15 January. The PAG and SAG hold separate press conferences. The PAG executive (their morale somewhat restored because of a torchlight procession through Alta last evening[39]) affirm that they have not given up; plans will be announced soon. Spokesmen for the 150 Saami who were at Zero Point are, in their meeting with the press, bitterly critical of the government and repeat their demand made on Tuesday evening. In Oslo, a SAG spokesman warns, "We now have our backs to the wall, and anything can happen."

Friday, 16 January. SAG spokesmen in Alta demand that the NSR AND NRL call an extraordinary joint meeting the next day.[40]

COMPARISON: OSLO (1979) AND ALTA (1981)

The Politics of Morality

As I suggested at the outset, the SAG's strategy in Oslo was to activate the politics of morality as a means of gaining power. It is obvious that such a morality has a strong strategic sense attached to it: it is also a politics of embarrassment (directed against the holders of power). Nor should it be overlooked that the cost of failure in this strategy is likely to be minted in the same way: either one becomes a butt of ridicule or is simply ignored (as irrelevant or 'lunatic'). Instances of these alternative fates among the SAG and the PAG will be noted. And, as the account should have made clear, a politically helpful ingredient of moral opposition is entertainment (so much depends on effective presentation). Other likely properties will be added as we proceed.

Still, against these calculating, means-to-an-end considerations, the Ghandian dictum that a worthy end must be seen to be using worthy means will always be of considerable importance in the practice of moral opposition. For one thing, success depends on public sympathy.[41] Perhaps, then, a factor that helped the Oslo public to sympathize with the hunger strikers was that it seemed quite clear that Mikkel and his associates were not "professional protesters"—exactly the phrase applied to the demonstrators at Alta. Mikkel did not show artifice, but at Alta the PAG, and even the SAG, seemed calculating—and in consequence many people stopped to ponder the worthiness of the means employed. In short, concerning the PAG at Alta a common judgment was "it's that lot again" (from earlier anti-hydro development demonstrations), whereas SAG-at-Eidsvoll appeared as victims.

"This contest on our side is not one of rivalry or vengeance but of endurance. It is not those who can inflict the most but those who can suffer the most who will conquer," said Terence McSwiney, mayor of Cork.[42] Professor M would be familiar with McSwiney's words, though perhaps not L and, almost certainly, not Mikkel. Nonetheless, in beginning our comparison, the words serve well. The PAG 'muffed' the MacSwiney lines; the SAG 'spoke' them well. The PAG wished their actions to be suggestive of sacrifice and of moral rectitude too, but I think the dominant impressions of the public were rivalry (against the police) and hubris. SAG-at-Eidsvoll, in contrast, had succeeded rather easily in demonstrating that what mattered was not how long they could stay at Eidsvolls *plass*, but rather how long the government would force them to suffer. And it was really only in respect to them that the public in the south would concede that faith was kept with another Ghandian precept: that "the object . . . is to win a victory over conflict, not to triumph over the opponent" (Russell n.d.:8). As a consequence, SAG-at-Eidsvoll had much more success than the PAG (or the SAG) at Alta in persuading the public that it was the government that provoked a contest between the law and the demonstrators.[43]

With these general considerations in mind, let us take a closer look at what happened at Oslo and at Alta.

Symbolic Oppositions

In Oslo, the SAG put up their tent 'against' the parliament building, whereas the PAG had nothing 'against' their ice barrier and tents. In Oslo, the tent—the distinctive Saami *lavvo*—was out of context and yet not inauthentic; rather, it helped induce a scrambling effect in Norwegian/Saami relations. We can say together with Turner (1974:29) that parliament building and tent at Eidsvolls *plass* "engender[ed] thought in their co-activity." This, as well as the fact that men and women were fasting, awakened attention. The hunger strike itself was a necessary artifice that moved the Norwegian public around the tent into a "liminoid" state of mind and into "this gap between ordered worlds" where (to cite Turner again) "almost anything may happen." But a tent on a mountain does not arrest attention, for it is *in* context. What PAG-on-the-mountain were deprived of was a metonym (a smokestack, say, set against the natural beauty of the landscape) of the forces they were opposing. Further, the demonstrators on that bare mountainside were on a stage *empty of actors*, except for themselves, even though there was a full cast in the Alta area. The news-hungry media visited them periodically but there was little to see or listen to, other than Professor M and his associates huddled in their tent. The police—concerned to avoid situations out of which the demonstrators could construct symbolic oppositions that would excite sympathy—kept away from Zero Point until the morning of the last day. In Oslo, by contrast, a full cast of actors (Saami, their supporters and the police) were concentrated upon that single stage—Eidsvolls *plass*.

A consequence of those seven days at Eidsvolls *plass* was that the SAG's message (in part about the illegitimate behaviour of Parliament) was not delivered to Parliament by the seven Saami alone; had it been so, it would not have likely carried compulsion. Instead, the message was relayed through a series of 'teams,' and its legitimation was enhanced at each step: the SAG (team 1) spoke their lines, the crowd (team 2) expressed support and the mass audience (team 3) witnessed it all. The message, then, was 'delivered' to Parliament by these teams in concert. Now, the absence of a team 2 at Zero Point was, I suggest, a severe curtailment on the potential impact of that protest. For it is largely by way of this kind of an immediate audience—that participates and is seen doing so by the mass audience—that a protest group is brought nearer (or at least rendered less strange) to the general television audience; by the same token, the absence of a team 2 increases the likelihood of the protestors being disparaged (above).

Also, the difference in the way the police were handled in Oslo and in Alta probably has more to do with the presence or absence of a team 2 than with the otherwise obvious ethnic variable. Mikkel put his energy into obtaining the ambience he desired with the supporting Norwegian crowd, and the character of relations with the police followed largely from that. However, the PAG, in their circumstance at Alta and Zero Point, were overly dependent on challenges to the police for the stimulation of public attention, even though this brought the PAG into the field of physical and material opposition, rather than moral (i.e., boasts about the chains).

Personalities and the Work of Mediation

At Alta it was the police superintendent who was the pivotal and commanding figure, whereas at Oslo it had been the strike spokesman (but using a markedly different idiom of command). I perceive E in this way, rather than L of the PAG, because he recognized that his mandate was not only to remove the demonstrators from Zero Point but also to protect them (e.g., from the attacks of vigilantes); and because there seemed to be some expectation that his handling of the situation in Alta, and at Zero Point, could help determine whether the people of Alta would soon find relief from their condition of acute polarization. In short, E was in a position to pay some attention to principles and sentiments of justice, at the same time as he attended to the maintenance and restoration of law. I think it is particularly in this connection that one can understand the attention the media gave to E's use of means (a worthy goal should be accomplished by means that are themselves worthy); and E impressed upon the media his own concern with just this issue. I think E was conscious of the role that the media could play (if handled properly) as his alibi.

After deciding that work would be resumed on the access road and (probably in consultation with E) the date when this would happen, the government firmly defined the removal of all demonstrators from Zero Point as a police operation. Superintendent E, charged with this task, was himself a northerner and, quite as important, known to enjoy the outdoor pursuits valued by so many of the demonstrators (especially the "Norwegians"): salmon fishing in the summer, ptarmigan hunting in the autumn and skiing (sometimes with dog sleds) in the winter and spring.[44] Polite, reasonable and objective—while strong and thoroughly professional—his is not a public persona that incites passion; it is even difficult for a person to be indignant over what the superintendent says or does, and still retain his credibility. Thus E's personality lent credence to his claims that the police have no secrets, and would see that no one gets hurt. In place of the scrambling effect of SAG-at-Eidsvoll, E, I suggest, helped to relegitimate the institutional order[45] which the country chose to live by. I think he was seen by many Norwegians in the role of society's guardian against "anarchy" (a term frequently used with regard to aspects of the PAG's activities).

The police also applied several lessons learned from the summer and autumn of 1979. The first was that the control of passive resisters, and especially their physical removal, requires a large number of policemen. Superintendent E, this time, was practically given *carte blanche* regarding manpower (in fact, every fifteenth policeman in the country) and technical resources. A second lesson was that moral opposition needs something to work against, that is, to be symbolized against (dichotomization), and—as already noted—E tried his best not to oblige on this account. It also became clear that what serves least well in opposing moral opposition is crude, physical vigilante-type opposition (such as occurred at Zero Point in 1979), and what serves best is *moral support* of the forces of law and order: this was provided in a limited way by the citizens who called themselves the "Committee for Order and Work in Alta." Another lesson learned was that the police should be in possession and control of the 'timetable' for the entire episode—including the demonstrators' side of it—and that the timetable should be publicly announced at an early date. This was done at Alta in 1981 and it meant, in effect, that the PAG were at Zero Point on time granted by E (and would be removed when that time expired). Quite a different situation—bestowing moral advantage on the demonstrators—had prevailed in Oslo in 1979.

Turning now to E's opponents (see Figure 1), it can be assumed that Professor M was the most newsworthy of all the principals

(E included); the placing of L, however, is more complicated. In the sense that he was so like E—a local, a sportsman, quiet but strong and confident, obviously not corruptible—he was E's rival. Indeed, in the eyes of many throughout Norway, L too was a "hero." Both men represented core Norwegian values although in different ways, for L stood for the values of local autonomy and individualism.

However, in his defence of these values L demonstrated a zeal (a fanaticism, some called it) that (1) is rather un-Norwegian (at least in politics), and (2) leads him to defy the core value of parliamentary authority. This aspect of L's political persona represented itself in bolder relief in his partnership with Professor M. It is difficult to conclude otherwise than that the gross effect of this partnership was to E's advantage. The PAG's strength depended upon a populist appeal that was democratically accented. Broad sectors of the public saw L, either in respect to his lifestyle or his insistence upon local autonomy, or both, as embodying the appropriate values; but for many people the attachment of a distinguished or notorious (all according to one's point of view) academic wing to the PAG signalled social elitism and liminality.[46] It was also important for the PAG that the movement be seen as making practical sense, but "the professors" (a label of which the press was particularly fond) were widely associated with radical politics and utopianism.[47]

This difficulty, or even contradiction, in the PAG's ideological presentation of itself exacerbated the embarrassment which the movement suffered over the "freeze to death" statement. L said it at a PAG press conference—more as a challenge to the police than anything else;[48] but the media were immediately interested in what Professor M thought about it. M deprecated the idea that there was a "death gang." But the occasion for moral instruction remained: by staying chained as long as possible (even after the tents were removed), "we will show the Norwegian public that this matter is important" (*Dagbladet* 9 January). What had been suffered as elitism about this element was now, I would gauge, widely seen as hubris: "the professors" at Zero Point were telling their countrymen (comfortably settled in front of television sets) where the *real* Norwegian values lay in this situation.

Yet what L and M were saying up at Alta *seemed* to be similar

Figure 1. Mediation (as viewed by television audiences)

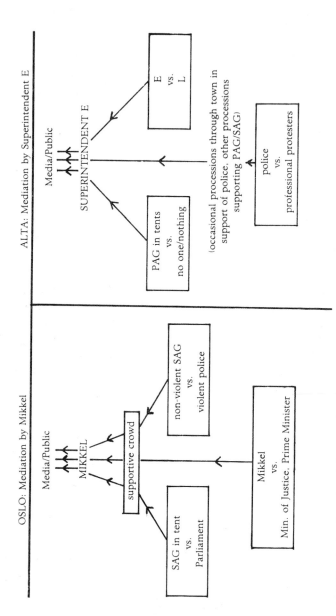

NOTE: *My thanks to Nigel Rapport for help with this figure.*

to what SAG-at-Eidsvoll had done and said. But the reactions were extremely different: Mikkel was accepted by the Oslo crowd and the television viewers as their moral 'tutor'; and far from provoking indignation, the determination of the hunger strikers to die for their cause, if necessary, unleashed a flood of sympathy. In short, for the public the meanings of the PAG and SAG statements *were* different;[49] and in this way, more than any other, the public showed that it considered the PAG as Norwegian (and constrained accordingly) and the SAG as Saami (and licensed accordingly).[50]

The predicament of PAG was not made any less by M's attempt to retrieve the situation by the self-deprecatory comment that "none of us has come here to die . . . *we'll just be a little uncomfortable,*[51] that's all. The river is worth that much." The media, and then the public, were able to make light of the PAG's high avowals and —with evident delight—to laugh at the professor. By this time, too, the rhetorical absurdity involved in *dying* for a river which, by the very slogan of the PAG, must itself *live* had begun to sink in. Furthermore, the public now knew that the will of the PAG was not unbreakable (and some PAG members were furious about that: see Hansen and Pihlström, 1981:58).

Still, the PAG's rhetoric included repeated references to the chains that were going to help hold Zero Point against the police— the chains, at any rate, should be inviolable (but see note 37). Although SAG-at-Eidsvoll had drawn sympathy from the crowd because of the police—they had made a point of *not* challenging the police; but this is exactly what the PAG—with few options available—ended up doing. Even as their challenge became a boast, that boast was about a physical property (strength of chains) and not a moral one. There is a double irony in this: first, that a demonstration against technology should come to depend (even for its expressive purposes) on technology,[52] and secondly, that the role thus given to the police was to free the demonstrators from their chains! The difference between this and the 'freeing' of SAG-at-Eidsvoll should be noted: the SAG broke their fast because the government heeded them, but the chains were broken for the PAG by a government that did not heed them.

In Oslo the media participated; in Alta they interpreted—and this difference in role at the two locations is not fortuitous. At

Eidsvolls *plass* the participatory role followed as a consequence of the 'concentrated' stage and, in particular, Mikkel's mediating skills. He was not only the spokesman of the seven, orchestrating the interaction between them and their Norwegian supporters, but also the effective master of his performance. He (1) extemporized what he said (there was no script, no aforehand knowledge of what he would say), just as the SAG collectively extemporized what they did (there was no precedent for the action: its context, then, as well as its text, was unique); (2) what Mikkel said and what was happening around the tent were intimately related and the flow was two-way; (3) whatever he said had to do with what we might call "real symbols": the parliament building and the prime minister were real (more real than, but every bit as symbolic as, the national flag); likewise Mikkel, symbol of the Saami cause, was a real Saami and, at Eidsvolls *plass*, only a Saami.[53] Something of the same can be said of the crowd that gathered there: they exhibited real affect; they had nothing to do with a 'rent a demo' demonstration; nor were they bystanders—they were participants. Their presence helped to divert attention away from representativeness (of the seven Saami) as an issue. In these circumstances, the role of the media became that of helping "the event spell its name" (Dayan and Katz 1981:12): in place of interpretation and editorializing, the media became actively engaged in endorsing and conveying the self-definition of the demonstration. The demonstrators had successfully defined for the media the context and meaning of what was happening.

By comparison, the shortcomings of the PAG at Alta and Zero Point are self-evident. First, so much of what they said was scripted—some of it was even old script from previous demonstrations against hydro developments elsewhere in the country. Second, their handling of the media suffered from the difficulties of communication between L and his team in Alta and M and his team at Zero Point. Third, far from monopolizing the attention of the public, the PAG had to compete for it against the police (e.g., the two series of press conferences; the sea voyage of MS Janina versus the 'occupation' of a bare mountainside). Fourth, the performative capacity of the PAG was impoverished by the lack of on-site interaction: it was precisely at Zero Point, the spot chosen by the PAG as the locus of its moral protest that there was little dramatic structure as one day followed another. Finally, at Eidsvolls *plass*, the majority of the viewing public was manouevred into a strong relationship of dependence upon the performance—and hence upon the SAG; but at Zero Point, because there was no team 1 - team 2 interaction, large sectors of the viewing public retained their independence: as January 14 edged closer, the demonstrators were increasingly held *accountable to* the public for their actions.

In these circumstances, the media resumed their normal interpretive (*contra* participatory) role in which they define the context and meaning of what is happening (Dayan and Katz 1981; Paine 1983). Notable here was the series of interviews—some with front-line principals, others with functionaries (whose involvement with the unfolding events could well be routine and/or indirect) and yet others with randomly selected members of the general public. What the television cameras failed to do, however, was to splice in shots of, say, the tents at Zero Point, the PAG in Alta, the police and the "police ship", bringing various elements of the dispersed 'cast' on stage together. Had television done this, its mediating role would have edged toward the participatory—the team 2 factor would have become apparent, the viewing audience would have been exposed to suggestions of symbolic oppositions (see Figure 2)—and Zero Point, prior to the massive police operation, would not have been so isolated contextually and dramaturgically. As it was, so much of the meaning of Zero Point was "not ascribed to the event but rather perceived during its unravelling" (Dayan and Katz, p. 15).[54]

Figure 2. Presence and Absence of Symbolic Opposition in Oslo and Alta

OSLO	ALTA	
tent vs. parliament bldg.	tent vs. ____	____ vs. ship

SAG at Alta

It was not, of course, just at Zero Point that the SAG and PAG were in association: at Eidsvolls *plass*, PAG membership was the nucleus of the supportive crowd, and there was a momentary reversal of the historical relation of power between Norwegians and

Saami. For the SAG managed to focus directly upon the issue of Saami rights (to land and water) without becoming entangled in Norwegian interests. To the contrary, it was the Norwegians who found themselves entangled in Saami interests; this is what being master of one's own performance meant for the SAG.[55] But at Zero Point, the situation was quite different: the PAG and SAG were represented to the public (especially by the PAG) as being in partnership, and the issue of nature conservancy joined to that of Saami rights. But this 'packaging' of issues induced questions and doubts, even confusion, among broad sectors of the public. For example, Professor M declared that his primary concern was Saami rights, and yet the publicized slogan of the PAG at Zero Point was about protecting the river. Other differences with the earlier situation were that at Zero Point the PAG had the larger profile (than the SAG), and they were perceived as steadily losing control to Superintendent E.

And so the SAG ran the risk of 'contamination' through its association with the PAG. This was the principal reason for the Saami delaying their arrival at Zero Point until the last hours; in this way they at least distinguished themselves from the "professional protestors" who had been there a week or more. Beyond contamination, there was the risk (at Zero Point) of the SAG's being "used" (as was often suggested by the media) by the PAG; and beyond this, the need arose to recognize that the goals of the SAG and the PAG were separate and could even be at odds with each other.[56]

The following episode highlights the issue. A well-respected member of the SAG was asked by the PAG leadership to join one of the chain gangs at Zero Point in order to demonstrate (to the government) PAG - SAG solidarity. She consented, but reluctantly (for she had intended to be part of the Saami contingent in front of the ice barrier). As she sat with them, chained, the Norwegians began to sing their national anthem, whose opening verse is *Ja, Vi elsker dette landet* ("Yes, We love this country"). Her reaction was visceral—it is not *their* country to love (it is Saami-land, says the SAG). She was unchained and joined her fellows in front of the ice barrier in time to be removed by the police.

CONCLUSIONS

The Moral Basis of Make-Believe

To denote the hunger strike as drama, as we have done, implies its 'separation' from everyday reality: and my first contention is that make-believe was important to the impact the SAG had achieved at Oslo.[57] The seven Saami momentarily became "the Saami" and their *lavvo* the summarizing symbol of Saami culture. However, there was also a strong moral component to the drama: that the Saami fasted made an enormous impact on the public. Yet the evidence presented also strongly suggests that the success of the hunger strike owed much to the dramatic staging of the event at Eidsvolls *plass*. In short, (1) drama needs make-believe, (2) make-believe needs a moral basis, and (3) moral protest needs a dramatic structure. These conditions were largely unfulfilled at Alta: large sectors of the public believed they discerned artifice and artificiality, as well as much that was familiar—and they did not believe.

The 'separation' of drama is achieved, in the first place, through a reduction in social roles and the introduction of a symbolic relationship: "Since all are 'players,' they all hold to the same definition of the play reality . . . . Thus . . . *the social self is superfluous*" (Handelman 1977:185; emphasis added). This was precisely the state of affairs achieved by the SAG in Oslo and between them and the crowd of supporters. It freed 'the self,' as well as freeing discourse, from constraints otherwise placed by the social structure. The heightening of reflexivity and distancing from subjectivity that happened there "permit[ted] one to gain unusual perspective on oneself in relation to others, and on oneself in relation to principles of order" (Handelman 1982:163). We recognized, for instance, the scrambling effect of the SAG and the debate begun among Norwegians about their society. Also helping to sustain the make-believe at Eidsvolls *plass* was the fact that although the SAG presented a political challenge, relations between Mikkel (in particular) and the crowd were mutually enacted in terms of a moral order—and were thus perceived by the viewing public. That is, much attention was given to metacommunication.[58] We emphasized Mikkel's "tutoring" of the Norwegian crowd and the popular endorsement given to the symbolic placing of the tent across from parliament: out of context politically *but not morally,* it successfully raised doubts over the validity of the political order.

At Zero Point, in contrast, there was a breakdown in the make-believe. The tents on the mountainside were "in context" in the sense of being unremarkable; and so attention immediately shifted to—and stayed with—the persons inside the tents, particularly Professor M. According to the media and comments that I heard personally, broad sectors of the public were never at ease with M's presence at Zero Point. He was perceived as playing a role. His presence there was anticipated—it was a predictable role. The reason for his being seen in this light was that the public had some knowledge (however vague and inaccurate it might have been) of M in other roles, such as "professor," "intellectual," "radical," "from Oslo," and the like. In short, M was unable to satisfy the first requirement set out above: his social self remained important. The paradox is that by not being able to dissociate himself from everyday realities, he suffered from a loss of authenticity at Zero Point. Whereas the public had accepted Mikkel's, they *rejected* Professor M's questioning of the validity of ordinary experience (i.e., the principles and practice that Parliament had applied to the Alta/Kautokeino issue). It was also the case that M, in trying to say something to his fellow Norwegians, was seen to be preaching: this implies a conscious and direct attempt to rearrange their common experience, but his fellow Norwegians would not grant him that privilege. And Mikkel? His audience accepted his speaking to them from another culture and that his concern was, in the first place, not the rearrangement of their experience but their acceptance of his.

Finally, the public questioned the morality—and registered disbelief—concerning suggestions that persons would die for a river. Indeed, it is here that the contrast is greatest between the ways the SAG and PAG handled the public (see Figure 3). A secondary point (it reminds us of the importance dramatic structure has for moral protest) is that whereas the timing (and other contextual aspects) of the SAG's announcement of a hunger strike imparted to it the character of a performative act (see note 53), PAG's equivalent statement became associated with a political threat that would be implemented some time in the future following certain unfavourable (as judged by the PAG) actions by the police.

Figure 3. Terms of Confrontation

OSLO	ALTA
SAG: prepared to die if we may not live as Saami	PAG: prepared to die for a river that must live
vs.	vs.
Police: will prevent disturbance of the peace	Police: will prevent death

The Political Significance of the SAG

Culture itself was politicized by the SAG at Eidsvolls *plass;* symbolic references to "Saami" became the basis of a practical strategy for the attainment of political rights. A similar political mission has been recognized for carnivals, but carnivals are "set apart in time and space from other activities" (Manning, 1983). The SAG, in contrast, *usurped* time and space and *intruded,* unbidden and unheralded, upon the routines, consciences and, above all, the imaginations of the citizens and politicians of Oslo—and eventually of the whole country. They decided to challenge the authority of Parliament; and the issue they selected was nothing less than the gross inadequacy of ordinary democratic rules and procedures in providing a minority people, the Saami, with a fair deal. We have discussed at length how they set up the challenge. Only by such 'revolutionary' means, the SAG believed, would their cause ever be noticed by the general public, and only then would it be taken seriously by the politicians.

The SAG may not have appreciated the power of the metaphor they created when they put their tent outside the parliament building,[59] but they knew that they had to step outside the ordinary democratic process, and they also understood something about Norwegian sentimentality. Yet they could not have anticipated the extent and strength of the popular response, or even all the reasons for it. Of course the response assured media attention, but what soon became the most compelling reason for this attention was the public's amazement over their own response to the hunger strike. Nor had this response only to do with sympathy for the Saami (though sympathy was widespread): the action by the SAG also sparked issues that the public believed had to do with Norwegian society generally (mentioned previously).

It was in direct response to the demonstration in Olso that the government charged a Commission of Inquiry to report on the status, actual and desired, of the Saami; the SAG's action also forced the government to a painful realization of its need to take the NSR seriously. What this means is that the lasting significance of the Oslo demonstration (regardless of the fact that the dam project was not halted) was to place two new and troubling questions on the Norwegian political agenda: "Who are Saami? What are Saami rights?" The important thing about these questions is that they implicitly assert: "There *are and will be* Saami! There *are* special Saami rights!" These questions have superceded the traditional Norwegian question (with its implicit negative assertion): Why would anyone wish to remain "a Lapp" (a term of contempt and even of abuse)? The explicit Norwegian assertion had always been that Lapps would become Norwegians.

Relations with the government were put under strain again in 1981 by the decision to renew work on the hydro project before the commission had completed its inquiries; nevertheless, Saami ethnopolitics has gone beyond the SAG interlude of individuated action into a new phase of institutional negotiations with the government under NSR leadership. The NSR also has work to do on another front. The SAG were concerned exclusively with winning the sympathetic attention and support of the majority (Norwegian) population; however, the task of giving political force to the moral claim of Saami rights is a more formidable one still. Common cause has to be established among the (sorely divided) Saami population itself, and whereas the SAG operated with a suspension of the rules of representativeness, the NSR finds itself continuously constrained by this political factor.

I conclude with a postscript. The opposition to the damming of the river did not cease with the 'fall' of Zero Point on 14 January 1981. Mikkel himself (not at Zero Point in 1981) started a hunger strike in Oslo on 26 January, which continued until 24 February. However, this painfully long fast won little sympathy and even less political attention. Mikkel's situation had begun to be analogous to Professor M's. He had gone into this new hunger strike with a public persona (this allowed the public to define what Mikkel was up to; indeed, they defined Mikkel), and Mikkel, the Saami, began to lose ground to Mikkel, the hunger striker (even a sad clown).[60] The episode points to the hard political probability that any act of moral opposition has a short life. It is not only that the public becomes bored but also that the necessary cognitive simplification, affective heightening and perceptions of society in moral (rather than political) terms, cannot be sustained. What had been a transcending experience of the general public becomes reduced to an experience that is different, in the sense of being without bearing to ordinary life (Handelman 1982:185). The case of Mikkel also suggests that in public politics (as opposed to theatre, proper, and public acts of commemoration) there is little chance of *re-enacting* a communicative event—for its circumstances will have changed in the interlude.

And what consequences does this have for Fourth World politics where, as was said at the beginning, so much depends on the ability to attract the broadest public by leaps of the imagination and events of particular force? All depends on whether the ethnodrama, before it burns itself out, manages to create a furor sufficient to pressure the government. Often this does not happen. For the SAG in 1979 it did.

Notes

1. This essay continues my account of contemporary Saami/Norwegian relations that was begun in ''Norwegians and Saami: Nation-State and Fourth World'' (Paine, 1985) where discussion centres upon two decades of ethnopolitics prior to the crisis discussed here; other essays will follow. I am indebted to Noel Dyck and Nigel Rapport for particularly searching comments (many of which I have incorporated) on different drafts of this essay; my thanks also to Ivar Björklund, Terje Brantenberg, Harald Eidheim, Don Handelman, Andreas Hompland, Elihu Katz and Sonia Kuryliw Paine.

2. My views stem from Blau's ''indirect competition'' (1964) and Schwimmer's ''symbolic competition'' (1972). Substituting ''moral'' for ''symbolic'' and ''opposition'' for ''competition'' brings us nearer to the phenomenon in question here.

3. Put another way, moral opposition is commonly connected with a basic disparity between the professed values of a group and the facilities at their command for the protection and propagation of these values.

4. An earlier version of this essay referred to ''cultural dramas,'' but this could be taken as meaning that Fourth World politics are *merely*

cultural and therefore unable to address *real* issues of political consequence. This would make a travesty of our whole argument.

5. *Norges vassdrags- og elektrisitetsvesen* (NVE).

6. NRL (*Norsk Reindriftssamers Landsforbund*), an organization of Saami reindeer owners, and NSR (*Norske Samers Riksforbund*), representing the interests of all Saami in Norway irrespective of livelihood.

   In the spring of 1979, a group of NSR members, complaining that the organization no longer represented the "ordinary" Saami, formed a new association: SLF (*Samenes Landsforbund*). Concerning the Alta/Kautokeino project, SLF insisted upon respect for parliamentary principle (the necessity of the project is regretted but opposition to it must stop).

7. Alta council by 30 votes to 15 and Kautokeino council by 12 votes to 5, but the provincial council votes in favour (24 to 11).

8. The voting is 90 to 36, but all except three of the votes against the project come from the four smaller political parties (Agrarian, Christian, Liberal, and Socialist) while Labour and Conservative vote *en bloc* in favour.

9. Reductions in the total scope of the project did not lead to a slackening or softening of opposition to it; the contrary took place. In Saami circles, there was (and is) considerable worry over problems that the access road were expected to bring to reindeer management in the area, and also about consequences for the community of Masi of an all-male Norwegian labour force (150 to 200 persons) billetted in the terrain for a period of five years. These issues are discussed in Paine 1982, which includes maps of the region, the river and the dam site.

10. Compiled from national and regional newspapers and personal interviews in winter 1980-81.

11. Tents have been pitched from time to time on the lawns outside the White House in Washington and outside Parliament House in Canberra. Note should also be taken of the moral significance of the periodic general assemblies on different continents of the World Council of Indigenous Peoples (WCIP): one was held in North Sweden in 1977 and it certainly contributed to the upbeat mood perceptible among Saami activists at this period (something that the Norwegian public would be in ignorance of).

12. In connection with their peaceful placard-bearing demonstrations during the 1970s, the villagers of Masi spoke of "the men in black uniforms," that is, the police who came (Paine 1982:83). In Oslo, at the end of the decade, the "dark" imagery was extended to members of Parliament.

13. The national headlines on Monday, 8 October, concerned a strike (and demonstration) by the country's lorry-drivers; by mid-week they

were no longer newsworthy—SAG and their Norwegian supporters had captured the headlines.

14. Denmark, Iceland, Norway, and Finland. The council has a section concerned with Saami affairs.

15. Brought by several parties, including Saami reindeer-owners. Judgment was given in December 1980: the court rejected (but only by a majority of 3 to 2) the plaintiffs' plea that the Board was proceeding illegally. This judgment was immediately brought before the Supreme Court, which, in 1982, found unanimously in favour of the Board (Paine 1982:6).

16. The citations in this paragraph are from *Finnmark Dagblad* (16, 17 and 18 Oct.) and *Dagbladet* (18 Oct.).

17. I owe this formulation—which I believe serves so well—to an essay on the nature of religious experience (Geertz 1975:93, 114).

18. "The meaning of the demonstration was not only a symbolization of Saami culture and of ethnic difference, in which case it could have been interpreted merely as a theatrical performance of a folkloristic content. It was also a purposeful action to attain a reinterpretation of Norwegian responsibilities towards the Saami people" (Thuen 1983:22).

19. See Paine, in press.

20. And so it was that the SAG gained, rather than lost, from their eventual agreement to move their tent off Eidsvolls *plass* to the other side of Karl Johansgate.

21. "It not only demands that we say 'no' to the organization of experience as it is given to us in pre-ordained categories; it also requires us to rearrange cognition into new forms and association" (Brown 1976:176).

22. See Thuen (1983) for an analysis along similar lines; and Paine (1981) on political uses of metaphor and metonym.

23. I see the relation of "polemic metaphor" to the customary notation of metaphor to be of the same order as that of "negative reciprocity" to reciprocity (cf. Sahlins 1972).

24. This part of my analysis builds upon Eidheim's discussion (1971:68ff.) of "complementarization" and "dichotomization" in interethnic relations.

25. Schwimmer (1972:50) associates symbolic competition with "revelation" (as "answers" to "failures of justice") and with (p. 123 f.) "reversal of scaling" whereby the moral/conceptual order of the majority is subordinated to the ordinarily weak one of the minority: hence among the Cree of the James Bay area (Feit, this vol.), the opposition between Indian and white values "had a transform where 'Indian' meant predictable and secure, and 'white' unpredictable and

insecurity-provoking'' (Salisbury 1977:182). All this appropriately connotes the effect that Mikkel had on the Norwegian scene.

26. The ethnography is rich and complex, and will be treated elsewhere.

27. Located at Stille (Stilla).

28. Whereas in 1979 the slogan had read: LA ELVA LEVE (LET THE RIVER LIVE).

29. The government also appointed a separate commission to inquire into the cultural (as opposed to legal) status of Saami in Norway. (As of this writing in summer 1983, the Saami Rights Commission has not presented any findings to Parliament.)

30. It should be borne in mind throughout this account that Norwegians have always been divided over the issue of hydro development. But it is really only in the north today that the issue is still alive, for the south has its hydro energy. What is it—some people ask—that delays hydro development in the north: "internal colonialism" (of the north by the south)? the nature-conservationist lobby? the Saami "radicals"? Those who raise such questions constitute a powerful pro-hydro lobby. But the forces arraigned ideologically against hydro development are also strong and numerous; thus the PAG could claim 72 local branches, between 13,000 and 15,000 members and a good budget at the beginning of 1981 (Hansen and Pihlström 1981:50). The town of Alta was sorely divided over the issue of the river, and also over the way that the PAG became involved in it on a national scale. Little wonder, then, that the Saami organizations (NSR and NRL) were wary of becoming overly identified with the opponents of hydro development. Another factor that they took into account was the traditional hostility of many Alta people toward Saami, including present members of the PAG.

31. Compiled from my field notes in Alta, supplemented by national and provincial newspapers and a published account by two Norwegian journalists (Hansen and Pihlström 1981).

32. They all eventually arrived. The other two are professors of philosophy and law (see narrative for 12 Oct. 1979, above), respectively. M's field is the sociology of law.

33. He held several but this was the only one I attended. (When press cards had to be shown, I managed by waving, with suitable nonchalance, a card bearing my photograph.)

34. In 1979 the mayor of Kautokeino belonged to the Norwegian Conservative party. The present mayor belongs to what is known as "the Saami list" (Samelistan) as distinct from the lists of the Norwegian parties.

35. According to Hansen and Pihlström (p. 21), the government anticipated this judgment, and the date it would be delivered, when planning their own timetable at Alta.

36. There were frequent radio newsflashes from Zero Point and Alta throughout the day.

37. The metal belts of the chain gang had successfully (in rehearsal) withstood hydraulic tongs with a pressure of 70 tons, and the police knew that. However the PAG had been advised that their chains would not withstand the use of grinding wheels, but it was thought that the police would consider their use too risky against belts fitted so tightly to the body. However, *they were used*— with an asbestos sheet shielding the body from flying sparks. Then, after a number of people had been cut loose in this fashion, the police actually found the key that opened the belts, so that they were saved the labour of cutting loose those who were still chained. (Hansen and Pihlström, pp. 96, 129, 131, 135).

38. Figures supplied by the PAG. The number of demonstrators actually booked by the police was 601, and each was fined 3,000 kroner, giving a total of 1.8 million kroner; however, only 2 persons paid the fine (court summons' awaiting the remainder).

39. This attracted over 1,500 supporters—even though many others were still at Zero Point or in the temporary care of the police.

40. No meeting was called, but the demand itself was a foretaste of the turbulence that beset Saami political circles throughout 1981 (which I will describe elsewhere).

41. Horowitz's (1980) essay on terrorism is suggestive of a range of differences and similarities between it and the kind of politics of morality that I am discussing here. Particularly *à propos* is his note on the fineness of the distinction between being perceived as "heroes" or as "scoundrels . . . who coat their venal acts with an ideological gloss" (p. 142).

42. Spoken at his inauguration in 1920, the mayor's words had a prophetic impact on the Irish republican movement. McSwiney died the following year as a hunger striker. I am grateful to Mary Russell (n.d.) for this and other references to hunger strikes.

43. Cf. George Bernard Shaw's comments on the McSwiney case in *Doctor's Delusions.*

44. I was unable to confirm the persistent rumours that the superintendent's father-in-law was among those at Zero Point in '79; yet should it be baseless in fact, the rumour still tells us how E, even when in the role of policeman, is perceived locally. I suggest that the message of the rumour is something like: "even in the way that this public controversy has divided his family, he's one of us." That the Norwegian government sometimes pays attention to the importance of casting is suggested by the fact that E's predecessor, known for

his critical views regarding the handling of the hydro development, was moved to a post in the south.

45. But not the legitimacy of the politicians who are, almost universally, condemned for their mishandling of the Alta/Kautokeino affair from its beginning over a decade earlier.

46. My choice of the term derives from Turner (1969); however, I use it simply in contradistinction to *everyday* attitudes, values and style—which is less than the use Turner himself puts it to.

47. That two of them were professors of law naturally became an additional cause for scepticism, cynicism and indignation.

48. There is this account from L: "The same thought had occurred to me: perhaps I would stay there even after they had taken the tent down. Then the courier came with a letter from the people at Zero Point in which they proposed the same. So with that we decided to tell [the press]. If a catastrophe followed, it would be the responsibility of the police. I admit that the wording was too dramatic and it was one of the few times that we allowed ourselves to be egged on at a press conference" (Hansen and Pihlström pp. 56-67). Cf. narrative for 7 Jan., above.

49. Indeed, were one to believe *Dagbladet* commenting upon the PAG at Alta, the value of human life had not been used as a political weapon by SAG-at-Eidsvoll: "Never in modern Norwegian history has anyone put forward threats about suicide as a counter in a political battle" (editorial, 9 Jan.).

50. See note 30 for a relevant background factor.

51. *Ha det litt ekkelt.*

52. True, the hunger strikers at Eidsvolls *plass* had joined themselves with a chain while they slept at night in their tent; but (i) it was a thin chain attached to their person or clothing, and (ii) its purpose was to prevent any one of their number from being removed from the tent without the others knowing. It was incidental to the demonstration.

53. Mikkel's rhetoric is an example of illocutionary power (Austin 1962) whereby to say something is to do something; see Paine, 1981, for a discussion of its application to politics.

54. Dayan and Katz (1981 *passim*) elaborate this point and distinguish (in respect to different genres of television production) between the sceptical, inquisitive glance of *journalism* and the essential act of endorsement of *broadcasting*.

55. As masters of their own performance, the SAG were "in control" (symbolically and interactionally) and the PAG (of team 2) were "under control" (cf. Heelas 1981:39-63). But it is unlikely that the Norwegians, whether in the crowd (team 2) or in the viewing public

(team 3), saw it in these terms; I suggest that their perception of what was happening focused upon the *empathetic* interaction between the SAG and their immediate circle of supporters.

56. Locally, competition over natural resources between villagers of the Alta area and others (including reindeer pastoralists) farther upstream has, from time to time, generated a good deal of ill feeling; this situation has also often been viewed locally in Saami versus non-Saami terms (see narrative for 5 and 8 Jan.). Nor are the conservationist aims of the PAG easily reconcilable with the practice of extensive reindeer pastoralism in the same area.

57. Professor M (personal communication, July 1983) challenges this mode of analysis. He is concerned that the centrality given to the notion of "play" and the dramaturgical model will (i) "have political implications of a sort we would both dislike," (ii) "take away the authenticity of the participants" and (iii) "make both the problems and the participants less serious."

58. Or Bateson's "communication about communication" (1951:209) in which "the subject of discourse is the relationship between the speakers" (1972:178), thereby heightening a "mutual awareness of perception" (1951:208).

59. Though the artist in the group had depicted the scene months before.

60. This time there were five hunger strikers and it seemed at first as though they were going to try to re-enact the public drama of 1979. But as it turned out, their fast took place in a room lent them by the Student Christian Association of Oslo University. Thus removing themselves from the public gaze, they sagaciously avoided having to ask the public to take up their cause once more. But this arrangement also meant that the hunger strikers were left alone to pit the moral force of their powerlessness, and of their pain, against the government. Portraying the hunger strike as "political" (something they had not succeeded in doing in 1979), the government did not yield. How this hunger strike was concluded will be described elsewhere, along with an analysis of the variety of events that followed the fall of Zero Point.

Representation and the 'Fourth World': A Concluding Statement

8

NOEL DYCK

Our primary concern in this volume has been to elucidate the processes and the mechanisms by which aboriginal peoples' interests are represented to governments in three Western liberal democratic states. We began by identifying some of the general analytical issues raised by minority indigenous peoples' dealings with the nation-state in Canada, Australia and Norway. We then considered ethnographic case studies that examined particular aspects of the strategies, resources and processes of representation, ranging in topic from the negotiation of land claims to the establishment of formal structures of representation to the politics of moral opposition. Our efforts throughout have intentionally been exploratory rather than definitive. Yet even at this stage it may be prudent to formulate some broader propositions about minority indigenous peoples' dealings with governments in countries such as Canada, Australia and Norway and about the general nature of Fourth World representation.

The minority indigenous peoples examined in this volume share four important characteristics. First, they are minority populations that have no hope of ever prevailing within their respective national societies on the basis of numbers: there is little possibility of them ever achieving their ends through the ballot box. Second, they are peoples who are recognized as being ethnically different from other segments of national populations by virtue of their aboriginal or indigenous status. This ethnic distinction originally reflected differences between aboriginal peoples and immigrant settlers in terms of their economic ways of life and in some cases continues to do so. On the other hand, differences between minority indigenous communities and majority populations may also be based primarily upon social and cultural factors. Third, aboriginal peoples within contemporary nation-states tend to suffer not only from a lack of political power but also from economic subjugation and social and cultural stigmatization. In short, the loss of traditional subsistence activities in the course of the historical settlement of their territories by immigrants has for the most part stranded aboriginal peoples at the bottom of local and national socio-economic hierarchies. Finally, minority indigenous peoples are located within nation-states that make little or no provision for the exercise of rights beyond those provided by legislatures in the form of citizenship. Aboriginal peoples' claims for special rights fly in the face of this charter premise of the nation-state.

Together these characteristics suggest that the notion of a "Fourth World"—at least as it may exist within these three countries—might most usefully be envisioned as comprising not so much discreet groups of people or specified aboriginal societies as complex political, economic and ideological *relations* between modern nation-states and a distinctive category of people. From this perspective it is possible to specify four salient properties of Fourth World relations. The first is that relations between aboriginal peoples and nation-states are not recent inventions, but well established (though by no means unchanging) phenomena. As Wolf (1982) has noted, the anthropological assumption that aboriginal peoples until recently possessed neatly bounded and self-perpetuating cultures or "designs for living" amounts to a tacit erasure of hundreds of years of colonial history. In effect, the mythology of the "only-recently-departed pristine primitive" ignores relationships and involvements that have been instrumental in shaping the lives of minority indigenous peoples within settler societies. The historicity of Fourth World relations obliges us to bear in mind that we may discover at least some of the causes of the present in the past.

A second property of these relations is that both in the past and in the present these have hinged largely upon an ideological dimension. This is not to deny the vital significance of economic factors to social and political relationships but to accord appropriate recognition of the subjective basis and moral premise inherent in

Fourth World relations. Although the stigmatization of aboriginal peoples went hand in hand with the economic expansion of the Western European world, we cannot safely assume a simple correlation between economic and ideological factors. State authorities in Canada, Australia and Norway have historically justified the appropriation of native lands and framed their treatment of aboriginal peoples in terms of a larger mission of tutelage whereby indigenous peoples would be transformed into civilized beings. This ubiquitous enterprise has yielded complicated histories of state practices toward indigenous peoples; indeed, at different times governments have adopted courses of action that not only reversed past policies but which would also contradict future official assumptions concerning the appropriate relationship between aboriginal peoples and the nation-state. These inconsistencies in the historical record today offer aboriginal representatives a valuable resource with which to scrutinize and contest government leaders' public stands concerning the legitimacy of native peoples' claims for special status and land rights.

Third, relations between aboriginal peoples and the nation-state in Canada, Australia and Norway should not be treated merely as a variant of interethnic relations because of the basic asymmetry of the parties involved—a people (or peoples) vs. a state (Paine 1985). Yet in order for aboriginal peoples to escape being categorized as ''just another ethnic minority'' by government officials and, thereby, to promote and protect their claims for special status and rights within national societies, they must seek simultaneously to make themselves both like and unlike the national societies they deal with. On one level they must constantly demonstrate fundamental cultural differences between themselves and members of the majority population; on another they must transcend the cultural plane in order to negotiate and assert a complementarity of status between themselves and governments. In short, a continuing aspect of aboriginal peoples' dealings with national governments involves a striving for recognition of a unique constitutional status and treatment within societies that have been determined to maintain only a single category of citizenship.

Fourth, aboriginal peoples in Canada, Australia and Norway both suffer and pose ''problems'' because of their ideological, economic and (often) geographical distictiveness. The determination of aboriginal communities—if not of all persons of aboriginal ancestry—to retain a separate identity and preserve their integrity often places them at odds with the assumptions and administrative arrangements of the nation-state. At the same time, the poverty of so many indigenous people brings them into intimate contact with the agencies of the welfare state. Since minority indigenous peoples have both encountered and posed ''problems'' in the past and seem likely to continue to do so in the future, it follows that an examination of the particular ways in which these ''problems'' are defined and dealt with by the state can tell us much about the dynamics of Fourth World relations. Indeed, histories of minority indigenous peoples' dealings with governments reveal that the distinctive aboriginal communities that make up the Fourth World are perennially on the edge of extinction, assimilation and crisis, in large part due to the ''solutions'' imposed by governments in accordance with their views of the ''native problem.''

In consequence, the ability of aboriginal communities to discover effective means of articulating their interests vis-à-vis the nation-state is a chronic concern and an essential condition for their survival as aboriginal communities. Nor is it simply a matter of selecting leaders who can catch the ears of government officials, for, as Weaver's essay (this volume) shows, governments may have as much need of aboriginal representatives as these leaders have of receiving official recognition from governments. Further, as Feit (this volume) argues, Fourth World representation entails two spheres that need to be distinguished at least in analytical terms: the field of relations between aboriginal representatives and those whom they represent as well as the relations of representatives to those to whom representations are made. Feit goes on to show that quite different expectations and criteria for evaluating the representatives' performance may exist within these two fields. Beckett's essay (this volume), on the other hand, suggests that acts of representation entail a form of structural alienation, and that for representation to occur there must be a discontinuity between two parties. This raises the possibility that the activities of representatives may serve to reinforce rather than narrow the gap between minority indigenous peoples and national governments, thus creating a continuing demand for the representatives' services.

The representation of aboriginal peoples' interests, especially in the formulation and adjudication of land claims, may also involve non-aboriginal personnel including anthropologists. Sansom (this volume) makes a compelling argument for anthropologists' need to adopt what he calls "processual modelling," a mode of analysis that pays attention not only to the formal structure of aboriginal social organization, but also to the processes by which labile and often fluctuating aboriginal communities are composed and recomposed over time. There is also, as Weaver's essay (this volume) indicates, considerable variation and flexibility in governments' criteria for assessing what comprises legitimate representation or "representivity" on the part of aboriginal leaders and organizations. Weaver's contention that representivity comprises a political resource that governments can either ascribe or deny to aboriginal leaders offers a valuable proposition that might usefully inform future investigations.

The potential for aboriginal representatives to establish themselves as political actors—in arenas from which they would otherwise be excluded—by adopting symbolic stands over issues about which they otherwise would have no chance of making their position known, is clearly illustrated in Sanders' essay (this volume). The value of moral opposition as an instrument of minority indigenous peoples' representation is also demonstrated by Paine's analysis (this volume) of an instance of ethnodrama where the conjunctions of physical powerlessness and moral power were turned to good representational effect. Paine identifies the particular significance of public drama in Fourth World politics and demonstrates how aboriginal peoples in countries such as Norway use drama to express their version of reality and thereby possibly to rearrange the experience and influence the actions of others.

These findings about the processes and strategies by which aboriginal peoples in three Western liberal democracies seek to manage their dealings and represent their interests to the agencies of the nation-state, and about the means by which governments have sought to exercise control of these representations, constitute the politics of representation in the Fourth World—or at least in that part of the Fourth World that exists in the Western, industrialized "First World." These concerns lie at the heart of minority indigenous peoples' struggles to survive as aboriginal peoples and of governments' efforts to reconcile demands for special aboriginal status and rights with the existing institutional arrangements and ideological foundations of Western nation-states.

References

ABORIGINAL LAND COMMISSIONER
  1981 *Finness River Land Claim.* Report by the Aboriginal Land Commissioner to the Minister for Aboriginal Affairs and to the Administrator of the Northern Territory. Canberra: Australian Government Publishing Service.

ABORIGINAL LAND RIGHTS COMMISSION
  1974 *Second Report.* Canberra: Australian Government Publishing Service.

ANDERSON, MYRDENE
  1981 "Broker Boundaries: Axles of Information and Energy Management in a Fourth World Crisis." Purdue University (typescript).

ASCH, MICHAEL
  1984 *Home and Native Land. Aboriginal Rights and the Canadian Constitution.* Toronto: Methuen.

AUSTIN, J. L.
  1962 *How To Do Things with Words.* Oxford: Clarendon Press.

BARGER, W. K.
  1980 "Inuit and Cree Adaptation to Northern Colonialism." In Ernest L. Schusky (ed.), *Political Organization of Native North Americans.* Washington: University of America.

BARTH, F.
  1969 "Introduction." In F. Barth (ed.), *Ethnic Groups and Boundaries.* Oslo: Universitetsforlaget.

BATESON, GREGORY
  1951 "Information and Codification: A Philosophical Approach." In Jurgen Ruesch and Gregory Bateson (eds.), *Communication. The Social Matrix of Psychiatry.* New York: Norton.

  1972 *Steps to an Ecology of Mind.* New York: Ballantine Books.

BEAVER, JACK
   1979 *To Have What is One's Own: Report from the President.* Ottawa: National Indian Socio-Economic Development Committee.

BECKETT, JEREMY
   1967 "Elections in a Small Melanesian Community." *Ethnology,* 6(3):332-44.

   1971 "Rivalry, Competition and Conflict among Christian Melanesians." In C. Jayawardena and L. R. Hiatt (eds.), *Anthropology in Oceania: Essays Presented to Ian Hogbin.* Sydney: Angus and Robertson.

   1977 "The Torres Strait Islanders and the Pearling Industry: A Case of Internal Colonialism." *Aboriginal History,* 1(1):77-104.

   1978 "Mission, Church and Sect: Three Types of Religious Commitment in Torres Strait. In J. Boutilier *et al.* (eds.), *Mission, Church and Sect in Oceania.* Ann Arbor: University of Michigan Press.

BEE, ROBERT and RONALD GINGERICH
   1977 "Colonialism, Classes and Ethnic Identity: Native Americans and the National Political Economy." *Studies in Comparative International Development,* 12:70-93.

BERGER, THOMAS
   1977 *Northern Frontier, Northern Homeland: The Report of the Mackenzie Valley Pipeline Inquiry.* 2 Vols. Ottawa: Department of Supply and Services.

BERKES, F., I. LARUSIC and H. A. FEIT
   1972 "A Case Study in Northern Quebec." In Berkes *et al.* (eds.), *Environmental Aspects of the Pulp and Paper Industry in Quebec* (2nd ed.). Montreal: Terra Nova.

BERNDT, RONALD M.
   1971 "The Concept of Protest within an Australia Aboriginal Context." In Ronald M. Berndt (ed.), *A Question of Choice.* Perth: University of Western Australia.

BLAU, P. M.
   1964 *Exchange and Power in Social Life.* New York: John Wiley.

BLEAKLEY, J. W.
   1961 *The Aborigines of Australia.* Brisbane: Jacaranda Press.

BLU, KAREN
   1980 *The Lumbee problem: The Making of an American Indian People.* Cambridge: Cambridge University Press.

BODLEY, JOHN H.
1982 *Victims of Progress* (2nd Ed.). Menlo Park, California: Benjamin/Cummings.

BOREHAM, P., M. CASS and M. MCCALLUM
1979 "The Australian Bureaucratic Elite: The Importance of Social Backgrounds and Occupational Experience." *The Australian and New Zealand Journal of Sociology*, 15(2):45-55.

BRAND, STEWARD
1973 "Both Sides of a Necessary Paradox." *Harpers*, 247(1482):20-37.

BRODY, HUGH
1975 *The People's Land: Eskimos and Whites in the East Arctic.* Markham, Ontario: Penguin Books of Canada.

BROOKES, E. H. and J. B. MACAULAY
1958 *Civil Liberty in South Africa.* Cape Town: Oxford University Press.

BROWN, RICHARD A.
1976 "Social Theory as Metaphor: On the Logic of Discovery for the Sciences of Conduct." *Theory and Society*, 3(2):169-98.

BURKE, JAMES
1976 *Paper Tomahawks: From Red Tape to Red Power.* Winnipeg: Queenston House.

CANADA
1980 *The Canadian Constitution 1980: Proposed Resolution Respecting the Constitution of Canada.* Ottawa: Publications Canada.

1981a *Text of Proposed Constitutional Resolution Filed by the Deputy Attorney General of Canada with the Supreme Court of Canada on April 24, 1981.* Ottawa: Department of Justice.

1981b *The Canadian Constitution 1981: A Resolution Adopted by the Parliament of Canada, December 1981.* Ottawa: Publications Canada.

CARDINAL, HAROLD
1969 *The Unjust Society: The Tragedy of Canada's Indians.* Edmonton: Hurtig.

1977 *The Rebirth of Canada's Indians.* Edmonton: Hurtig.

CASTILE, GEORGE P. and GILBERT KUSHNER (eds.)
1981 *Persistent Peoples: Cultural Enclaves in Perspective.* Tucson: University of Arizona Press.

CHRETIEN, JEAN
1972 Statement, *House of Commons Debates*, 116(41):1736-39, 1746.

COHEN, ANTHONY P.
1982 "Belonging: The Experience of Culture." In A. P. Cohen (ed.), *Belonging: Identity and Social Organisation in British Rural Cultures.* St. John's, Nfld.: Institute of Social and Economic Research, Memorial University.

COOMBS, H. C.
1978 *Kulinma: Listening to Aboriginal Australians.* Canberra: Australian National University Press.

COOPER, JAN E.
1976 "The Politics of Consultation with Aboriginals." Unpublished M.A. thesis, Department of Sociology, University of Essex, England.

CUMMING, PETER A.
1977 *Canada: Native Land Rights and Northern Development.* Copenhagen: International Working Group for Indigenous Affairs, Document 26.

CUNNISON, I.
1959 *Luapula Peoples of Northern Rhodesia: Custom and History in Tribal Politics.* Manchester: Manchester University Press for the Rhodes - Livingstone Institute.

DAWSON, HELEN JONES
1975 "National Pressure Groups and the Federal Government." In A. Paul Pross (ed.), *Pressure Group Behaviour in Canadian Politics.* Toronto: McGraw-Hill Ryerson.

DAYAN, DANIEL and ELIHU KATZ
1981 "Electronic Ceremonies: Roles of Television in a Royal Wedding, the Experience of Not Being There." Hebrew University of Jerusalem (typescript).

DENING, G.
1980 *Islands and Beaches: Discourse on a Silent Land, Marquesas 1774-1880.* Honolulu: University Press of Hawaii.

DEPARTMENT OF INDIAN AFFAIRS AND NORTHERN DEVELOPMENT (DIAND)
1968 *Choosing a Path.* Ottawa: Queen's Printer.

1969 *[The White Paper] Statement of the Government of Canada on Indian Policy 1969.* Ottawa: Queen's Printer.

DESY, PIERRETTE
1968 "Fort George on Tsesa-sippi — Contribution à une étude sur la désintégration culturelle d'une communauté indienne de la baie James." Thèse de doctorate. Paris.

DIAMOND, BILLY

1977 *Highlights of the Negotiations Leading to the James Bay and Northern Quebec Agreement.* Val d'Or: Grand Council of the Crees (of Quebec).

1981 "Interview." In R. Wittenborn and C. Biegert (eds.) *James Bay Project - River Drowned by Water.* Montreal: Museum of Fine Arts.

DOMMERGUES, PIERRE

1976 "L'Affaire de la Baie James." *La Monde diplomatique.* No. 272, November 1976.

DUNCAN, LEITH

1974 "Protest and Aborigines: An Initial View." In Donald E. Edgar (ed.), *Social Change in Australia.* Melbourne: Cheshire.

DYCK, NOEL

1981 "The Politics of Special Status: Indian Associations and the Administration of Indian Affairs." In Jorgen Dahlie and Tissa Fernando (eds.), *Ethnicity, Power and Politics in Canada.* Toronto: Methuen.

1983 "Representation and Leadership of a Provincial Indian Association." In A. Tanner (ed.), *The Politics of Indianness: Case Studies of Native Ethnopolitics in Canada.* St. John's, Nfld.: Institute of Social and Economic Research, Memorial University.

EIDHEIM, HARALD

1971 *Aspects of the Lappish Minority Situation.* Oslo: Universitetsforlaget.

ELLIOTT, JEAN LEONARD (ed.)

1983 *Two Nations, Many Cultures: Ethnic Groups in Canada* (2nd Edition). Scarborough, Ontario: Prentice-Hall.

EVANS, RAYMOND, KAY EVANS and KATHRYN CRONIN

1975 *Exclusion, Exploitation and Extermination: Race Relations in Colonial Queensland.* Sydney: Australia and New Zealand Book Company.

EVANS-PRITCHARD, E. E.

1961 *Anthropology and History.* Manchester: Manchester University Press.

FEDERAL-PROVINCIAL TASK FORCE

1971a "A Preliminary Study of the Environmental Impacts of the James Bay Development Project, Quebec." (typescript)

1971b "A Summary of the Preliminary Study of the Environmental Impacts of the James Bay Development Project, Quebec." [In English and Cree syllabics]. (typescript)

FEIT, HARVEY A.

1979 "Political Articulations of Hunter-Gatherers to the State." *Inuit Studies,* 3:37-52.

1980 "Negotiating Recognition of Aboriginal Rights: History, Strategies and Reactions to the James Bay and Northern Quebec Agreement." *Canadian Journal of Anthropology*, 1(2):159-72.

1982 "The Future of Hunters within Nation State: Anthropology and the James Bay Cree." In Eleanor Leacock and Richard Lee (eds.), *Politics and History in Band Societies*. Cambridge: Cambridge University Press.

FELDMAN, K. D.
1980 "Ethnology and the Anthropologist as Expert Witness in Legal Disputes: A Southwestern Alaskan Case." *Journal of Anthropological Research*, 36:245-57.

FOSTER, CHARLES R. (ed.)
1980 *Nations Without a State: Ethnic Minorities in Western Europe*. New York: Praeger.

GARIGUE, PHILLIP
1957 "The Social Organization of the Montagnais-Naskapi." *Anthropologica*, 4:107-35.

GEERTZ, C.
1966 *Agricultural Involution: the Process of Ecological Change in Indonesia*. Berkeley and Los Angeles: University of California Press.

1975 *The Interpretation of Cultures*. London: Hutchinson.

GOURDEAU, ERIC
1974 *Le processus décisionnel de la conception et la réalisation du développement nordique au Canada. Un d'espèce: la Baie de James*. Rapport pour le compte du conseil des Sciences du Canada (Ottawa).

GOVERNMENT OF CANADA
1980 "Canada's Native Peoples and the Constitution, Background Material." Government of Canada: Federal Provincial Relations Office.

GRABURN, NELSON H. H.
1981 "1,2,3,4 . . .: Anthropology and the Fourth World." *Culture*, 1(1):66-70.

GRAYSON, J. PAUL (ed.)
1980 *Class, State, Ideology and Change*. Toronto: Holt, Rinehart and Winston.

GRILLO, R. D. (ed.)
1980 *"Nation" and "State" in Europe: Anthropological Perspectives*. New York: Academic Press.

GUMBERT, M.
1981 "Paradigm Lost: An Analysis of Anthropological Models and Their Effect on Aboriginal Land Rights." *Oceania*, 52:103-23.

GUSFIELD, JOSEPH R.
1981 *The Culture of Public Problems: Drinking-Driving and the Symbolic Order.* Chicago: University of Chicago Press.

HADDON, ALFRED CORT
1904-1935 *Reports of the Cambridge Anthropological Expedition to Torres Strait*, Vols. 1-6. Cambridge: Cambridge University Press.

HANDELMAN, DON
1977 "Play and Ritual: Complementary Frames of Metacommunication." In A. Chapman and H. Foot (eds.) *It's a Funny Thing, Humour.* London: Pergamon.

1982 "Reflexivity in Festival and other Cultural Events." In Mary Douglas (ed.), *Essays in the Sociology of Perception.* London: Routledge and Kegan Paul.

HANSEN, JAN DITLEV and KJELL PIHLSTRÖM
1981 *Stormen om Stilla.* Bodö: Egil Trohaugs Forlag.

HARRIS, STEWART
1972 *This Our Land.* Canberra: Australian National University Press.

1979 *'It's Coming Yet . . .' An Aboriginal Treaty Within Australia Between Australians.* Canberra: Aboriginal Treaty Committee.

HAWTHORN, H. B.
1966 *A Survey of the Contemporary Indians of Canada.* Vol. 1. Ottawa: Queen's Printer.

1967 *A Survey of the Contemporary Indians of Canada.* Vol. 2. Ottawa: Queen's Printer.

HEELAS, PAUL
1981 "The Model Applied: Anthropology and Indigenous Psychologies." In Paul Heelas and Andrew Lock (eds.), *Indigenous Psychologies.* London: Academic Press.

HENRIKSEN, GEORG
1983 "Contrasting Prophecies of Indian-White Relations and the Lack of Political Mobilization among the Naskapi." In Reidar Gronhaug (ed.), *Transaction and Signification.* Bergen: Universitetsforlaget.

HIATT, L.
1976 *The Role of the National Aboriginal Consultative Committee: Report of the Committee of Inquiry.* Canberra: Department of Aboriginal Affairs.

HOBBES, T.
1914 (1651) *Leviathan*. London: J. M. Dent.

HONIGMANN, JOHN J.
1962 *Social Networks in Great Whale River. Notes on an Eskimo, Montagnais-Naskapi, and Euro-Canadian Community*. Ottawa: National Museum of Canada.

1964 "Indians of Nouveau-Québec." In Jean Malaurie and Jacques Rousseau (eds.), *Le Nouveau-Québec. Contribution à l'étude l'occupation humaine*. The Hague: Mouton.

HOROWITZ, IRVING LOUIS
1980 *Taking Lives: Genocide and State Power*. New Brunswick, N.J.: Transaction Books.

HOWARD, MICHAEL C. (ed.)
1978 *"Whitefella Business": Aborigines in Australian Politics*. Philadelphia: Institute for the Study of Human Issues.

1982 *Aboriginal Power in Australian Society*. Honolulu: University of Hawaii Press.

HYMAN, JACQUELINE
1971 "Conflicting Perceptions of Exchange in Indian-Missionary Contact." Unpublished M.A. thesis, Department of Anthropology, McGill University.

INDIAN CHIEFS OF ALBERTA
1970 "Citizens Plus." [The Red Paper] Presented to Prime Minister Pierre Trudeau, June 1970. Exerpt published in Waubageshig (ed.), *The Only Good Indian*. Toronto: New Press.

INDIANS OF QUEBEC ASSOCIATION (IQA)
1972 (1969) "Brief on Indians of Quebec Territorial Rights." *Recherches amérindiennes au Québec*, 2(4-5):13-27.

1974 *Our Land, Our People, Our Future*. Caughnawaga: Indians of Quebec Association.

JACKSON, KEITH
1973 "Arrested Development - Problems of Maori Representation." In K. Jackson (ed.), *New Zealand: Politics of Change*. Wellington: Reed.

JAMES BAY COMMITTEE (JBC)
1972a *James Bay Development: Progress or Disaster?* Montreal: James Bay Committee.

1972b *L'aménagement de la baie James: Progrès ou désastre?* Montréal: Le Comité pour la défense de la baie James.

JAMES BAY TASK FORCE
   1972 "The James Bay Power Project—A Protest." Press release by the James Bay Task Force, Indians of Quebec Association and Northern Quebec Inuit Association, December 1972.

JAYAWARDENA, CHANDRA
   1968 "Ideology and Conflict in Lower Class Communities. *Comparative Studies in Society and History*, 10(4):412-46.

JOHNSON, WILLIAM D.
   1962 *An Exploratory Study of Ethnic Relations at Great Whale River*. Ottawa: Department of Northern Affairs and National Resources, Northern Co-ordination and Research Centre.

JULL, P.
   1982 *A Perspective on the Aboriginal Rights Coalition and the Restoration of Constitutional Aboriginal Rights*. IWGIA Newsletter. Copenhagen: International Work Group for Indigenous Affairs.

KERNAGHAN, KENNETH
   1978 "Representative Bureaucracy: The Canadian Perspective." *Canadian Journal of Public Administration*, 21(4):489-511.

KERR, A. J.
   1950 *Subsistence and Social Organization in a Fur Trade Community. Anthropological Report on the Ruperts House Indians*. Report to the National Committee for Community Health Studies.

KNIGHT, ROLF
   1968 *Ecological Factors in Changing Economy and Social Organization Among the Rupert House Cree*. Ottawa: National Museum of Canada, Anthropology Papers No. 15.

KORNBERG, ALLAN, H.D. CLARKE and A. GODDARD
   1980 "Parliament and the Representational Process in Contemporary Canada." In Harold D. Clarke, *et al.* (eds.), *Parliament, Policy and Representation*. Toronto: Methuen.

KUPFERER, HARRIET J.
   1966 "Impotency and Power: A Cross-Cultural Comparison of the Effect of Alien Rule." In Marc J. Swartz, Victor W. Turner and Arthur Tuden (eds.), *Political Anthropology*. Chicago: Aldine.

LACASSE, ROGER
   1983 *Baie James. Une épopée*. Montréal: Société pour Vaincre la Pollution.

LAJAMBE, HELEN (ed.)
   1972 *La baie James, c'est grave, grave, grave*. Montréal: Société pour Vaincre la Pollution.

LARUSIC, IGNATIUS
1971 [1972] "The Reactions of the Waswanipi Indians at the Announcement of the James Bay Project." Unpublished English version of "La réaction des Waswanipis à l'announce du projet de la baie James." *Recherches amérindiennes au Québec*, 1(4-5):15-21.

1972 "The Influence of the Indians of Quebec Association in Waswanipi." Report to the Department of Secretary of State. Montreal: McGill University, Programme in the Anthropology of Development.

LARUSIC, IGNATIUS, SERGE BOUCHARD, ALAN PENN, TAYLOR BRELSFORD, JEAN-GUY DESCHENES
1979 *Negotiating a Way of Life: Initial cree Experience with the Administrative Structure Arising from the James Bay Agreement.* Montreal: SSDCC for Department of Indian and Northern Affairs, Policy Research and Evaulation Group.

LASLITT, P.
1977 *Family Life and Illicit Love in Earlier Generations.* Cambridge: Cambridge University Press.

LEACH, E.
1977 "In Formative Travail with Leviathan." *Anthropological Forum*, 4:190-97.

LEGER, YVES
1971 [1972] "The James Bay Project: The Other Side of the Coin." Unpublished translation of "Le projet de la baie James: l'envers de la médaille." *Recherches amérindiennes au Québec*, 1(4-5):36-42.

LIPS, JULIUS E.
1947 *Naskapi Law (Lake St. John and Lake Mistassini Bands). Law and Order in a Hunting Society.* Philadelphia: Transactions of the American Philosophical Society, New Series, Vol. 37, Part 4.

LONEY, MARTIN
1977 "A Political Economy of Citizen Participation." In Leo Panitch (ed.), *The Canadian State: Political Economy and Political Power.* Toronto: University of Toronto Press.

LONG, J.A., L. LITTLE BEAR and M. BOLDT
1982 "Federal Indian Policy and Indian Self-Government: An Analysis of a Current proposal." *Canadian Public Policy*, 8:189-99.

LOVEDAY, PETER
1970 "Pressure Groups." In Venturino G. Venturini (ed.), *Australia: A Survey.* Wiesbaden: Otto Harrassowitz.

1975 "Australian Political Thought." In Richard Lucy (ed.), *The Pieces of Politics*. Sydney: Macmillan.

MADDOCK, K.
1980 *Anthropology, Law and the Definition of Australian Aboriginal Rights to Land*. Nijmegen: Instituut voor Volksrecht.

1981 "Walpiri Land Tenure: A Test Case in Legal Anthropology." *Oceania*, 52:85-102.

MALOUF, ALBERT
1973 *La Baie James indienne. Texte intégral du jugement du juge Albert Malouf*. Montréal: Editions du Jour.

MANNING, FRANK
1983 "Text, Strategy and Celebration." In Frank Manning (ed.), *Bread and Circuses. Festivity and Public Performance in Contemporary Societies*. Ohio: Bowling Green University Popular Press.

MANUEL, GEORGE and M. POSLUNS
1974 *The Fourth World: An Indian Reality*. Toronto: Collier-Macmillan.

MATTHEWS, TREVOR
1976 "Interest Group Access to the Australia Government Bureaucracy." In *Report of the Royal Commission on Australian Government Administration*. Vol. 2. Canberra: Government Printer.

1977 "Australian Pressure Groups." In Henry Mayer and Helen Nelson (eds.), *Australian Politics: A Fourth Reader*. Melbourne: Longman Cheshire.

MAYER, ADRIAN C.
1966 "The Significance of Quasi-Groups in the Study of Complex Societies." In M. Banton (ed.), *The Social Anthropology of Complex Societies*. London: Tavistock (ASA Monograph No. 4).

MCCALL, GRANT
1980 "Four Worlds of Experience and Action." *Third World Quarterly*, 2(3):536-45.

MCDONALD, RICHARD, HEDLEY DIMOCK, HUBERT GUINDON and NORMAN CHANCE
1965 *A Community Development Study Regarding the Life of the Cree Indians the Mistassini-Chibougamau Region of Quebec*. Montreal: Sir George Williams University Centre for Human Relations and Community Studies.

MCROBIE, ALAN D.
1978 "Ethnic Representation: The New Zealand Experience." In Stephen Levine (ed.), *Politics in New Zealand*. Boston: George Allen & Unwin.

MCWHINNEY, EDWARD
1982 *Canada and the Constitution, 1979-1982.* Toronto: University of Toronto Press.

MORANTZ, TOBY
1982 "Northern Algonquian Concepts of Status and Leadership Reviewed: A Case Study of the Eighteenth-Century Trading Captain System." *Canadian Review of Sociology and Anthropology,* 19(4):482-501.

MURPHY, ROBERT F.
1971 *The Dialectics of Social Life.* London: George Allen and Unwin.

NATIONAL INDIAN BROTHERHOOD (NIB)
1973 *Contemporary Indian Protests, Reference Aids—Bibliographies, Volume 3, James Bay Hydro-Electric Project (April 24, 1971 - May 1, 1973).* Ottawa: National Indian Brotherhood.

NATIVE COUNCIL OF CANADA (NCC)
1981 *Native People and Constitution of Canada.* Ottawa: Mutual Press.

PAINE, ROBERT (ed.)
1977 *The White Arctic: Anthropological Essays on Tutelage and Ethnicity.* St. John's: Institute of Social and Economic Research, Memorial University.

1981 *Politically-Speaking: Cross Cultural Studies of Rhetoric.* St. John's: Institute of Social and Economic Research, Memorial University and Philadelphia: ISHI.

PAINE, ROBERT
1981 "When Saying is Doing." In R. Paine (ed.), *Politically Speaking: Cross-Cultural Studies of Rhetoric.* St. John's: Institute of Social and Economic Research, Memorial University, and Philadelphia: ISHI.

1982 *Dam a River, Damn a People? Saami (Lapp) Livelihood and the Alta/Kautokeino Hydro-Electric Project and the Norwegian Parliament.* IWGIA Document 45. Copenhagen: International Work Group for Indigenous Affairs.

1983 "News Show Politics and the Absent Anthropologist." In Frank Manning and Marc-Adelard Tremblay (eds.), *Consciousness and Inquiry: Ethnology and Canadian Reality.* Ottawa: Museum of Man, Mercury Series.

1985 "Norwegians and Saami: Nation-State and Fourth World." In Gerald Gold (ed.), *Minorities and Mother Country Imagery.* St. John's: Institute of Social and Economic Research, Memorial University.
In press "The Claim of Aboriginality." *Anthropologica.*

PANITCH, LEO (ed.)

1977 *The Canadian State: Political Economy and Political Power.* Toronto: University of Toronto Press.

PARSONS, T.

1951 *The Social System.* Glencoe: The Free Press.

PARTI QUEBECOIS

1972 *L'affaire de la baie James.* Québec: Les éditions du Parti québécois.

PERKINS, CHARLES

1975 *A Bastard Like Me.* Sydney: Ure Smith.

PETERS, E. L. P.

1960 "The Proliferation of Segments in the Lineage of the Bedouin of Cyrenaica." *Journal of the Royal Anthropological Institute,* 90:29-53.

PONTING, J. RICK and ROGER GIBBINS

1980 *Out of Irrelevance: A Socio-Political Introduction to Indian Affairs in Canada.* Toronto: Butterworths.

PORTER, JOHN

1965 *The Vertical Mosaic.* Toronto: University of Toronto Press.

POTHIER, ROGER

1967 *Relations inter-ethniques et acculturation à Mistassini.* Quebec: Université laval, Centre d'Etudes Nordiques, Travaux Divers, 9.

PRESTON, RICHARD

1968 "When Leadership Fails: The Basis of a Community Crisis." *The Northland,* 24(3):7-9.

1971 "Functional Politics in a Northern Indian Community." *Proceedings of the 38th International Congress of Americanists,* (3):169-78.

1975 *Cree Narrative: Expressing the Personal Meanings of Events.* Canadian Ethnology Service, Paper No. 30, Mercury series. Ottawa: National Museums of Canada.

1983 "Algonquian People and Energy Development in the Subarctic." McMaster University Research Program for Technology Assessment in Subarctic Ontario, Research Report No. 4.

PROSS, A. PAUL

1975 "Pressure Groups: Adaptive Instruments of Political Communication." In A. Paul Pross (ed.), *Pressure Group Behaviour in Canadian Politics.* Toronto: McGraw-Hill Ryerson.

1981 "Pressure Groups: Talking Chameleons." In M. Whittington and G. Williams (eds.), *Canadian Politics in the 1980s.* Toronto: Methuen.

ROYAL COMMISSION ON AUSTRALIAN GOVERNMENT AD-MINISTRATION (RCAGA)
1976 "Non-statutory Bodies." In *RCAGA*, Vol. 1. Canberra.

RECHERCHES AMERINDIENNES AU QUEBEC
1971 *La Baie James des amérindiens.* R.A.Q. 1(4-5). [Unpublished English version prepared by the Programme in the Anthropology of Development, McGill University, May 1972].

RICHARDSON, BOYCE
1972a *Baie James: Sans Mobile Légitime.* Montréal: Editions l'Etincelle.

1972b *James Bay: The Plot to Drown the North Woods.* San Francisco: Sierra Club.

1975 *Strangers Devour the Land. The Cree Hunters of the James Bay Area Versus Premier Bourassa and the James Bay Development Corporation.* Toronto: Macmillan.

ROBBINS, RICHARD H.
1967 "The Two Chiefs: Changing Leadership Patterns Among the Great Whale River Cree." Paper read at the Northeastern Anthropological Association, Montreal, 2 April 1967.

ROGERS, EDWARD S.
1963 *The Hunting Group—Hunting Territory Complex Among the Mistassini Indians.* Ottawa: National Museum of Canada, Bulletin No. 195.

1965 "Leadership among the Indians of Eastern Sub-Arctic Canada." *Anthropological,* N.S. 7:263-81.

ROULAND, NORBERT
1978 *Les Inuits du Nouveau Québec et la Convention de la Baie James.* Québec: Association Inuksiutiit katimajit et Centre d'Etudes Nordiques, Université Laval.

ROWLEY, CHARLES D.
1972a *The Destruction of Aboriginal Society.* Vol. 1. Sydney: Penguin.

1972b *Outcasts in White Australia.* Vol. 2. Sydney: Penguin.

RUSSELL, MARY
n.d. "A History of the Irish Hunger-Strike." School of Peace Studies, University of Bradford (typescript).

SAHLINS, MARSHALL
1972 *Stone Age Economics.* New York: Aldine.

SALISBURY, RICHARD
1977 "A Prism of Perceptions: The James Bay Hydro-Electric Project."

In Sandra Wallman (ed.), *Perceptions of Development*. London: Cambridge University Press.

SALISBURY, RICHARD F., FERNAND FILLON, FARIDA RAWJI and DONALD A. STEWART

1972 *Development and James Bay. Social Impacts of the James Bay Hydro-Electric Scheme*. Montreal: Programme in the Anthropology of Development, McGill University.

1983 "Les Cris et leur consultants." *Recherches amérindiennes au Québec*, 13(1):67-69.

SAM, JOSIE

1968 [1967] [Letter to] "Rt. Hon. J. G. Diefenbaker, Leader of the Queen's Loyal Opposition, House of Commons, Ottawa, Canada." *The Northland*, 24(3):9.

SANDERS, DOUGLAS

1973 "The Nishga Case." *B.C. Studies*, 19:3-20.

1975 "Family Law and Native People." Law Reform Commission of Canada, 99-102.

1977 *The Formation of the World Council of Indigenous Peoples*. IWGIA Document No. 29. Copenhagen: International Work Group for Indigenous Affairs.

1980 "Indians, the Queen and the Canadian Constitution." *Survival International Review*, 6. London: England.

1982 "Discussion Paper on Membership and Representation within the World Council of Indigenous Peoples." Unpublished Manuscript.

1983 "The Re-Emergence of Indigenous Questions in International Law." Unpublished Manuscript.

SANSOM, B.

1976 "Humpty Doo Claim." Report submitted to the Northern Land Council, July 1976.

1980 "Statement of the Finniss River Land Claim." Exhibit No. 125 in the Finniss River Land Claim.

1981a "Processural Modelling and Aggregate Structures in Northern Australia." In L. Holy and M. Stucklik (eds.), *The Structure of Folk Models in Social Anthropology*. ASA Monograph No. 20. New York: Academic Press.

1981b *The Camp at Wallaby Cross*. Canberra: Australian Institute for Aboriginal Studies.

SAVOIE, DONAT
   1971 [1972] "The Dorion Report and the Territorial Rights of the James Bay territoriaux des Indiens de la baie James." *Recherches amérindiennes au Québec,* 1(4-5):32-35.

SCHAPERA, I.
   1955 *Handbook of Tswana Law and Custom.* London: Oxford University Press for the International African Institute.

SCHWIMMER, E. G.
   1972 "Symbolic Competition." *Anthropologica,* N.S., 14(2):117-55.

SCOTT, COLIN
   1983 "The Semiotics of Material Life Among Wemindji Cree Hunters." Unpublished Ph.D. thesis, Department of Anthropology, McGill University.

SPENCE, J. A.
   1972 *Consequences of Existing Impoundment Projects as Relevant to the Proposed James Bay Hydro-Electric Development Scheme.* Montreal: James Bay Committee.

SPENCE, J. A. and G. C. SPENCE
   1972 *Ecological Considerations of the James Bay Project.* Montreal: James Bay Committee.

SPICER, EDWARD H.
   1971 "Persistent Cultural Systems: A Comparative Study of Identity Systems That Can Adapt to Contrasting Environments." *Science,* 174:795-800.

SSDC
   1982 *Etude des retombées sociales et économiques sur les communautés autochtones du territoire NBR.* Montréal: Sociéte d'énergie de la baie James.

STANNER, W. E. H.
   1965 "Aboriginal Territorial Organization: Estate, Range, Domain and Regime." *Oceania,* 36:1-26.

   1979 *White Man Got No Dreaming.* Canberra: Australian National University Press.

STEWARD, J.
   1938 *Basin Plateau Aboriginal Socio-Political Groups.* Washington: Smithsonian Institute, Bureau of American Ethnology, Bulletin No. 120.

STOKES, EVELYN (ed.)
   1981 *Maori Representation in Parliament.* Hamilton, New Zealand,

University of Waikato, Centre for Maori Studies and Research, Occasional Paper No. 14.

STOLJAR, S. J.
1973 *Groups and Entities.* Canberra: Australian National University Press.

SUPPLY AND SERVICES CANADA
1978 *A Time for Action: Toward the Renewal of the Canadian Federation.*

1981 *In All Fairness; A Native Claims Policy.*

1982 *Outstanding Business; A Native Claims Policy.*

SUTTON, P.
1980 "Notes on some aspects of traditional Aboriginal land takeovers marked by conflict." Exhibit No. 664 in the Finniss River Land Claim.

TATZ, COLIN
1979 *Race, Politics in Australia: Aborigines, Politics and Law.* Armidale, N.S.W.: University of New England Press.

THUEN, TROND
1983 "Meaning and Transaction in Saami Ethnopolitics." In Reidar Grönhaug (ed.), *Transaction and Signification.* Bergen: Universitetsforlaget.

TRUDEAU, PIERRE ELLIOTT
1978 *A Time for Action: Toward the Renewal of the Canadian Federation.* Ottawa: Minister of Supply and Services.

TRUDEL, PIERRE
1982 "Les Cris et les structures administratives de la C.B.J.: 'La négociation d'un mode de vie'' (1ere partie). *Recherches amérin diennes au Québec,* 12(3):230-33.

1983 "Les Cris et les structures administratives de la C.B.J.: 'La négociation d'un mode de vie'' (2e partie). *Recherches amérindiennes au Québec,* 13(1):61-66.

TURNER, V. W.
1957 *Schism and Continuity in an African Society.* Manchester: Manchester University Press for the Rhodes-Livingstone Institute.

1969 *The Ritual Process: Structure and Anti-Structure.* Chicago: Aldine.

1974 *Dramas, Fields, and Metaphors.* Ithaca: Cornell University Press.

VINER, IAN
1977 "Ministerial Statement on National Aborigial Conference."

Australia, House of Representatives, Debates, May 30, 1977, 2104-2111.

WARNER, W. L.
1937 *A Black Civilization*. New York: Harper and Brothers.

WATKINS, M.
1977 *Dene Nation - The Colony Within*. Toronto: University of Toronto Press.

WEAVER, SALLY M.
1981 *Making Canadian Indian Policy: The Hidden Agenda, 1968-70*. Toronto: University of Toronto Press.

1982 "The Joint Cabinet/National Indian Brotherhood Committee: A Unique Experiment in Pressure Group Relations." *Canadian Public Administration*, 25:211-39.

1983 "Australian Aboriginal Policy: Aboriginal Pressure Groups or Government Advisory Bodies?" Parts I and II. *Oceania*, 54:1-22; 85-108.

1985 "Struggles of the Nation-State to define Indigenous Ethnicity: Canada and Australia." In Gerry Gold (ed.), *Minorities and Mother Country Imagery*. St. John's, Nfld.: Institute of Social and Economic Research, Memorial University.

WHITTINGTON, M.S. and R. VAN LOON
1976 *The Canadian Political System*. Toronto: McGraw-Hill Ryerson.

WITTENBORN, R. and C. BIEGERT
1981 *James Bay Project—A River Drowned by Water*. Montreal Museum of Fine Arts.

WOLF, ERIK R.
1982 *Europe and the People Without History*. Berkeley, Los Angeles, London: University of California Press.

WOODWARD, A. E.
1973 *Aboriginal Land Rights Commission: First Report July 1973*. Canberra.

1974 *Aboriginal Land Rights Commission: Second Report April 1974*. Canberra.

WORSLEY, PETER
1967 *The Third World*. London: Weidenfeld and Nicolson. Press.

WUTTUNEE, WILLIAM
1971 *Ruffled Feathers*. Calgary: Bell Books.

List of Contributors

Jeremy Beckett, Senior Lecturer in Anthropology, University of Sydney, Sydney, New South Wales, Australia

Noel Dyck, Associate Professor of Anthropology, Simon Fraser University, Burnaby, British Columbia, Canada

Harvey Feit, Associate Professor of Anthropology, McMaster University, Hamilton, Ontario, Canada

Robert Paine, Henrietta Harvey Professor of Anthropology, Memorial University of Newfoundland, St. John's, Newfoundland, Canada

Douglas Sanders, Professor of Law, University of British Columbia, Vancouver, British Columbia, Canada

Basil Sansom, Professor of Anthropology, University of Western Australia, Nedlands, Western Australia, Australia

Sally M. Weaver, Professor of Anthropology, University of Waterloo, Waterloo, Ontario, Canada

ISER Publications

Other